Lecture Notes in Computer Science   14414

Founding Editors

Gerhard Goos
Juris Hartmanis

The series Lecture Notes in Computer Science (LNCS), including its subseries Lecture Notes in Artificial Intelligence (LNAI) and Lecture Notes in Bioinformatics (LNBI), has established itself as a medium for the publication of new developments in computer science and information technology research, teaching, and education.

LNCS enjoys close cooperation with the computer science R & D community, the series counts many renowned academics among its volume editors and paper authors, and collaborates with prestigious societies. Its mission is to serve this international community by providing an invaluable service, mainly focused on the publication of conference and workshop proceedings and postproceedings. LNCS commenced publication in 1973.

Haniel Barbosa · Yoni Zohar
Editors

Formal Methods: Foundations and Applications

26th Brazilian Symposium, SBMF 2023
Manaus, Brazil, December 4–8, 2023
Proceedings

Springer

Editors
Haniel Barbosa (iD)
Universidade Federal de Minas Gerais
Belo Horizonte, Brazil

Yoni Zohar (iD)
Bar-Ilan University
Ramat Gan, Israel

ISSN 0302-9743   ISSN 1611-3349   (electronic)
Lecture Notes in Computer Science
ISBN 978-3-031-49341-6   ISBN 978-3-031-49342-3   (eBook)
https://doi.org/10.1007/978-3-031-49342-3

This Springer imprint is published by the registered company Springer Nature Switzerland AG
The registered company address is: Gewerbestrasse 11, 6330 Cham, Switzerland

Paper in this product is recyclable.

Preface

This volume contains the papers presented at SBMF 2023: the 26th Brazilian Symposium on Formal Methods. After three consecutive virtual events due to the COVID-19 pandemic, we were happy to have SBMF again as an in-person event, held at Manaus, Brazil, from December 6 to December 8, 2023, with satellite events on December 4 and December 5, 2023.

The Brazilian Symposium on Formal Methods (SBMF) is an event devoted to the development, dissemination, and use of formal methods for the construction of high-quality computational systems, aiming to promote opportunities for researchers and practitioners with an interest in formal methods to discuss the recent advances in this area. SBMF is a consolidated scientific-technical event in the software area. Its first edition took place in 1998, and it reached the jubilee 25th edition in 2022. The proceedings of recent editions have been published mostly in Springer's Lecture Notes in Computer Science series as volumes 5902 (2009), 6527 (2010), 7021 (2011), 7498 (2012), 8195 (2013), 8941 (2014), 9526 (2015), 10090 (2016), 10623 (2017), 11254 (2018), 12475 (2020), 13130 (2021), and 13768 (2022).

The conference included four invited talks, given by Artur d'Avila Garcez (City, University of London, UK), Stéphane Graham-Lengrand (SRI International, USA), Chantal Keller (Université Paris-Saclay, France), and Vince Molnár (BME-FTSRG, Hungary). A total of 9 papers were presented at the conference and are included in this volume, with 7 of them as regular papers and 2 of them as short papers. They were selected from 16 submissions (12 regular, 4 short) that came from 7 different countries: Brazil, Spain, the UK, France, the USA, South Africa, and Argentina. The Program Committee comprised 36 members from the national and international community of formal methods. Each submission was reviewed by three Program Committee members (single-blind review). Submissions, reviews, deliberations, and decisions were handled via EasyChair, which provided good support throughout this process.

We are grateful to the Program Committee for their hard work in evaluating submissions and suggesting improvements. We are very thankful to the general chair of SBMF 2023, Edjard Mota (Universidade Federal do Amazonas, Brazil), who made everything possible for the conference to run smoothly. SBMF 2023 was organized by the Universidade Federal do Amazonas (UFAM), and promoted by the Brazilian Computer Society (SBC). We would further like to thank SBC for their sponsorship, and Springer for agreeing to publish the proceedings as a volume of Lecture Notes in Computer Science.

December 2023

Haniel Barbosa
Yoni Zohar

Organization

General Chair

Edjard Mota   Universidade Federal do Amazonas, Brazil

Program Committee Chairs

Haniel Barbosa   Universidade Federal de Minas Gerais, Brazil
Yoni Zohar   Bar-Ilan University, Israel

Steering Committee

Gustavo Carvalho   Universidade Federal de Pernambuco, Brazil
Volker Stolz   Western Norway University of Applied Sciences,
                             Norway
Sérgio Campos   Universidade Federal de Minas Gerais, Brazil
Marius Minea   University of Massachusetts Amherst, USA
Vince Molnár   Budapest University of Technology and Economics,
                             Hungary
Lucas Lima   Universidade Federal Rural de Pernambuco, Brazil

Program Committee

Yoni Zohar   Bar-Ilan University, Israel
Haniel Barbosa   Universidade Federal de Minas Gerais, Brazil
Katalin Fazekas   TU Wien, Austria
Mathias Preiner   Stanford University, USA
Daniela Kaufmann   TU Wien, Austria
Edjard Mota   Universidade Federal do Amazonas, Brazil
Maurice ter Beek   ISTI-CNR, Italy
Vince Molnár   Budapest University of Technology and Economics,
                             Hungary
Mathias Fleury   University of Freiburg, Germany
Leila Ribeiro   Universidade Federal do Rio Grande do Sul, Brazil
Luís Soares Barbosa   University of Minho, Portugal
Volker Stolz   Høgskulen på Vestlandet, Norway
Nils Timm   University of Pretoria, South Africa
Thierry Lecomte   ClearSy System Engineering, France
Lucas Lima   Universidade Federal Rural de Pernambuco, Brazil
Marcel Oliveira   Universidade Federal do Rio Grande do Norte, Brazil
Gustavo Carvalho   Universidade Federal de Pernambuco, Brazil
Márcio Cornélio   Universidade Federal de Pernambuco, Brazil

Clark Barrett	Stanford University, USA
Juliano Iyoda	Universidade Federal de Pernambuco, Brazil
Sergio Campos	Universidade Federal de Minas Gerais, Brazil
Adenilso Simao	University of São Paulo, Brazil
Ahmed Irfan	SRI International, USA
Leopoldo Teixeira	Universidade Federal de Pernambuco, Brazil
David Déharbe	ClearSy System Engineering, France
Michael Leuschel	University of Düsseldorf, Germany
Giselle Reis	Carnegie Mellon University-Qatar, Qatar
Rohit Gheyi	Universidade Federal de Campina Grande, Brazil
Augusto Sampaio	Universidade Federal de Pernambuco, Brazil
Armin Biere	University of Freiburg, Germany
Sophie Tourret	INRIA and MPI for Informatics, France
Natarajan Shankar	SRI International, USA
Sidney C. Nogueira	Universidade Federal Rural de Pernambuco, Brazil
Cesare Tinelli	University of Iowa, USA
Lucas Cordeiro	University of Manchester, UK
Clare Dixon	University of Manchester, UK

Additional Reviewers

Levente Bajczi
Laura Bussi
Bence Graics
Lars Michael Kristensen

Invited Talks and Tutorial

Neurosymbolic AI to Achieve Trustworthy AI

Artur d'Avila Garcez

City, University of London, UK

Abstract. Current advances in Artificial Intelligence (AI) and Machine Learning (ML) have achieved unprecedented impact across research communities and industry. Nevertheless, concerns around trust, safety, interpretability and accountability of AI were raised by influential thinkers. Many identified the need for well-founded knowledge representation and reasoning to be integrated with Deep Learning (DL). Neurosymbolic AI has been an active area of research for many years seeking to do just that, bringing together robust learning in neural networks with reasoning and explainability via symbolic representations. Our focus is on research that integrates in a principled way neural-network learning with symbolic AI. In this keynote I will review the research in neurosymbolic AI and computation, and how it can help shed new light onto the increasingly prominent role of safety, trust, interpretability and accountability of AI. We also identify promising directions and challenges for the next decade of AI research from the perspective of neurosymbolic computation. Over the past decade, AI and in particular DL has attracted media attention, has become the focus of increasingly large research endeavours and has changed businesses. This led to influential debates on the impact of AI in academia and industry. It has been argued that the building of a rich AI system, semantically sound, explainable and ultimately trustworthy, will require a sound reasoning layer in combination with deep learning. Parallels have been drawn between Daniel Kahneman's research on human reasoning and decision making, and so-called "AI systems 1 and 2" which would in principle be modelled by deep learning and symbolic reasoning, respectively.

We seek to place 20 years of research in the area of neurosymbolic AI, known as neural-symbolic integration, in the context of the recent explosion of interest and excitement around the combination of deep learning and symbolic reasoning. We revisit early theoretical results of fundamental relevance to shaping the latest research, such as the proof that recurrent neural networks compute the semantics of logic programming, and we identify bottlenecks and the most promising technical directions for the sound representation of learning and reasoning in neural networks. As well as pointing to the various related and promising techniques, we aim to help organise some of the terminology commonly used around AI, ML and DL. This is important at this exciting time when AI becomes popularized among researchers and practitioners from other areas of Computer Science and from other fields altogether, psychology, cognitive science, economics, medicine, engineering and neuroscience.

I will survey some of the prominent forms of neural-symbolic integration. We address neural-symbolic integration from the perspectives of distributed and localist forms of representation, and argue for a focus on logical representation based on the assumption that representation precedes learning and reasoning.

We delve into the fundamentals of current neurosymbolic AI methods and systems and identify promising aspects of neurosymbolic AI to address exciting challenges for learning, reasoning, validation and explainability. Finally, based on all of the above, we propose a list of ingredients for neurosymbolic AI and discuss promising directions for future research to address the challenges of AI.

Collaborating Reasoners: Theory Combination Beyond Nelson-Oppen

Stéphane Graham-Lengrand

SRI International, USA

Abstract. The Nelson-Oppen scheme constitutes a cornerstone of SMT-solving by providing a systematic recipe for interfacing theory-specific reasoners. In this scheme, the reasoners can simply be black boxes whose only requirements are to be decision procedures for (quantifier-free) satisfiability in their respective theories. To make them collaborate, extra properties are required of the theories to be combined, rather than of the reasoners; for instance, the theories should be disjoint in that they only share the equality symbol.

In this talk, we will range over the design and the benefits of several alternative schemes where reasoners collaborate by answering more complex queries than pure satisfiability queries and/or by satisfying stronger requirements than simply being decision procedures for their underlying theories. Among such designs are the CDSAT scheme where completeness and termination of reasoners are stated in a combination-aware form, as well as several schemes, like QSMA, that rely on the reasoners' ability to produce over-and under-approximations of the input formula. The benefits include the support of non-disjoint theory combinations, additional freedom in the lemmas to be learned, new techniques for interpolation, and new techniques for supporting quantifiers.

`Sniper`: **Automated Reasoning for Type Theory**

Chantal Keller

Université Paris-Saclay, France

Abstract. For formal proofs to become mainstream in software and hardware development, as well as mathematical formalization, automation plays an essential role. Many systems already enjoy a high degree of automation, such as deductive verification tools for proof of programs. In the case of interactive theorem proving, provers based on Higher Order Logic now often provide hammers, which are very powerful tools that call many external automated provers in parallel and propose a meaningful proof script if possible.

For interactive provers based on Type theory, though, attempts to build hammers have given good results, but appear to be less powerful and hardly predictable than for Higher Order Logic. More generally, in such systems, a variety of automatic tactics are available, but expertise is still required to use them: one needs to know when they apply, how to combine them, and apparently small changes in a goal can completely break a tactic. We give non-exhaustive examples in the Coq proof assistant:

- the `Micromega` plugin provides various tactics to reason about integer linear arithmetic, but it is non trivial to apply them when integers live in types out of Coq's standard library, and by design it cannot be applied modulo congruence;
- the `CoqHammer` plugin provides tactics to call various first-order provers, as well as to reconstruct their proofs, but it lacks theory reasoning such as integer arithmetic, and it is very hard to predict when the provers or proof reconstruction will succeed;
- the `SMTCoq` plugin provides tactics to call various SMT solvers and reconstruct their proofs, but it is limited to goals expressed in Boolean logic and with a very specific shape;
- ...

We analyze these difficulties in this way.

- Tactics for general automation (such as `CoqHammer`) are very hard to predict because there is a gap between Type theory and first-order logic that prevents anticipating if solvers and proof reconstruction will succeed.
- Tactics for more specific automation (such as `Micromega` and `SMTCoq`) are easier to predict, but apply to very specific goals, and expertise is needed to obtain or recognize such goals.

`Sniper`: **Compositional Pre-processing**

To reconcile the two methods, we propose a new approach that makes use of existing tactics for specific automation and tries to combine them to obtain predictive and extensible general automation. This approach is being implemented in the Coq plugin `Sniper`[1], whose development is under progress.

It is based on the following architecture:

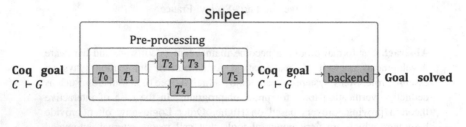

`Sniper` pre-processes goals before calling an automatic tactic dedicated to specific automation (called *backend* in the figure) such as `SMTCoq` or `Micromega`. The key idea is that pre-processing is not a monolithic transformation, but it is a dynamic composition of fine-grained transformations (called T_1 to T_5 in the figure) that can be taken from a pool; the backend can also be any tactic that (partially) solves a given class of problems. By *dynamic*, we mean that the transformations that are used, the order in which they are applied, and the chosen backend are not fixed, but depend on the original goal.

The advantages of this approach are the following.

- It is adaptive, and can thus apply to a variety of goals.
- It should be quite predictive from the pools of transformations and backends.
- It is compositional, and contributors can easily add new transformations or backends to extend the tactic. Note that more powerful backends such as `CoqHammer` can also be used, as they become more predictive if goals are pre-processed into specific classes of problems.
- Fine-grained transformations tackle one aspect of Coq logic at a time, which make them easy to produce partial proofs (such as Coq tactics do); and partially preserve goal's structure, making some automatic backends such as `SMTCoq` more likely to succeed.

As of writing, the implementation of `Sniper` already provides a library of around fifteen certifying transformations designed for this architecture, and a prototype tactic `snipe`. Work in progress consists in making `Sniper` dynamic (as explained above) and designing an API for contributors to easily add new transformations and backends.

---

[1] https://github.com/smtcoq/sniper.

Acknowledgments. Sniper is common work with Louise Dubois de Prisque, Pierre Vial and Valentin Blot. It relies on SMTCoq, which is the work of many smart people, who are listed here: https://github.com/smtcoq/smtcoq/blob/coq-8.13/AUTHORS. We also thank Enzo Crance, Denis Cousineau, Assia Mahboubi and Kazuhiko Sakaguchi for fruitful discussions on this work.

References

1. Armand, M., Faure, G., Grégoire, B., Keller, C., Théry, L., Werner, B.: A modular integration of SAT/SMT aolvers to Coq through proof witnesses. In: Jouannaud, J.P., Shao, Z. (eds.) Certified Programs and Proofs. CPP 2011. LNCS, vol. 7086, pp. 135–150. Springer, Berlin (2011). https://doi.org/10.1007/978-3-642-25379-9_12

2. Besson, F.: Fast reflexive arithmetic tactics the linear case and beyond. In: Altenkirch, T., McBride, C. (eds.) Types for Proofs and Programs. TYPES 2006. LNCS, vol. 4502, pp. 48–62. Springer, Berlin (2007). https://doi.org/10.1007/978-3-540-74464-1_4

3. Blanchette, J.C., Kaliszyk, C., Paulson, L.C., Urban, J.:Hammering towards QED. J. Formalized Reasoning **9**(1),101–148 (2016). https://doi.org/10.6092/issn.1972-5787/4593

4. Blot, V., et al.: Compositional pre-processing for automatedreasoning in dependent type theory. In: Krebbers, R., Traytel, D.,Pientka, B., Zdancewic, S. (eds.) Proceedings of the 12th ACM SIGPLANInternational Conference on Certified Programs and Proofs,CPP 2023, Boston, MA, USA, January 16–17, 2023, pp. 63–77. ACM(2023). https://doi.org/10.1145/3573105.3575676

5. Czajka, L., Kaliszyk, C.: Hammer for Coq: automation for dependenttype theory. J. Autom. Reason. **61**(1–4), 423–453 (2018).https://doi.org/10.1007/s10817-018-9458-4

6. Desharnais, M., Vukmirovic, P., Blanchette, J., Wenzel, M.: Seventeenprovers under the hammer. In: Andronick, J., de Moura,L. (eds.) 13th International Conference on Interactive TheoremProving, ITP 2022, August 7–10, 2022, Haifa, Israel.LIPIcs, vol. 237, pp. 8:1–8:18. Schloss Dagstuhl - Leibniz-Zentrumfür Informatik (2022). https://doi.org/10.4230/LIPIcs.ITP.2022.8,https://www.dagstuhl.de/dagpub/978-3-95977-252-5

7. Filliâtre, J.C., Paskevich, A.: Why3 — where programs meet provers. In: Felleisen, M., Gardner, P. (eds.) Programming Languages and Systems. ESOP 2013. LNCS, vol. 7792, pp. 125–128. Springer, Berlin (2013). https://doi.org/10.1007/978-3-642-37036-6_8

8. Sakaguchi, K.: Micromega tactics for mathematical components(2019–2022), https://github.com/math-comp/mczify

9. Swamy, N., et al.: Dependent types and multimonadiceffects in F. In: Symposium on Principles of ProgrammingLanguages (POPL)

Formal Methods in Systems Engineering - Verifying SysML v2 Models

Vince Molnár

BME-FTSRG, Hungary

Abstract. Formal methods have been successfully applied to several fields in engineering, including software, hardware, and communication protocols. Systems engineering is an interdisciplinary field that focuses on how to design, integrate, and manage complex systems over their lifecycles. Models in systems engineering may capture the specification of both software and hardware components, but also processes, physical aspects, and even expected user behavior, as well as abstract descriptions of scenarios in which the system is expected to operate. Due to the integration aspect, there is a heavy emphasis on the interplay between these various viewpoints. Even though there would be plenty of use cases to apply formal methods, V&V in systems engineering is still typically performed in the form of manual reviews, and only smaller components and their implementations are analyzed with automated formal verification tools.

The Systems Modeling Language (SysML) is the de facto standard modeling language for designing and developing complex systems. The second version of SysML is a complete redesign, including changes like moving away from UML, adding an expression language, and adopting a 4D ontology-like semantics based on classification and logic. Many of these changes make SysML v2 more suitable for formal analysis than its predecessor. At the same time, the ever-increasing complexity and the increasingly popular notion of executable modeling are creating demand to automate analysis tasks. Automation is expected to save time and resources for engineers and reduce manual errors, especially in the engineering of critical systems.

In this tutorial, we provide an overview of use cases of formal methods in systems engineering, then introduce the fundamentals of the SysML v2 language, focusing on its declarative 4D semantics and how it handles temporal aspects. We take a look at formal verification approaches from the perspective of the new language, including new techniques devised for parallel programs, as well as model generation. Model execution is a central topic in the community around the new standard, so we dedicate some time to present the ongoing efforts related to execution, semantics, and formal methods. Finally, we present an early prototype for model checking SysML v2 models and discuss the challenges and open problems in the field.

Formal Methods in Systems Engineering-verifying SysML v2 Models

Contents

Specification and Modeling Languages

A Formal Model for Startups Financial Transactions

Rodrigo Stevaux$^{(\boxtimes)}$ ⑩ and Ana C. V. de Melo$^{(\boxtimes)}$ ⑩

Institute of Mathematics and Statistics, University of São Paulo, São Paulo, Brazil
{roehst,acvm}@ime.usp.br

Abstract. This paper proposes a formal model for a subset of the startup finance transaction space. The initial version of the provided domain is the result of an industry coalition effort to make the data model standard.

The data definition explains how this domain can be modeled syntactically. We refined this first model with semantics on transactions by using the Alloy formal modeling language and analyzer, aiming for a more expressive and correct model by capturing domain invariants. As a result, the new model is machine-checkable for important safety integrity criteria.

This research contributes to the field of formal methods by demonstrating how to progress from a semi-formal specification to a formal one, evaluating the results, and providing a case study of a real-world domain.

Keywords: Formal methods · Financial modeling · Alloy

1 Introduction

Capitalization tables are essential documents required for conducting **venture capital** investments in **startup companies**. A capitalization table depicts the ownership structure of a company, and this structure is subject to change over time due to new investments, transfers, and acquisitions. The cost and risk associated with validating **capitalization tables** have a significant effect on the business market. According to the accounting firm KPMG [3], 38,644 **venture capital** transactions were closed in 2021, with each transaction requiring tens of hours of attorneys and accountants.

Errors in **capitalization tables** can be costly and may lead to potential legal disputes. **Capitalization tables** are typically maintained in spreadsheets, a method that is error-prone and difficult to audit. Spreadsheets do not adhere to a standard format, requiring all parties involved in a transaction to agree on a uniform format before exchanging data (or lose time disambiguating the data). Validating the **transactions** that led to the current **capitalization table** is the only method to assure that a **capitalization table** accurately reflects the correct stakes of each **stakeholder**.

H. Barbosa and Y. Zohar (Eds.): SBMF 2023, LNCS 14414, pp. 3–19, 2024.
https://doi.org/10.1007/978-3-031-49342-3_1

Due to the inherent difficulties associated with maintaining **capitalization tables** in spreadsheets, a number of companies now provide **capitalization table** management as a service. These companies offer a web-based interface for managing **capitalization tables** in an attempt to streamline the process and reduce errors. However, the underlying data models are proprietary, and the criteria for updating the **capitalization tables** are often not explicitly defined.

The Open Cap Table Coalition [1], comprised of industry members such as venture capital funds, law and accounting firms and cap table management service providers is currently working on a standard for **capitalization tables** to address these issues, called Open Cap Table Format (OCF). The standard is based on a publicly available data model that can be used to develop software systems that handle the **capitalization tables**' data structure. Nevertheless, the data model still lacks a formal specification of the criteria for updating the **capitalization tables**. We can see that many users ask questions on how exactly to interpret the rules. In the discussion forum in the Open Cap Table Format's GitHub repository, multiple questions have been asked seeking for clarification on how to interpret the data in the original format, as well as how to model different real world scenarios in the format.

The proposed standard models **securities** as entities and **transactions** as events. This is a pattern commonly known as event sourcing [6]. The current state of any **capitalization table** must be computed by replaying all events on an initial state, but the standard provides no clear guidance on the semantics of each type of transaction. This is an unfortunate consequence of the syntax-focused semantics of the selected technology, JSON Schema, which cannot accommodate the specification of transaction rules.

Very importantly, we found no previous work that specifically addresses the problem of specifying the semantics of **capitalization tables** transactions, although there is related work on financial modeling, legal modeling and smart contract verification.

There is related work on the formal specification of financial derivatives such as Simon Peyton Jones' work on the specification of financial contracts [13]. However, this work is focused on the specification of derivative contracts, not equity transactions. Catala [11] is a language for writing legal texts in a source code based on a logic language with semantics for resolving conflicts between clauses. However, Catala is not focused on the specification of financial transactions. In the field of smart contracts, verification of contracts is an active area of research, including the use of dependent types.

But we are very interested in modeling the global correctness of the system, and not only individual contracts. We found no work that focuses on the semantics that are specific to capitalization tables as a whole and the transactions that affect them. In this sense, TLA$^+$ [10] is a specification language that allows the specification of systems as a whole but is considerably more complex than Alloy.

Based on the Open Cap Table Format, the current work proposes using Alloy [7] to provide formal semantics for transactions to maintain the consistency of **capitalization tables** over time. Our work does characterize the **capitalization table** as whole, and provides rules for validating individual transactions, and is machine checkable.

2 Capitalization Tables and the Need for Specifications

A **capitalization table** is a table that shows a company's ownership stakes. The ownership stakes of a fictitious company's founders, angel investors, funds, and employees are illustrated bellow. Additionally, the table displays the number of shares issued, the type of security, the price per share, and the date of issuance. The capitalization table is used to calculate the ownership of each shareholder.

Stakeholders have interests in different **asset classes**, resulting in some shares and % ownership at a given cost. The cost might be different for different investors as they invest at different times, as a company's value might fluctuate.

Asset class	Stakeholder	Shares	Cost	% Ownership
Common stock	Founders	700	0	70%
Preferred stock	Angel investors	50	80	5%
Preferred stock	Funds	150	300	15%
Options	Employees	100	0	10%
Total		1000	350	100%

A typical use of **capitalization tables** is to follow investments in a company over time. In **startup companies**, for example, investments appear in stages: each stage requiring the achievement of certain objectives and milestones. The amount of investment can vary depending on the stage [12]: Seed/Startup financing, Early-stage financing, Mid-stage financing and Later-stage financing. From a computer science perspective, **a capitalization table is the state of a system, and financing operations are transitions of that state.**

Each round of **staged financing** is defined in contracts that define business rules. It is common for the investors of each round to have different rights and obligations. Conversions, transfers, vesting, and other events can only occur under specific conditions, and those conditions must always be validated to prevent the company's ownership structure be misrepresented. All these business rules and conditions are potentially complex to validate.

2.1   The Open Cap Table Format (OCF)

JSON Schema is a specification for JavaScript Object Notation (JSON) data that defines the structure and constraints of JSON data. JSON is a lightweight data interchange format that is widely used in web applications and APIs due to its simplicity and readability. JSON Schema (RFC8259 [2]) enables developers to specify the structure and constraints of JSON data. Taking into account these characteristics, the Open Cap Table Coalition [1] employs JSON Schema to provide the Open Cap table Format (OCF), which incorporates data communication standards and concepts. Our work is based on the following commit:

```
git clone https://github.com/Open-Cap-Table-Coalition/Open-Cap-Format-OCF
git checkout 20f3ede62d1f5bdbef16ae1edfa98c34fbda2610
```

The Open Cap Table format defines a package, or set, of JSON files, for storing data on transactions and business entities. Adopting the format means being able to export the **capitalization table** data according to the format. The Manifest file contains metadata about the other files, which contain data. The data files either contain immutable entities which participate in **transactions** or the transactions themselves, which are the events that change the state of the entities. The data files are: Issuers, Stakeholders, Stock classes, Stock legend templates, Stock option plans, Vesting terms and Transactions.

Although the OCF specifies a set of *files* by defining its contents as JSON documents with associated JSON Schema, it is built on top of a conceptual model that underlies the data. The schemas are organized according to two principles:

- Technical building blocks: *enums*, *types* and *objects*
- Conceptual blocks: *entities*, **transactions**, *conversion mechanisms, rights and triggers*, and *vestings*

Technically, types (in OCF terminology) define structures (expected keys and associated validation) that are reused in primitive objects (in the sense of JSON objects and documents) and in Enum (enumerations of constant values).

The OCF has three key logical components:

Transaction & tracing	Transactions that are linked by **security** identifiers (i.e., the issuance and cancellation of a **security** refer to a common **security** identifier)
Vesting	Composable rules for both schedule-based and event-based vesting
Convertible securities	Composable rules for converting securities, typically applied in the case of **debt** that can be converted to stock shares

In the current research, these three logical components are defined. For the lack of space, this paper focus on the presentation of the **Transaction & tracing** component and its related properties.

Transaction Tracing System. Since a **capitalization table** is a snapshot taken after a collection of **transactions** have been accumulated, one component of the OCF is the support for traceable **transactions**. **Transactions** are objects recorded in the **transactions** file which refer to **securities**. A **security** is a financial **asset** that can be bought and sold. Stocks, options, and **debt** notes are all a kind of **security**. The key ideas behind the transaction tracing systems are:

– Securities have an *initial* and a *terminal* transaction.
– Issuances (including re-issuances) and **exercises** are initial **transactions**.
– Cancellations, retractions, repurchases are terminal **transactions**.
– Transfers are both initial and terminal **transactions**, as they extinguish the initial **security** and create a new **security** (the result security).
– Partial cancellations are possible by extinguishing the original **security** and generating a new **security** with the remaining balance.
– Partial transfers are possible by extinguishing the original **security** and generating a new **security** with the remaining balance

To compute the state of a **security**, it is necessary to trace all transactions associated with it. The state of a **security** is equal to the sum of all issuances subtracted by the sum of all cancellations, repurchases, and transfers. This sequence of transactions makes the financial system auditable and traceable.

Advantages and Limitations of the OCF. The choice of designing patterns in OCF results in a data model that can fulfill the requirements of auditability (in special regarding transaction tracing) and flexibility. JSON Schema can syntactically validate data, which is sufficient for a file or data exchange format. However, JSON Schema lacks expressiveness in terms of sets, relations, and logic. It cannot reason about relational properties of instances or even distinguish between incorrect and correct transaction traces. All these validations are not included in the original OCF model.

By employing a more robust modeling framework, such as Alloy with the Alloy Analyzer, we can improve the OCF's validation and expressiveness. This should preserve the available business knowledge and data structure in the OCF while adding knowledge about the constraints on financial transactions.

3 Consistency of Capitalization Tables - Alloy Model

We developed an Alloy model based on the OCF that encompasses the OCF structure and the semantics of transactions permitted in financial systems. In this section, we explore the portion of the Alloy model that ensures the consistency of **transactions** that affect capitalization tables.

The main factors considered in selecting Alloy as the appropriate formal approach were simplicity, suitability for high-level design, and accessibility to business experts.

We considered languages with dependent types and other specification languages. Languages with dependent types such as Agda [15] are less accessible to programmers and out of reach for business experts. The TLA$^+$ model checker [10] has a can reason about ordering of operations, but we discovered that it has a much more complicated language and tooling than Alloy, which means that learning curve is higher. Conversely, these other options would have provided stronger assistance for arithmetic.

Alloy is a lightweight formal method, comprised of a language, a small standard library and a very practical graphical interface.

Alloy excels at enabling high-level design, and the Alloy Analyzer is user-friendly, capable of providing quick feedback to the user, and all features are easily discoverable and accessible. Especially when sharing our findings and concepts with stakeholders who might not have a strong background in formal methodologies, its visualization skills are invaluable.

A sample of Alloy's syntax is given in the listing below. The listing shows a very basic model requiring that a security is owned by a single investor (portfolios do not overlap).

```
sig Company { securities : set Security }
sig Investor { portfolio : set Security }
sig Security { owner : Investor, issued : one Company }
pred isInvestor[inv : Investor, co : Company] {
    some inv.portfolio & co.securities
}
fact { no inv1, inv2 : Investor | some inv1.portfolio & inv2.portfolio }
```

3.1   The Model Overview

A **capitalization table** tracks the ownership stakes and capital structure of a company. The **transactions** that typically affect a **capitalization table** include **issuances**, cancellations, and transfers of **securities** (see model overview in Fig. 1).

A **capitalization table** is built as new **transactions** are recorded. The Open Cap Table format proposes a "transaction tracing model" in which **securities** are identified with unique identifiers and **transactions** refer to those identifiers when issuing, canceling, or transferring **securities**.

The purpose of the transaction tracing model is to provide auditable **securities** traceability. The Alloy model then needs to conform to the requirements for a consistent model for capitalization tables and enforce certain properties.

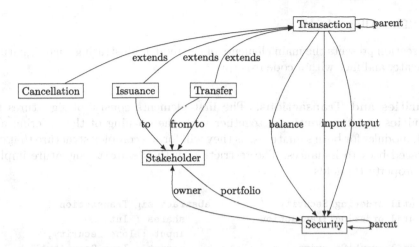

Fig. 1. Transaction tracing metamodel. The extends relation corresponds to inheritance. Other relations are fields of the signatures.

3.2   Expected Properties

A correct model is can only be considered correct if characterized with respect to a set of properties. In our case, we use two sets of properties: structural properties and accounting properties. The properties cannot be expressed in JSON Schema, but are expected for a consistent model of capitalization tables. The Alloy model must ensure that these properties hold, as checked by the Alloy Analyzer.

Structural properties	
P1	All **securities** can be traced back to an Issuance
P2	All **transactions** can be traced back to an Issuance
P3	There can be no cycles in the **security** hierarchy. This guarantees that every **security** can be traced back to a root security
P4	There can be no cycles in the transaction hierarchy. This guarantees that every transaction can be traced back to a root transaction

Accounting properties	
P5	The number of shares in circulation should be less than or equal to the number of shares issued
P6	No **securities** can have a negative number of shares
P7	The sum of shares in all portfolios should be equal to the number of shares issued minus the number of shares canceled

3.3   The Alloy Model

This section presents the main elements of the model, illustrating each signature, predicate, and fact with a code excerpt.

Securities and Transactions. The first elements consist of signatures for **securities** and **transactions**, together with the opening of the ordering and graph modules for both signatures, as they will form a complex structure that can be traced back to issuances. The restriction in the Security signature implies that property P6 holds.

```
open util/ordering[Security]
open util/ordering[Transaction]

open util/graph[Security]
open util/graph[Transaction]

sig Security {
   shares : Int,
   source : one Transaction,
   use : lone Transaction,
   parent : lone Security,
   owner : Stakeholder
} {
   nonneg[shares]
}
```

```
abstract sig Transaction {
   shares : Int,
   input : lone Security,
   output : lone Security,
   balance : lone Security,
   parent : lone Transaction
} {
   pos[shares]
}
fact {
   use = ~input
}
fact {
   source = ~(output + balance)
}
```

The Transaction signature is given abstract because a Transaction is never instantiated directly; they may have different types of **transactions**, such as issuances, cancellations, and transfers. Those types of **transactions** are defined afterwards.

Two constraints are stated as facts to relate the use and source fields of **securities** to the input and output fields of **transactions**. The use field of a **security** is the transaction that uses the **security** as input. The source field of a **security** is the transaction that uses the **security** as output. The ~ operator to invert the binary relations is used for input and output because they denote the same relation with the opposite direction.

Transaction Types. We consider three types of transaction in the model because they subsume all other more specific types of transaction. Any transaction is a composition of creation and destruction of **securities**. Transfers, in particular, are a combination of an issuance and a cancellation.

```
sig Issuance extends Transaction {           one input
    to : Stakeholder                         one (Transaction <: parent)
} {                                        }
    no input                               sig Transfer extends Transaction {
    no balance                                 from : Stakeholder,
    one output                                 to : Stakeholder - from
    no (Transaction <: parent)             } {
}                                              one input
sig Cancellation extends                       one output
 ↪  Transaction {} {                           lone balance
    no output                                  one (Transaction <: parent)
    lone balance                           }
```

All **transactions** have parent, input, output, and balance fields, but each transaction uses only a subset of them. Additional fields, appearing after the signature, constraint the **transactions**. For instance, the Issuance transaction has a to field stating who will own the issued security, while the Transfer transaction has from and to fields stating who will transfer the **security** from and to.

Issuance Constraints. The behavior of the Issuance is encoded in a single fact. The first line equates the number of shares of the newly issued **security** to the number of the shares in the issuance, while the following lines bind other specific fields to their appropriate values.

```
fact {                                          iss.output.owner = iss.to
    all iss : Issuance {                        iss.output in
        eq[iss.output.shares,               ↪      iss.to.portfolio
 ↪      iss.shares]                             }
        iss.output.source = iss         }
```

Cancellation Constraints. The case for a cancellation is more complex because it must distinguish between partial and complete cancellations. This is done by comparing the number of shares in the cancellation and in the cancelled security, and giving different constraints for each case. It is encoded in a single fact.

```
fact {
    all can : Cancellation {
        lt[can.shares, can.input.shares] implies {
            // In this case, the transaction is partial.
            can.input.use = can
            can.balance.source = can
            eq[can.balance.shares, sub[can.input.shares, can.shares]]
            lt[can.input, can.balance]
            can.balance.owner = can.input.owner
            can.balance in can.input.owner.portfolio
            can.balance.parent = can.input
            can.parent = can.input.source
        } else {
```

```
                can.input.use = can
                eq[can.input.shares, can.shares]
                can.parent = can.input.source
                no can.balance
            }
        }
    }
```

The constraints are now more detailed to ensure the balancing of shares, and the fields used to relate **securities** and **transactions** in a graph.

Transfer Constraints. Here, no new logic needs to be introduced, but we now use all three fields (`input`, `output`, and `balance`) if a partial transfer is performed.

```
fact {
    all xfer : Transfer {
        lt[xfer.shares, xfer.input.shares] implies {
            // In this case, the transaction is partial.
            xfer.input.use = xfer
            xfer.output.source = xfer
            xfer.balance.source = xfer
            eq[xfer.output.shares, xfer.shares]
            eq[xfer.balance.shares, sub[xfer.input.shares, xfer.shares]]
            lt[xfer.input, xfer.output]
            lt[xfer.input, xfer.balance]
            xfer.output.owner = xfer.to
            xfer.input.owner = xfer.from
            xfer.balance.owner = xfer.from
            xfer.from.portfolio = xfer.from.portfolio + xfer.balance
            xfer.to.portfolio = xfer.to.portfolio + xfer.output
            xfer.output.parent = xfer.input
            xfer.balance.parent = xfer.input
        } else {
            xfer.input.use = xfer
            xfer.output.source = xfer
            eq[xfer.output.shares, xfer.shares]
            eq[xfer.shares, xfer.input.shares]
            lt[xfer.input, xfer.output]
            xfer.output.owner = xfer.to
            xfer.input.owner = xfer.from
            xfer.to.portfolio = xfer.to.portfolio + xfer.output
            xfer.output.parent = xfer.input
            no xfer.balance
        }
    }
}
```

The required bookkeeping in a structural Alloy model can become complex. As we add more constraints to our model, we can rely on the Alloy Analyzer to ensure that it remains consistent.

3.4   Model Properties

The hypothesis for proving the properties of the system will be based on the ordering provided by the `ordering` module for **transactions** and **securities**. In the ordering, there is a consistent pattern for parents to always come before their children.

```
pred orderingOfSecurities {          pred orderingOfTransactions {
    all sec : Security {                 all tx : Transaction {
      some sec.parent implies {            some tx.parent implies {
        lt[sec.parent, sec]                  lt[tx.parent, tx]
      }                                    }
    }                                    }
}                                    }
```

Properties. The properties described in this section are the expected features that are required to provide consistency in cap tables during transaction updates, as previously defined in Sect. 3.2.

To support the main features of the model, a set of functions to query the number of shares in different contexts and also to trace the lineage of **securities** need to be defined.

```
fun lineage[sec : Security] :  set Security { sec.*(Security <: parent) }
fun depth[sec : Security] : Int { #lineage[sec] }
fun aliveSecurities : set Security { { sec : Security | no sec.use } }
fun deadSecurities : set Security { { sec : Security | some sec.use } }
fun issuedShares : Int { sum iss : Issuance | iss.shares }
fun cancelledShares : Int { sum can : Cancellation | can.shares}
fun transferredShares : Int { sum xfer : Transfer | xfer.shares }
fun aliveShares : Int { sum sec : aliveSecurities | sec.shares }
fun deadShares : Int { sum sec : deadSecurities | sec.shares }
```

The lineage of **securities** is defined using the * transitive closure operator, showing a succinct definition embedded in Alloy. This relationship has no possible equivalent in JSON Schema. The # operator returns the number of elements of a relationship. The other expressions are based on "set" comprehension expressions. Another group of functions supports accounting identities (related to the number of shares).

The first property of the model states that if the **securities** are ordered, then the graph of **securities** forms a forest. A forest is a collection of trees, which is a stronger condition than merely being a directed acyclic graph. Similarly, a property for **transactions** is defined. Requiring the graph to be a forest implies it is acyclic, as required by properties P3 and P4.

```
check { orderingOfSecurities => forest[~(Security <: parent)] }
check { orderingOfTransactions => forest[~(Transaction <: parent)] }
```

These properties cannot be modelled in JSON Schema, since we need to compare values in two different documents (in JSON Schema parlance). But they can be clearly expressed in Alloy.

The number of shares in circulation can only increase as new shares are issued, since cancellations always decrease the number of shares in circulation. Transfers have no effect on the number of shares in circulation, since they only change the ownership of the shares. We reflect this in the Alloy model by defining the `issuedShares`, `cancelledShares`, and `aliveShares` functions. The specification and implementation of the accounting identities is straightforward. It is also *critical*. Any design that can in principle violate these identities is an invalid design. Accounting checks satisfy properties P5 and P7.

```
cancelledSharesAlwaysLessThanIssued : check { lte[cancelledShares,
↪    issuedShares] }

nonNegativityOfIssuedShares : check { nonneg[issuedShares] }

nonNegativityOfCancelledShares : check { nonneg[cancelledShares] }

aliveLessThanIssued : check { lte[aliveShares, issuedShares] }
```

Another important property for all those financial systems regards investor portfolios: they must all be disjoint.

```
check {
    all o1, o2 : Stakeholder {
        some o1.portfolio & o2.portfolio implies o1 = o2
    }
}
```

Another property that we check is that all floating shares are owned. This property rules out the possibility that the system issues shares without assigning them to an owner. This sort of mistake can happen because companies have both the concept of an authorized quantity of shares and the number of shares that the company actually issued.

```
fun portfolioShares[stakeholder : Stakeholder] : Int {
    sum sec : stakeholder.portfolio |
            (sec in aliveSecurities implies sec.shares else 0)
}

fun portfolioSharesAll : Int {
    sum stakeholder : Stakeholder | portfolioShares[stakeholder]
}

check { eq[aliveShares, portfolioSharesAll] }
```

The following check shows that properties P1 and P2 hold. Why is that? The lineage contains every transaction that affected a security, but our predicate only requires that one of those transaction is an issuance. But since the check must pass for *each and every security*, it works inductively from instances of size 1 and up.

```
securityOriginIsIssuance : check {
    all s : Security | some i : Issuance | i in lineage[s]
}
```

4   An Example with a Long Chain of Transactions

In this example, we demonstrate the system's behavior when multiple transactions and securities interact. We utilize the Alloy Analyzer's feature to create a scenario with a chain of transactions at a depth of 3. This is achieved by defining a predicate that generates this specific instance, showcasing the capabilities of the tool.

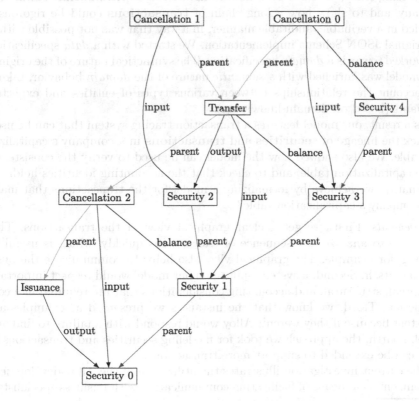

Fig. 2. A chain of **transactions** arising from a single issuance. Blue lines show the tree of securities, while orange lines show the tree of transactions.

```
run { some sec : Security | depth[sec] > 3 } for 5
```

The depth function is used to find the depth of a **security** in the graph of **securities**. The transitive closure operator ^ when applied to the **parent** relationship gives the lineage of any security, starting from an issuance. The depth is the size of the transitive closure of any security.

We reap the benefits of having a visualization from Alloy. Figure 2 shows the graph derived from the model. This is very useful for communicating the design to business people.

5   Conclusion

Alloy has been used in a wide range of applications in software engineering, database design, **security** analysis [4,5], multiagent negotiations [14]. It has also been applied to modeling beyond computer science, such as a model for central bank policy [8]. A model of the same-origin-policy used in web browsers can be found in the 500 Lines or Less open-source book [9]. There is a lack of existing models of **capitalization tables** in Alloy, as well as an absence of semantic models for this particular domain.

By using Alloy, we have been able to model the **capitalization table** of a company, and to show how a long chain of **transactions** could be rigorously modeled in a verifiable, auditable manner, in a way that was not possible within the original JSON Schema implementation. We started with a *data* specification and worked towards a *domain* specification. The syntactical nature of the original *data* model was enriched with a *semantic* nature of the *domain* behavior, taking into account the relationships between various types of entities and expected invariants (based on domain knowledge).

As a result, our model features a transaction tracing system that can be used to track the lineage of **securities** and **transactions** in a company's capitalization table. We also showed how the model can be used to verify the consistency of the capitalization table, and to check that the accounting identities hold.

What do we achieve by formalizing a model for the transactions that make up a company's capitalization table?

Achievements. First, we get a clear graphical view of the transactions. This allows one to analyze any sequence of transactions quickly, which is useful in auditing, for example. The graphical view also helps to communicate the business rules itself. Second, a system built upon our model would respect important conceptual, structural, and accounting considerations that are required in a correct design. Third, we know that the instances we presented as examples are consistent because if they weren't Alloy would respond with a failure to find any model. Fourth, the approach we took for modeling securities and transactions in Alloy can be extended to support more transactions.

The current investigation illustrates the utilization of the Alloy development environment as a means of facilitating communication with business specialists[1].

---

[1] The author holds a position in a private company and uses Alloy daily to sketch specifications.

Business professionals have the skills of comprehending Alloy models, although they may not always be able to compose them. This readability serves as a means to reconcile the disparity between technical modeling and comprehension within the commercial context.

Limitations. While Alloy offers numerous advantages for modeling and verification, it's important to also consider its limitations, especially when making an informed choice of tool for a specific problem domain.

Alloy's approach to problem-solving relies on bit blasting to transform problems into satisfiability (SAT) instances. This method inherently limits its support for integers. The intricacies of integer arithmetic can sometimes be lost or inadequately represented during this transformation. Another notable limitation is the performance of Alloy for larger scopes. As the instance size grows, the running times for checks increase significantly. These limitations, however, don't overshadow Alloy's strengths but provide a comprehensive understanding of where the tool excels and where it might require additional considerations.

The model we have developed also has inherent limitations. In our model, Alloy version 5 was used. Alloy has incorporated Electrum, an extension that encompasses linear temporal logic (LTL), starting from version 6. It is very likely that Linear Temporal Logic (LTL) can more effectively articulate our understanding of events and states, while also capturing a greater number of domain features. Furthermore, given the current framework, it is necessary to conduct all checks on the complete model synchronously. This phenomenon has an important impact on the overall performance. Implementing verification mechanisms on local components would result in improved productivity. Currently, a novel model incorporating these features is being developed.

Future Work. The comprehensive clarification of the semantic aspects of the principles we have formulated can be confirmed by examining legal documents. The model that is being offered is a first step toward a more thorough and expansive formalization of business contract laws. The purpose of this formalization is to make it easier to reason logically about the regulations and to make sure software systems accurately apply them. The aforementioned procedure holds substantial significance within the context of advancing secure smart contracts. The creation of a software tool that enables the production of legal contracts using pre-existing formal templates will effectively bridge the gap between software developers and lawyers responsible for preparing contracts for businesses.

Glossary

asset An asset is something that can eventually generate cashflows. Because not all future cashflows are known with certainty, the value of an asset must be discounted to reflect the risk that those cashflows do not meet expectations.

asset class An asset class is a group of securities that have similar characteristics. Stocks, bonds, and real estate are all asset classes.

capitalization table A capitalization table is a table that lists all the securities issued by a company. The capitalization table lists the number of shares issued, the type of security, the price per share, and the date of issuance. The capitalization table is used to calculate the ownership of each shareholder.

debt Debt is a loan that must be repaid. Companies might raise funds via equity issuances or debt issuances. Debt is issued as security in terms of the amount that was loaned, the interest rate, and the maturity date. Debt is safer than equity, and must be repaid before equity holders can receive any cashflows.

exercise Stock options are exercised and become stocks. The strike price is the price at which the stock options can be converted to equity. They can only be exercised after they have been vested.

issuance An issuance is the creation of a new security

security A security is a financial asset that can be bought and sold. Stocks, options and debt notes are all securities. Every security has an Issuer. A loan from a bank is not a security, because the bank can not generally sell the loan to another bank.

staged financing Staged financing is a financing strategy in which a company raises funds in stages. The first stage is typically called the seed round, with subsequent stages receiving a latin alphabet letter (such as Series A, Series B, etc.). Staged financing allows investors to reduce their risk by investing in stages, and allows the company to raise funds as it grows.

stakeholder A stakeholder is any person, legal or natural, with an economic interest in a company, including all debt, option and stock holders.

startup company A startup company is a new company that is searching for a business model as it grows. Startup companies are typically funded in stages and by specialized venture capital investors such as individual (angel) investors and funds. Startup companies usually aim for high growth and high returns, by choosing projects with higher risk.

transaction A transaction refers to the issuance, change, transfer and cancellation of securities. A transaction is typically initiated by a stakeholder, and must be approved by the company. Most transactions involve a cost, with money changing hands in the opposite direction of the securities.

venture capital Venture capital is a form of private equity financing that is provided by venture capital firms to startups and early-stage companies that have been deemed to have high growth potential or which have demonstrated high growth

References

1. Open Cap Table Coalition (OCT) – opencaptablecoalition.com. https://www.opencaptablecoalition.com/. Accessed 27 May 2023
2. Bray, T.: The JavaScript object notation (JSON) data interchange format. RFC 8259, IETF (2017). http://tools.ietf.org/rfc/rfc8259.txt
3. Caines, D.: Global venture capital investment shatters records. kpmg.com. https://kpmg.com/xx/en/home/media/press-releases/2022/01/global-venture-capital-annual-investment-shatters-records-following-another-healthy-quarter.html. Accessed 10 June 2023
4. Carpio, R., Alsmadi, I.: Websites security policies implementation using alloy analyzer. SSRN Electron. J. (2021). https://doi.org/10.2139/ssrn.3939856
5. Chen, C., Grisham, P., Khurshid, S., Perry, D.: Design and validation of a general security model with the alloy analyzer. In: First Alloy Workshop 2006, Portland, Oregon, USA (2006)
6. Evans, E.: Domain-Driven Design: Tackling Complexity in the Heart of Software. Addison-Wesley (2004)
7. Jackson, D.: Alloy: a lightweight object modelling notation. ACM Trans. Softw. Eng. Methodol. **11**(2), 256–290 (2002). https://doi.org/10.1145/505145.505149
8. Johnson, J., Alsmadi, I.: Formal modeling of banking policies using alloy analyzer. SSRN Electron. J. (2021). https://doi.org/10.2139/ssrn.3939880
9. Kang, E., Perez De Rosso, S., Jackson, D.: 500 lines or less - the same-origin policy. https://aosabook.org/en/500L/the-same-origin-policy.html. Accessed 23 May 2023
10. Lamport, L.: Specifying Systems: The TLA+ Language and Tools for Hardware and Software Engineers. Addison-Wesley Longman Publishing Co., Inc. (2002)
11. Merigoux, D., et al.: Catala. INRIA, ENS, OCamlPro, ENS, Lyon (2022). https://catala-lang.org/
12. Metrick, A.: Venture Capital and the Finance of Innovation, 3rd edn. John, Nashville (2021)
13. Peyton Jones, S., Eber, J.M., Seward, J.: Composing contracts: an adventure in financial engineering (functional pearl). In: Proceedings of the Fifth ACM SIGPLAN International Conference on Functional Programming, ICFP 2000, pp. 280–292. Association for Computing Machinery, New York (2000). https://doi.org/10.1145/351240.351267
14. Podorozhny, R., Khurshid, S., Perry, D., Zhang, X.: Verification of multi-agent negotiations using the alloy analyzer. In: Davies, J., Gibbons, J. (eds.) IFM 2007. LNCS, vol. 4591, pp. 501–517. Springer, Heidelberg (2007). https://doi.org/10.1007/978-3-540-73210-5_26
15. Wadler, P.: Programming language foundations in Agda. In: Massoni, T., Mousavi, M.R. (eds.) SBMF 2018. LNCS, vol. 11254, pp. 56–73. Springer, Cham (2018). https://doi.org/10.1007/978-3-030-03044-5_5

A Haskell-Embedded DSL for Secure Information-Flow

Cecilia Manzino[✉] and Gonzalo de Latorre

Departamento de Ciencias de la Computación, Universidad Nacional de Rosario,
Rosario, Argentina
ceciliam@fceia.unr.edu.ar

Abstract. This paper presents a domain specific language, embedded in Haskell (EDSL), for enforcing the information flow policy *Delimited Release*. To build this language we use Haskell extensions that will allow some kind of dependently-typed programming.

Considering the effort it takes to build a language from scratch, we decided to provide an information-flow security language as an EDSL, using the infrastructure of the host language to support it.

The decision of using Haskell as the implementation language is because it has a powerful type system that makes it possible to encode the security type systems of the embedded language at the type level and also because it is a general purpose language.

The implementation follows an approach where the type of the abstract syntax of the embedded language was decorated with security type information. This way, typed programs will correspond to secure programs, and the verification of the security invariants of programs will be reduced to type-checking.

The embedded security language is designed in a way that is easy to use. We illustrate its use through two examples: an electronic purchase and a secure reading of database information.

Keywords: dependently-typed programming · Haskell · information flow type systems · declassification

1 Introduction

Ensuring the confidentiality of information manipulated by computing systems has become of significant importance in recent years [2]. Traditional security mechanisms such as access control [1] or cryptography do not provide end-to-end protection of data. To complement these security mechanisms, techniques that examine information flows between inputs and outputs of systems have become a subject of study. In this context security polices arise for guaranteeing that confidential information cannot be released to public data. Non-interference [3] is an example of an information flow policy. A program satisfies this property when the final value of any public variable is not influenced by a variation of confidential inputs during its execution.

H. Barbosa and Y. Zohar (Eds.): SBMF 2023, LNCS 14414, pp. 20–35, 2024.
https://doi.org/10.1007/978-3-031-49342-3_2

A remarkable feature of this property is that it can be enforced statically by the definition of an information flow type system ([4,7]).

However, some realistic applications must allow intentional information release as part of its intended behavior and non-interference is very restrictive for this. To make security languages practical, mechanisms for declassifying or releasing information in a controlled manner have been studied ([6,8,11]).

The critical part of these mechanisms is to ensure that declassification is used safely.

An information flow policy, named *Delimited Release* was introduced by Sabelfeld and Myers [6] to guarantee that the intentional release of information, marked in programs under expressions *declassify*, cannot be used to infer more information than it should. They also define a type system that enforces this security property on typed programs.

The results about information flow security are mostly theoretical. Two languages based on information flow were implemented: Jif [5] (a variant of Java) and Flow Caml (based on Ocaml).

Other works investigate the way of expressing restrictions on information-flow providing control-flow primitives as a library, avoiding the work of producing a new language from scratch. In this line, Li and Zdancewic [12] implemented an embedded security sublanguage which provides a security property, in Haskell. Informally, the security property can be stated as: "code running at privilege l_p cannot observe information of label l if $(l \sqsubseteq l_p)$". Their implementation is based on arrows. Whereas Russo, Claessen and Hughes [10] provide information-flow security also as a library in Haskell but their implementation is based on monads. The intention of the authors is to show that the same goals can be achieved with monads instead of arrows.

In this work, we propose an EDSL in Haskell for providing information-flow security. To achieve our goal, we follow a different approach than the one used by the forementioned authors. Our implementation is based on the use of generalized algebraic data types (GADTs), for representing the terms of the embedded language together with the typing rules that guarantee the security property. Then, programs constructed with this data type are secure by-construction. Since the constructors of the GADT are a direct implementation of the typing rules, the type system must be syntax-directed. We give a syntax-directed formulation of the type system that guarantee Delimited Release to make this implementation possible.

The rest of the paper is organized as follows. Section 2 presents the syntax, semantic and security type system of the embedded language. Section 3 presents the implementation of the EDSL, while Sect. 4 gives some example programs that illustrate its use. Section 5 presents some related works. Section 6 concludes.

The complete Haskell code of the EDSL is available in a GitHub repository[1].

---

[1] https://github.com/ceciliamanzino/EDSL-DR-.

2   A Security Language

In this section we will describe the syntax, semantics and type system of the language implemented as an EDSL. The language is a standard while language extended with the construct *declassify* which declassifies the security level of an expression. The type system enforces a security property named *delimited release*. This security property together with type system that enforces it were defined in [6], here we present a syntax directed version of the type system.

2.1   Syntax

The expressions and statements of the language are defined by the following abstract syntax:

$$e ::= \text{val} \mid x \mid e_1 \text{ op } e_2 \mid \text{declassify}(e, l)$$
$$s ::= x{:=}e \mid \text{skip} \mid s_1; s_2 \mid \text{if } e \text{ then } s_1 \text{ else } s_2 \mid \text{while } e \text{ do } S$$

where $e \in$ **Exp** (expressions), $s \in$ **Stm** (statements), $x \in$ **Var** (variables), val $\in$ **Num** $\cup \{true, false\}$ (integer and boolean literals), $l \in \mathcal{L}$ (security lattice) and op ranges over arithmetic and boolean operations on expressions.

The semantics of this language is completely standard. The unique expression that is not standard is $\text{declassify}(e, l)$, which is used for declassifying the security level of the expression e to l. At the semantic level $\text{declassify}(e, l)$ is equivalent to e.

The meaning of expressions and statements is given relative to a memory $s \in M = \textbf{Var} \to \textbf{Num} \cup \{true, false\}$, which contains the current value of each variable. We assume that the semantics for expressions is given by an evaluation function denoted by $\langle M, e \rangle \Downarrow val$. For statements, we define a big-step semantics whose transition relation is written as $\langle M, s \rangle \Downarrow M'$, meaning that the evaluation of a statement s in an initial memory M terminates with a final memory M'.

2.2   Non-interference

We assume that each variable has associated a security level, which states the degree of confidentiality of the value it stores. A type environment $\Gamma : \textbf{Var} \to \mathcal{L}$ maps each variable to a security type, where $(\mathcal{L}, \sqsubseteq)$, is a bounded lattice of security levels with meet ($\sqcap$) and join ($\sqcup$) operations, and top ($\top$) and bottom ($\bot$) values. The bottom value represents the least security level (public data) whereas the top value represents the highest security level (private data).

Non-interference [3] is a security property that guarantees the absence of illicit information flows during execution of a program. A program satisfies this security property when final values of low level security variables are not influenced by a variation of the initial values of the high level security variables. This property can be formulated in terms of program semantics.

Two memories M_1 and M_2 are l-equivalent, written $M_1 \approx_l M_2$, when they coincide in the variables with lower security level than l. While, two program configurations $\langle M_1, s_1 \rangle$ and $\langle M_2, s_2 \rangle$ are indistinguishable at level l, written $\langle M_1, s_1 \rangle \approx_l \langle M_2, s_2 \rangle$, if whenever $\langle M_1, s_1 \rangle \Downarrow M_1'$ and $\langle M_2, s_2 \rangle \Downarrow M_2'$ for some M_1' and M_2' we have that $M_1' \approx_l M_2'$. Two expression configurations $\langle M_1, e_1 \rangle$ and $\langle M_2, e_2 \rangle$ are indistinguishable, written $\langle M_1, e_1 \rangle \approx \langle M_2, e_2 \rangle$, if $\langle M_1, e_1 \rangle \Downarrow val$ and $\langle M_2, e_2 \rangle \Downarrow val$ for some val.

Now, the security property can be formalized as follows:

Definition 1. *(Non-interference) A statement s satisfies non-interference if, for all level l, we have:*

$$\forall M_1 \; M_2 \,.\, M_1 \approx_l M_2 \Rightarrow \langle M_1, s \rangle \approx_l \langle M_2, s \rangle$$

A positive feature of non-interference is that it can be enforced statically by the definition of an information-flow type system ([4,7]). But its use in some computing systems could be too restrictive. For example, if we consider a password checking program, on every attempt to login there is a release of information about the user's password, or if we want to send encrypted secret information to a public place there is also an information leakage.

Even though it is necessary to relax the notion of non-interference and have mechanisms that are able to release information in a controlled manner, questions about how to prevent attacks arise. For example, an attacker could take advantage of these mechanisms for releasing data to extract more information than intended.

Sabelfeld and Myers [6] introduce a new security property, named *Delimited Release* that guarantees that the realease of information (marked in programs via expressions `declassify`) cannot be used to construct attacks. They also presented a security type system that enforces this property.

2.3   Delimited Release

The intention behind this property, is to express that only explicitly declassified information is released and no other information. More specifically, the property establishes that a program is secure if updates to variables that are latter declassified, occur in a manner that an attacker cannot use them to infer more information than the data that has already been released by declassification.

The security property is formalized as follows:

Definition 2. *(Delimited Release) Suppose the statement s contains within it exactly n declassify expressions* `declassify`$(e_1, l_1) \ldots,$ `declassify`(e_n, l_n). *Statement s is secure if for all security levels l we have:*

$$\forall M_1, M_2.(M_1 \approx_l M_2 \wedge \forall i \in \{i \mid l_i \sqsubseteq l\}.\langle M_1, e_i \rangle \approx \langle M_2, e_i \rangle) \Rightarrow \langle M_1, s \rangle \approx_l \langle M_2, s \rangle$$

EXPRESSIONS

$$\Gamma \vdash val \; : \; l, \varnothing \qquad \text{(VAL)} \qquad \frac{\Gamma \vdash e_1 \; : \; l_1, D_1 \qquad \Gamma \vdash e_2 \; : \; l_2, D_2}{\Gamma \vdash e_1 \; op \; e_2 \; : \; l_1 \sqcup l_2, D_1 \cup D_2} \text{(OP)}$$

$$\Gamma \vdash v \; : \; \Gamma(v), \varnothing \qquad \text{(VAR)} \qquad \frac{\Gamma \vdash e \; : \; l, D}{\Gamma \vdash \texttt{declassify}(e, l_1) \; : \; l_1, Vars(e)}$$
$$\text{(DEC)}$$

STATEMENTS

$$\Gamma, pc \vdash \texttt{skip} \; : \; \varnothing, \varnothing \qquad \text{(SKIP)} \qquad \frac{\Gamma \vdash e \; : \; l, D \quad l \sqcup pc \sqsubseteq \Gamma(x)}{\Gamma, pc \vdash x := e \; : \; \{x\}, D} \text{(ASS)}$$

$$\frac{\Gamma, pc_1 \vdash s_1 \; : \; U_1, D_1 \qquad \Gamma, pc_2 \vdash s_2 \; : \; U_2, D_2 \qquad U_1 \cap D_2 = \varnothing}{\Gamma, pc_1 \sqcap pc_2 \vdash s_1; s_2 \; : \; U_1 \cup U_2, D_1 \cup D_2} \text{(SEQ)}$$

$$\frac{\Gamma \vdash e \; : \; l, D \qquad \Gamma, pc_1 \vdash s_1 \; : \; U_1, D_1 \qquad \Gamma, pc_2 \vdash s_2 \; : \; U_2, D_2 \qquad l \sqsubseteq pc_1 \sqcap pc_2}{\Gamma, pc_1 \sqcap pc_2 \vdash \texttt{if } e \texttt{ then } s_1 \texttt{ else } s_2 \; : \; U_1 \cup U_2, D \cup D_1 \cup D_2} \text{(IF)}$$

$$\frac{\Gamma \vdash e \; : \; l, D \qquad \Gamma, pc \vdash s \; : \; U, D_1 \qquad l \sqsubseteq pc \qquad U \cap (D \cup D_1) = \varnothing}{\Gamma, pc \vdash \texttt{while } e \texttt{ do } s \; : \; U, D \cup D_1} \text{(WHILE)}$$

Fig. 1. Syntax-directed Security Type System For Delimited Release.

2.4 Security Type System for Delimited Release

This section presents a type system that enforces Delimited Release. This version of the type system is based on the one given in [6] with the characteristic of being syntax-directed. The typing rules are shown in Fig. 1.

In this system, the typing judgement for expressions has the form $\Gamma \vdash e \; : \; l, D$, meaning that the expression e is typed in the security environment Γ, has security level l and effect D. The type system collects the variables that are declassified in e, in set D. Typing judgement for statements has the form $\Gamma, pc \vdash s \; : \; U, D$ which means that statement s is typable in a program counter pc, under security environment Γ and effects U and D. The program counter is the lower level of the variables assigned in s. The type system collects the variables that are declassified in s in the effect D and the updated variables in U.

The goal of the typing rules is to prevent improper information flows during program execution and to control the information that is declassified.

If a program doesn't contain the expression `declassify` and is typed in the security type system for Delimited Release, then it satisfies non-interference [3].

2.5   Safe Programs Examples

This section will show two short examples, that are common in the literature and that have already been introduced in [6]. These simple programs will help us understand the security property. In the next section we will implement these examples in our EDSL in Haskell.

Example 1. (Average salary)

Consider a simple program to calculate the average salary of n employees.

Suppose that variables $h_1, \ldots, h_n$ store the salaries of the employees. We can store the result of the average of these private variables in a public variable named avg by declassifying the information of this result but not other information (like the salary of one employee):

$$avg := \mathtt{declassify}((h_1 + \cdots + h_n)/n, low)$$

If we consider a lattice of two levels $\mathcal{L} = \{low, high\}$, where $\bot = low$ and $\top = high$ and an environment Γ, such $\Gamma(h_i) = high$ for $i \in \{1, \ldots, n\}$, and $\Gamma(avg) = low$ we can easily check that the program is typable in the type system for Delimited Release.

Now, we consider a malicious use of this program for leaking information of variable h_1 to avg:

$h_2 := h_1;$

$\ldots$

$h_n := h_1;$

$avg := \mathtt{declassify}((h_1 + \cdots + h_n)/n, low)$

This program is rejected by the type system, since the variables $h_2, \ldots, h_n$ which are under declassification in the last line were updated before.

Example 2. (Electronic wallet)

In this example we have a scenario where if a customer has enough money in their electronic wallet then a purchase is carried out.

Suppose that a private variable h stores the amount of money in a customer's wallet, a public variable l stores the amount of money spent in the session and a public variable k stores the cost of the purchase. The following code checks if $h \geq k$, for modifying the values of the variables l and h:

$$\mathtt{if}\ \mathtt{declassify}(h \geq k, low)\ \mathtt{then}\ (h := h - k; l := l + k)\ \mathtt{else}\ \mathtt{skip}$$

This program doesn't satisfy the non-interference property, since an assignment of the public variable l occurs under a high condition, but it is typable with type system for Delimited Release.

Now, we show a program that uses this code for leaking bit-by-bit the value of the secret variable k to l:

$l := 0;$
while $(n \geq 0)$
    $k := 2^{(n-1)};$
    if declassify$(h \geq k, low)$
    then $(h := h - k; l := l + k)$
    else skip;
    $n := n - 1$

This program is rejected by the type system for Delimited Release.

3 Implementation

In this section we will present the implementation of our EDSL.

In the following we will accompany the implementation of the embedded language together with concepts introduced by some Haskell extensions, like *promoted data types* [13], *singleton types* [14], *type families* [9] and GADTs. These extensions will enable us to program in Haskell in a similar way as we will do in a dependently typed language.

3.1 Security Types and Variables

For simplicity we consider just two security levels, but the implementation can be easily generalized to a lattice of security levels ordered by their degree of confidentiality. In such generalization we can use Haskell's type class mechanism for defining security lattices.

The security types *low* and *high* are represented by the following definition:

```
data SType = Low | High
```

This defines datatype SType with two values (or constructors): Low and High. In a dependently typed language, we could use the values Low and High in a GADT definition, but in Haskell, we must lift them to the type level. With the extension *promoted datatypes*, we can use them one level up. So we can use the type SType as a kind and the values High and Low as types. To distinguish the types from the values we must use a quote.

Then, the types 'Low and 'High have kind SType and there are only two types of kind SType.

However, later we will need a copy of these types as value level, so we will use a *singleton type* definition of SType.

```
data SeType (s :: SType) where
    L :: SeType 'Low
    H :: SeType 'High
```

The idea of *singleton types* is that we can use pattern matching on values to know at run time the type of the value, since each type in the definition has exactly one value of that type.

For example, the values Low and High have the same type SType, but L and H (which represent the same values as Low and High) have different types SeType 'Low and SeType 'High, respectively.

In this implementation, we will use both definitions to represent security levels. In a dependently typed language, such as Agda, we need just one definition.

The order of the security types is given by the following non-method class with instances:

```
class LEq (a :: SType) (b :: SType)
instance LEq 'Low x
instance LEq 'High 'High
```

Haskell's type system will choose the appropriate instance for a pair of types st and st' that satisfies st ≤ st'. If we see each instance of this class as a pair of a relation, we can observe that these pairs form an order relation. This implementation can be generalized to a lattice of security levels by defining a class with methods for meet and join operations, the order relation (≤), and the bottom and top values.

In the same way we define natural numbers as types:

```
data Nat = Zero | Succ Nat
```

```
data SNat (n :: Nat) where
    SZero :: SNat 'Zero
    SSucc :: SNat n  →  SNat ('Succ n)
```

For example,

```
two :: SNat ('Succ ('Succ 'Zero))
two = SSucc (SSucc SZero)
```

Similarly we can define any natural number, and all of them will have different types.

We will use natural numbers to represent variables of the language and lists of pairs of security types together with naturals to represent type environments.

A *type family* is essentially a function on types or it can also be seen as parametric types. They provide a functional style for programming at type-level in Haskell.

For looking up the security type associated to a variable in a given environment we will use the *type family* Lookup:

```
type family Lookup (env :: [(k,st)]) (n :: k) :: a where
    Lookup ('(n, st) ': env) n = st
    Lookup ('(m, st) ': env) n = Lookup env n
```

The first line introduce the signature of the type family. The word family distinguishes this definition from a standard type definition.

In this definition we use the constructor for pairs promoted to type '(,) and the constructor for list ': which is also promoted.

3.2 The Language

Generalized algebraic data types (GADTs) are a generalization of ordinary algebraic data types. This generalization is over the return type of the constructors for the data type, that must be an application of the data type being defined, as in any data type definition, but this application can be on an arbitrary type. This feature make GADTs useful for expressing invariants at the type level.

As example, consider the following GADT definition for terms of a small language for arithmetic and boolean expresions:

```
data Term a where
    T       :: Term Bool
    F       :: Term Bool
    Lit     :: Int  →  Term Int
    Add     :: Term Int  →  Term Int  →  Term Int
    IsZero  :: Term Int  →  Term Bool
    If      :: Term Bool  →  Term a  →  Term a  →  Term a
```

We use GADTs for representing expresions and terms of the security language.

The encoding is such that, the judgement $env \vdash e \ : \ st, d$ in our formal type system corresponds to the typing judgement e :: Exp env st d d' in Haskell. The parameter d' doesn't have its correspondence in the type system since it was added in the implementation for collecting the occurrences of variables in the expression. Each constructor of the GADT encode a typing rule.

```
data Exp :: [(Nat, SType)]  →  SType  →  [Nat]  →  [Nat]  →  * where
    Var :: SNat (n :: Nat)  →  Exp env (Lookup env n) '[] '[n]
    IntLit :: Int  →  Exp env 'Low '[] '[]
    BoolLit :: Bool  →  Exp env 'Low '[] '[]
    Ope :: Op  →
            Exp env st d var1  →
            Exp env st' d' var2  →
            Exp env (Join st st') (Union d d') (Union var1 var2)
    Declassify :: Exp env l' d vars  →
                    SeType l  →
                    Exp env l vars vars
```

the type Op represents integer and boolean operations for expresions:

```
data Op = Plus | Minus | Mult | Div | Exp | Mod | And | Or | Gt |
            GtE | Lt | LtE | Eq | Not Eq
```

The datatype Exp is parametrized by the type environment (which is of kind [(Nat , SType)]), the security type of the expression (of kind SType), the list of variables that were used under declassification and the list of variables used in the expression (both of kind [Nat]).

In the encoding, the maximum between two security types is computed by a type family Join and the append of two list is computed by a type family Union. Both definitions are available in the github repository.

To model statements we define the following GADT that is parametrized by the type environment, the program counter (represented as a security type) and two lists that represents the set of variables that were updated and the set of variables that were used under declassification.

Now the typing judgement $env, pc \vdash stm : u, d$ in our formal type system corresponds to the typing judgement `e :: Exp env st d d'` in Haskell. Each constructor of the data type definition corresponds to a rule of the type system shown in Fig. 1. This representation is possible because the type system is syntax-directed.

Since the type `Stm env pc u d` encodes the security typing rules, it is only possible to write terms that corresponds to secure programs.

```
data Stm :: [(Nat, SType)] → SType → [Nat] → [Nat] →  *  where
    Skip :: Stm env 'High '[] '[]

    Ass :: LEq st (Lookup env n) ⇒
           SNat (n :: Nat) →
           Exp env st d var →
           Stm env (Lookup env n) '[n] d

    Seq :: Intersection u1 d2 ~ '[] ⇒
           Stm env pc u1 d1   ›
           Stm env pc' u2 d2 →
           Stm env (Meet pc pc')(Union u1 u2)(Union d1 d2)

    If :: LEq st (Meet pc pc') ⇒
          Exp env st d vars →
          Stm env pc u1 d1 →
          Stm env pc' u2 d2 →
          Stm env (Meet pc pc')(Union u1 u2)(Union d(Union d1 d2))

    While :: (Intersection u1 (Union d d1) ~ '[], LEq st pc) ⇒
             Exp env st d vars →
             Stm env pc u1 d1 →
             Stm env pc u1 (Union d d1)
```

The minimum between two security types is computed by the type family `Meet`, while the intersection of two sets is computed by the type family `Intersection`.

In the constructors `While` and `Seq` we use type equality constraints of the form a ~ b in their type context, which means that types a and b must be the same. The restriction $U \cap (D \cup D_1) = \varnothing$ in the WHILE rule of the type system corresponds to the constraints `(Intersection u1 (Union d d1) ~ '[]` in the constructor `While`, and the restriction $U_1 \cap D_2 = \varnothing$ of SEQ rule corresponds to the constraint `Intersection u1 d2 ~ '[]`. These restrictions are necessary to ensure that variables that are used under declassification may not be updated before being declassified.

Some rules of the type system have restrictions of the form $l \leq l'$. In these cases these restrictions correspond to a constraint of the form LEq 1 1' in the implementation, and are used in order to prevent improper information flows.

3.3 Constructors

Programming directly with the constructors of the GADT can be cumbersome, so we define the constructors of our EDSL using the definition of Stm.

In order to construct programs with these constructors, we need to provide a form to construct an environment of security variables. Then, we need type-level lists of types of kind (Nat , SType). We represent environments with the following definition:

```
data HList :: [(Nat , SType)]  →  * where
    Nil :: HList '[]
    ( :-: ) :: (SNat n , SeType s)  →
             HList xs  →
             HList ('(n , s) ': xs)
```

We use this data type to have a copy of the environment at value level.

For example, we define an environment with three variables, variable zero has security level Low and variables one and two have security level High.

```
zero = SZero
one = SSucc zero
two = SSucc one

env = (zero, L) :-: (one, H) :-: (two, H) :-: Nil
```

The constructor var is used to declare a variable in a given context. The first argument is the type environment that will be used throughout the program, while the second is a natural number associated to the variable. The expression is only typable if the natural number belongs to the environment:

```
var :: HList env  →
       SNat (n :: Nat)  →
       Exp env (Lookup env n) '[] (n ': '[])
var en n = Var n
```

As example we define a low variable l that belongs to environment env:

```
l = var env zero
```

The constructors int and bool are used for literal integer and boolean values:

```
int :: Int  →  Exp env 'Low '[] '[]
int = IntLit

bool :: Bool  →  Exp env 'Low '[] '[]
bool = BoolLit
```

For example, the expressions int 3 and bool True represents the values 3 and True respectively.

The constructor for writing assignments is the following:

```
(=:) n exp = Ass n exp
```

Now, we can write a program which assigns the value 3 to the public variable zero:

```
Program1 = zero =: int 3
```

The other constructors of the language are defined as follows:

```
skip = Skip

iff s e1 e2 = If s e1 e2

while s e1 = While s e1

declassify :: Exp Env l' d vars →
              SeType l →
              Exp Env l vars vars
declassify e l = Declassify e l

(>>>) :: (Intersection u1 d2 ~ '[]) ⇒
         Stm Env pc u1 d1 →
         Stm Env pc' u2 d2 →
         Stm Env (Meet pc pc') (Union u1 u2) (Union d1 d2)
(>>>) s1 s2  = Seq s1 s2
```

To make programs look more concise, the list of operations was simplified:

```
plus    = Ope Plus
minus   = Ope Minus
mult    = Ope Mult
gt      = Ope Gt
gte     = Ope GtE
lt      = Ope Lt
lte     = Ope LtE
eq      = Ope Eq
neq     = Ope Not Eq
(/.)    = Ope Div
(&.)    = Ope And
(|.)    = Ope Or
```

4 Implementation of Examples

In this section we illustrate the practicality of the EDSL through the examples presented in Sect. 2.5. A larger example that implements a secure program for password checking can be found in the repository.

Example 3. Average salary

For writing this program we need an environment with four variables, 3 of them must be high since they will be used for storing the salaries of 3 employees, and the other must be low since it will store the average of the salaries.

```
env = (zero, L) :-: (one, H) :-: (two, H) :-: (three, H) :-: Nil
```

Then we can write the example as follows:

```
h1 = var env one
h2 = var env two
h3 = var env three
avgSalaries = zero =: declassify ((h1  +.  h2  +.  h3)
                                  /.  int 3) L
```

Now, if we try to define a program in our EDSL that is considered a laundering attack (since leaks information about the salary of one employee to the variable zero) as follows:

```
avgAttack = one =: h2   >>>
            three =: h2 >>>
            avgSalaries
```

we found that the program is rejected by Haskell's type system.

Example 4. Electronic wallet

To write this example we define an environment with three variables, the secret variable will be used to store the amount of money of the customer's electronic wallet, and the public variable will store the amount of money spent by the customer and the cost of the purchase.

```
env = (zero, H) :-: (one, L) :-: (two, L) :-: Nil
```

The secure program is written as follows:

```
h = var env zero
l = var env one
k = var env two
walletSecure = iff  (declassify (h >.  k) L)
                    (zero =: h  -.  k >>> one =: l  +.  k)
                    skip
```

While, the following attack is rejected by ghc:

```
walletAttack = one =: int 0 >>>
              (while (n  >.  int 0)
                     (two =: int 2 ^. n  -.  int 1) >>>
                     (iff (declassify (h  ≥ . k) L)
                          (zero =: h  -.  k >>> one =: l  +.  k)
                          skip ) >>>
                     three =: n  -.  int 1 )
```

This program leaks information bit-by-bit of the private variable h to l. It is rejected since the variable h (zero) that occurs under declassification is updated in the body of the loop.

5   Related Work

Security-typed programming languages have been studied in the last years to guarantee that confidential information cannot be released to public data. Jif [5] is a secure language that extends Java with support for information flow control and access control. While Flowcaml is a prototype implementation of an information flow analyzer for OCaml.

Rather than producing a new language, Li and Zdancewic [12] presented a library for information-flow security programming in Haskell based on arrows combinators and type classes. They use arrows for providing an interface that support programming constructs like sequential compositions, conditionals and loops. The library provides some information-flow control mechanisms likes dynamic security lattices and declassification.

Russo, Claessen and Hughes [10] showed that the same goals can be achieved using monads instead of arrows, which is a less general notion and most used by Haskell programmers. The monadic library guarantees that well-typed programs are non-interferent and also allows to specify declassification polices, which are enforced dynamically at run-time. These polices can be expressed using different combinators related to what, when, and by whom information is released.

Even if the arrow notation was eliminated in this library we found that the declassification combinators for generating escape hatches for downgrading information are difficult to use.

In this paper we provide information-flow security as a sublanguage in Haskell. A difference from the works mentioned above is that in this work the sublanguage provided is an imperative language, while in the others, information flow control is applied to programs of the host language. The approach we follow to achieve this is also different, in this work we attach security type information to the datatypes representing the abstract syntax of the sublanguage in such a way that we only deal with well-typed terms. To make it we use some extensions of Haskell that gives us the possibility to perform some kind of type-level programming.

6   Conclusion and Future Work

We presented an EDSL in Haskell for writting applications that require to enforce a security property that guarantee confidentiality of the information.

In the implementation we follow an approach for representing the security language using GADT to represent terms, where each constructor of the GADT is a direct implementation of a typing rule. This encoding guarantees that we can only write terms that corresponds to secure programs and the verification of that reduce to type checking.

Although type-level programming in Haskell is a bit tedious, we were able to encode the typing rules in the term's type of the embedded language in a not so difficult way. The user of the EDSL does not have to program at type-level, using the constructors provided, the implementation of the given examples could be written easily. We conclude that the EDSL is suitable for writing applications where the confidentiality of information must be required.

The decision of using Haskell instead of a dependently programming language like Adga or Idris is because Haskell is a general purpose language, and the user of the EDSL will not have to program at type-level for writing applications.

As future work we plan to add a constructor to the language for adding variables to the environment. We started working in this direction by defining a constructor:

```
newVar :: HList env →              --  actual environment
          SNat (n :: Nat) →        --  new variable
          SeType (st :: SType) →   --  security level
          Stm ('( n , st ) ': env) 'High '[] '[]
newVar en n st = Skip
```

This constructor changes the information about the security environment at type level. To use it we must find a way to have an unfixed environment in some of the constructors of the datatype Stm, like Seq.

Another future work is to address the formalization of other security policies. The property *delimited release* can capture *what* information is released, other security properties capture *who* releases information, *where* in the system information is released, and *when* information can be released [11]. The security property *robust declassification* [8], is a good candidate since it is orthogonal to *delimited release* (in the sence that control *when* information is declassified) and can be combining with this.

References

1. Lampson, B. W.: Protection. In: Proceedings of the 5th Princeton Conference on Information Sciences and Systems, Princeton (1971). Reprinted in ACM Operating Systems Review, vol. 8, no. 1, pp 18–24 (1974)
2. Denning, D.E.: A lattice model of secure information flow. ACM **19**(5), 236–243 (1976)

3. Goguen, J.A., Meseguer, J.: Security policies and security models. In: Proceedings of the IEEE Symposium on Security and Privacy, pp. 11–20 (1982)
4. Volpano, D., Smith, G.: A type-based approach to program security. In: Bidoit, M., Dauchet, M. (eds.) CAAP 1997. LNCS, vol. 1214, pp. 607–621. Springer, Heidelberg (1997). https://doi.org/10.1007/BFb0030629
5. Myers, A.C., Zheng, I., Zdancewic, S., Chong, S., Nystrom, N.: Jif: java information flow. Software release (2001). http://www.cs.cornell.edu/jif
6. Sabelfeld, A., Myers, A.C.: A model for delimited information release. In: Futatsugi, K., Mizoguchi, F., Yonezaki, N. (eds.) ISSS 2003. LNCS, vol. 3233, pp. 174–191. Springer, Heidelberg (2004). https://doi.org/10.1007/978-3-540-37621-7_9
7. Sabelfeld, A., Myers, A.C.: Language-based information-flow security. IEEE J. Select. Areas Commun. 21(1), 5–19 (2003)
8. Myers, A.C., Sabelfeld, A., Zdancewic, S.: Enforcing robust declassification. In: Proceedings of the IEEE Computer Security Foundations Workshop (2004)
9. Chakravarty, M.M., Keller, G., Jones, S.P., Marlow, S.: Associated types with class. In: POPL (2005)
10. Russo, A., Claessen, K., Hughes, J.: A library for light-weight information-flow security in Haskell. ACM Sigplan Not. 44(2), 13–24 (2008)
11. Sabelfeld, A., Sands, D.: Declassification: dimensions and principles. J. Comput. Secur. 17, 517–548 (2009)
12. Li, P., Zdancewic, S.: Arrows for secure information flow. TCS 411, 1974–1994 (2010)
13. Yorgey, B.A., Weirich, S., Cretin, J., Peyton Jones, S., Vytiniotis, D., Magalhães, J.P.: Giving Haskell a promotion. In: TLDI (2012)
14. Eisenberg, R.A., Weirich, S.: Dependently typed programming with singletons. ACM SIGPLAN Not. 47(12), 117–130 (2012)
15. Löh, A.: Applying type-level and generic programming in Haskell (2015)
16. Manzino, C., Pardo, A.: Agda formalization of a security-preserving translation from flow-sensitive to flow-insensitive security types. Electron. Notes Theoret. Comput. Sci. 351, 75–94 (2020)
17. De Latorre, G.: EDSL en Haskell para la programación segura respecto a la propiedad Delimited Release. Final year project. National University of Rosario, Argentina (2022)

CSP Specification and Verification of a Relay-Based Railway Interlocking System

P. E. R. Bezerra[1]([✉]), M.V.M. Oliveira[1]([✉]), Thierry Lecomte[2]([✉]),
and D.I. de Almeida Pereira[2]([✉]) [iD]

[1] DIMAp - Universidade Federal do Rio Grande do Norte, Natal, RN, Brazil
`paulo.rolim.074@ufrn.edu.br`, `marcel@dimap.ufrn.br`
[2] CLEARSY, Aix-en-Provence, France
`{thierry.lecomte,dalay.almeida}@clearsy.com`

Abstract. In previous work, we have presented a methodology for the specification and verification of relay-based Railway Interlocking Systems (RIS) based on their transient states. By using CSP as formal support, it is possible to use a model checker in order to analyse the safety of such critical systems as a way to improve their safety. However, this type of verification tends to consume a lot of computational resources, which hinders the use of this methodology for industrial systems. This work presents a proposal for a new methodology for the specification of RIS. In this work we rebuild the whole model by changing the notion of components, integrating them in the core of the model while keeping their interface visible to the end-user. In this context, it is possible to maintain the concepts of instantiating and combining components at the same time we reduce the number of components and states as a way to alleviate the time spent on model checking. Besides, we propose a new methodology of verification based on the decomposition of the model. Our new proposed approach supports the analysis of a bigger set of properties of these systems, like the analysis of the Ringbell Effect, short circuits, deadlocks, divergences, and components that cannot be activated at the same time. In order to evaluate our approach, a new industrial case study is modelled and analysed.

Keywords: CSP · Model-Checking · Railway Interlocking Systems

1 Introduction

A Railway Interlocking System (RIS) is a vital part of a railway signalling system that is responsible for detecting and controlling track-side equipment in a safe manner. Even though computer-controlled RISs are available [11], relay-based

M.V.M. Oliveira—This work is partially supported by INES (National Institute of Software Engineering), CNPq grant 465614/2014-0, CAPES grant 88887.136410/2017-00, and FACEPE grants APQ-0399-1.03/17 and PRONEX APQ/0388-1.03/14.

H. Barbosa and Y. Zohar (Eds.): SBMF 2023, LNCS 14414, pp. 36–54, 2024.
https://doi.org/10.1007/978-3-031-49342-3_3

RIS are still used in the majority of the installations [28]. It can be argued that this choice is a result of the historical success of this technology as well as its lower complexity and clear definition of fault modes [19]. Due to the potential dangers associated with the failure of these systems, they are classified as safety-critical systems. Thus, RISs must be safety-proved before their implementation and use; "Railway accident reports from recent incidents suggest that current signalling systems have design defects due to the commonly employed architecture" [31], highlights the need for formally proving the application logic correctness [10].

There is a strong recommendation in railway norms that formal methods should be utilised when developing railway systems [9]. These methods offer rigorous mathematical foundations for formal analysis and proofs. In this context, logical verification can be used to analyse the system safety based on unique combinations of electrical component states for every input configuration [3], hence, it is important that the system always reaches a stable state. However, transient states during system stabilisation pose potential safety concerns. The states between the input and the reaction of the components must be considered in order to truly guarantee the safety of the system. Besides, some specific electric circuit configurations can prevent the system from achieving a stable state, which impedes logical verification as the system is no longer considered reliable.

One example of such a configuration is the Ringbell Effect [4], where two relays activate and deactivate each other in a permanent cycle of events for a specific set of inputs. The continuous relay activation and deactivation cycle can lead to overheating and premature failure. This compromises system reliability and invalidates logical analysis, as stable states are not achieved. Considering intermediate states is crucial for ensuring safety and reliability in RISs.

Traditionally, relay-based RISs are verified by manual inspection, which is insufficient in a critical situation [13]. Some works in the literature have presented methodologies for the formal specification and verification of electrical circuits. In general, these studies are based on a logical analysis of the relationships between the electrical component states, allowing analysis of the outputs based on the inputs of the system [1,2,12,15,30]. It is therefore imperative that the system is reliable, i.e., every input set will result in a unique combination of electrical component states, during the execution of the system. To analyse transient states and cyclic behaviours, new modelling approaches are required for relay-based RISs verification. Process-based specification and verification using CSP enable the specification of component behaviours based on sequential events, facilitating the analysis of system transient states. An automated process-based verification has the potential to prevent safety, reliability, and implementation issues in RISs.

This work presents a new formal modelling approach for relay-based RISs using the process algebra CSP [14], since it has a strong support for the specification of the behaviour of components as well as their instantiation and composition. Besides, its support for concurrency specification and model-checking is essential in our project. All these benefits were successfully used in our previous works [5,18]. The models detailed in this work are based on the models presented in [4], where we discuss a first approach for using CSP to specify RISs. In this work, this idea is completely rebuilt in order to alleviate the analysis of the models by the model checker by integrating the components in the core of the model while keeping their interface visible to the end-user. In this context, the whole specification has been improved in order to support a more efficient analysis. Besides, new assertions are used in order to provide a more complete analysis of the system and a new verification approach based on the decomposition of the model is used, decreasing the time spent on verification. The evaluation of the model is made based on a new industrial case study.

The remainder of this paper is organised as follows. Section 2 focuses on the theoretical reference of this work, presenting some important information about relay-based Railway Interlocking Systems and CSP. Section 3 discusses related work and then our approach for the formal specification and analysis of RISs using CSP is detailed in Sect. 4. Our proposed verification strategy and the evaluation of our modelling approach are presented in Sects. 5 and 6, respectively. Section 7 presents an optimization designed to handle larger systems. Section 8 is then devoted to some conclusions and perspectives.

2 Theoretical Reference

2.1 Relay-Based RISs

Relay-based RISs are the implementation of the interlocking system logic using electrical circuits [27]. Signals and turnouts are controlled based on how electrical components respond to their electrification caused by the system's inputs. In these systems, the electrical current flux is controlled by relays, which are electromagnetic components composed of an electromagnet coil and a movable armature containing electrical contacts. When electrified, the relay coil produces a magnetic field that attracts the armature, changing the position of the contacts, which open or close circuits according to their initial positions.

Relay diagrams are generally used by railway infrastructure managers for describing the relay-based RIS. These models detail the system's physical structure, modelling the electrical connection between the components. A small example of a diagram is depicted in Fig. 1. Table 1 presents how some components used in relay-based RISs are depicted in relay diagrams. More details about these components are presented in [7] and in Sect. 4.

Table 1. Electrical Components of Relay-Based Diagrams.

⊟ ●╱●	Monostable relay and contat, respectively.
—●— +●—	Energy sources.
├ ●∥● ●⊥●	A junction, a capacitor and a button, respectively.
5s 15s	Blocks for timed activation and deactivation, respectively.

In the example depicted in Fig. 1, we consider that the electric energy flow departs from the positive energy sources P1 and P2, and arrives at the negative energy sources N1 and N2. Thereby it is possible to observe how a button (B1) can cause the electrification of another component (R2) when pressed down. Besides, one may also observe how components (relays, in this example) can be electrified based on the states of other components (contacts and buttons). The relays R1 and R2 control the positions of the contacts C1 and C2, respectively. When electrified, the relays raise the contacts, closing (C2) or opening (C1) them.

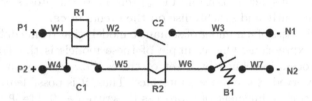

Fig. 1. The Ringbell Effect Example.

A Ringbell Effect occurs when two components activate and deactivate each other indefinitely in an infinite cycle of events. In Fig. 1, for instance, R2 closes C2 when activated, which activates R1. As a consequence, R1 opens C1, deactivating R2. The cycle begins again when C2 opens, deactivating R1 and closing C1. This is a dangerous behaviour as the constant movement of the contacts may cause the system to overheat and break.

Each company uses a different format of relay diagram with different information [1]. This work focuses on the models used by SNCF (Société Nationale des Chemins de fer Français), the French National Railway Company. More details about the French relay-based RISs modelling and implementation can be found in [20]. In the SNCF models, the behavioural safety properties differ from model to model and they are generally related to the way components be electrified together [1]. Thus, each electrical circuit model has specific safety properties that the system must meet and which were defined during model conception.

Nonetheless, the analysis of these systems regarding safety is generally made by manual inspection of the relay diagrams, which is not satisfactory in such a critical context. In order to analyse these systems, formal methods may be used.

2.2 Communicating Sequential Processes

The CSP language has a rich syntax that allows us to make a well-detailed specification of the RIS behaviour. The most basic constructors are processes and channels. For instance, one of the most basic processes is *STOP*, which represents a system break or a deadlock. Channels can have specific types, like integer, boolean, or even a set of proper definitions, called datatype. Processes can communicate through channels and this communication may have a value.

Processes are defined using the events that constitute them. An event is an atomic single action that a process may engage in. Every event consists of a communication channel and the information that it can transmit. In CSP, the declaration of a channel c is made by: "`channel c: T1.T2...Tn`", where c indicates the name of the channel and T1, T2, and Tn are the channel types.

Given an event a in the interface of a process P, the prefixing a -> P is initially able to perform a, after which it will behave like P. CSP also provides notations to describe different paths of behaviour. The external choice P [] Q initially offers the initial events of both processes, P and Q. The environment makes the choice of synchronisation.In P [| cs |] Q, the processes P and Q are executed concurrently and synchronise on the events in cs.

CSP also disposes of a number of semantic models that define different meanings for CSP expressions. One example of these models is the Traces Model, where each process is defined by a set of traces, i.e., the sequences of events that can be observed at the process interface. Thus, it is possible to infer that a process P is a trace refinement of a process Q (written as Q [T= P) if, and only if, every trace of P is a trace of Q.

CSP disposes of many tools that facilitate its use. For instance, the model checker FDR4 [29] is a tool that allows users to verify properties of the processes written in CSP based on the existing semantic models.

FDR4 uses an ASCII version of CSP as input: CSP_M [22]. More details about FDR and the CSP syntax and semantics can be found in [21,23].

In order to make verifications in FDR4, the user must write assertions about the processes and their properties. Then, the tool explores every possible behaviour of the process in order to check if the assertion is true. If the tool finds a counter-example to the assertion, it indicates the invalidity of the assertion and provides the counter-example. For instance, one may verify that a process P is deadlock-free using the assertion `assert P :[deadlock free]`.

3   Related Work

The literature contains many examples of methodologies for the formal specification and analysis of RISs, like [6,8,10,17,25]. However, despite the importance of analysing relay-based RISs, the literature regarding the formal specification of such systems is still scarce. This section presents some of the most important works in this field and how they compare with our work. Nonetheless, for a more complete literature review, a more curious reader may consult one of our previous publications: [1–4,7].

Although formal methodologies are the focus of this work, there are some informal models of interlocking systems that are worth citing. In [25,33] component-based models and graphs are used to represent the connection between components. This strategy is also used in our work. Nonetheless, formal specification and verification are still essential in such a safety-critical context. Regarding formal methodologies, the works presented in [1,2,12,26,30,32] use a more logical state-based approach to specify and analyse RISs. However, as transient states are not considered, they lack some important analysis of the properties of these systems.

The works that are closer to our proposal are the ones presented in [32] and [8]. While the former uses CSP for the RIS specification and analysis, the latter uses an approach that considers transient states. The work presented in [32] provides an important discussion about the use of CSP in this context and proposes some solutions to reduce the number of states when model-checking the systems. Nonetheless, its approach is based on control tables, which are at a different abstraction level compared to our relay-based modelling. Similarly, in [8], the model is at another abstraction level, focusing on the electrical properties of the system, requiring information like voltage and amperage, which are generally presented in the Italian relay diagrams. Our work focuses on the interlocking logic, ignoring the electrical properties of the system.

4 CSP Specification of Relay-Based RISs

When modelling a relay-based RIS, it is necessary to take into account the system structure and behaviour. The former defines how the electrical components are physically connected by wires. The latter defines the rules for the components electrification based on the system structure and on each component-specific behaviour. A system structure is essential for determining the behaviour of the system in this context, as each type of electrical component behaves in an invariable manner regardless of its position within the system. This formalisation of relay-based RISs is grounded on the relay-diagrams provided by SNCF and the concepts about their functioning as described in [1,20,24].

Our specification is divided into four parts: the "general.csp" script is where all the functions responsible for the behaviour of each component are located; the "problem.csp" script is where the components are listed, instantiated and composed to build the system to be modelled; the "functions.csp" script contains some auxiliary functions essential for the behavioural specification; and finally, the "assertions.csp" script lists the assertions defined to verify safety and reliability of the installed system in addition to standard "FRD4" assertions that verify the existence of deadlock, livelock and nondeterminism. The auxiliary functions and other details are not discussed in this paper due to space limitations. Nonetheless, the complete specification is provided elsewhere[1].

4.1 The Model Interface

Although the way we formalise the system behaviour has been completely transformed compared to its last version [4], the interface of the model remains almost the same. In the file "problem.csp", one may list the components that are used in the model and compose them in order to describe the system structure. As the behaviour of each component is invariable, the end-user of our model may only

---

[1] https://www.dimap.ufrn.br/~marcel/research/RIS/SBMF2023.

concern with describing the system structure. Nonetheless, the system behaviour remains transparent and available in the "general.csp" file for the more curious users. This latter part of the specification is detailed in the next section.

The components used in a case study may then be listed inside a datatype following the format: `datatype IDS = C1_id | C2_id |...| Cn_id`, listing all the components `Cx_id` used in the system. Then, one must group these components inside separate sets. For instance, inside the set of positive energy sources, one may add the components `P1_id` and `P2_id`: `POSITIVE_IDS = P1_id, P2_id`. As part of modelling the system structure, one must also model the relation between the components as presented in the relay diagram. In this context, the connection between components is defined in a function `CONNECTIONS` that relates pairs of components that are connected by wires; and other relations are defined by simple functions supported by CSP_M, as presented below.

```
CONNECTIONS = { {P1_id,R1_id},{R1_id,C2_id},
                {C2_id,C2_ENDPOINT_id},{C2_ENDPOINT_id,N1_id} }
RELAY_OF(C2_ENDPOINT_id) = R2_id
```

In this example that represents part of diagram in Fig. 1, the components `P1_id`, `R1_id`, `C2_id` and `N1_id` are connected by wires according to the couples presented inside the `CONNECTIONS` function, and then the contact `C2_id` is related to the relay `R2_id` according to the simple function `RELAY_OF`. This strategy is also used to define other information like the blocks connections, the activation and deactivation time, the contacts connections at each position and other important structural information presented inside the relay diagrams.

Another important information presented in the "problem.csp" file is the initial state of the system. For instance, the variable `INITIAL_OPEN_COMPONENTS` defines a set of component ("ids") whose initial states represent disconnections in the system. The behavioural specification utilises this set to determine the initial state of the system. As the other control functions are executed, this set is dynamically updated at each new intermediate system state. Its initial instantiation is depicted below, that represents the initial state of Fig. 1:

```
INITIAL_OPEN_COMPONENTS = {B1_id, C2_ENDPOINT_id}
```

Other structural functions and sets defined in this part of the specification and used in the model are discussed in the next section, which presents the behaviour of the system based on its structure. For a complete list of the required structural information, we advise consulting the provided commented case study specification, which is discussed later in this paper.

4.2   The Path Master Process

In a previous version of this model, each component had a separate behaviour that could be composed to form the complete system. In this new version, every component behaviour is integrated into a unique process: the `PATH_MASTER`. This process is the most important part of our specification, through it, we may monitor the system connections and keep track of the paths of electrified components.

The information described in the "problem.csp" is used in the PATH_MASTER as the basis for the description of the system behaviour. As a common CSP strategy, the PATH_MASTER process calls the auxiliary process PATH_MASTER_AUX with a list of constant inputs. These inputs are, in this context, the initial state of the system as defined by the user in the system interface in the form of sets: INITIAL_OPEN_COMPONENTS, INITIAL_POSITIVES, INITIAL_NEGATIVES, CAPACITOR_IDS, INITIAL_CHARGES, TIME_DEACTIVATION_SETTING and TIME_ACTIVATION_SETTING. These sets contain the components that are initially open, the positive and the negative energy sources, the "id" of capacitors, their charges and the deactivation and activation settings of blocks, respectively.

```
PATH_MASTER = PATH_MASTER_AUX(INITIAL_OPEN_COMPONENTS, INITIAL_POSITIVES,
                 INITIAL_NEGATIVES, CAPACITOR_IDS, INITIAL_CHARGES,
                 TIME_DEACTIVATION_SETTING, TIME_ACTIVATION_SETTING)
```

As the core of the specification, the PATH_MASTER has the role of controlling the system execution by allowing the components states to evolve. In this context, this process contains a choice between updating the system inputs or evolving the time or the states of the components. Based on this choice, the PATH_MASTER executes sub-processes and functions responsible for the execution of the system behaviour. As a recursive process, after executing the chosen events, the process calls itself with the parameters updated. For instance, in order to update the system inputs, the PATH_MASTER_AUX calls the INPUTS() process, which has the function of receiving all inputs from the environment and updating each input component state. Then this process calls PATH_MASTER_AUX again with the list of open components updated.

A button is one example of input, it may close and open a connection. In the INPUTS() process, a channel press communicates with the environment through the event press?id?ns, receiving a button id and its status ns. Then, this process calls the function update_buttons(open_components, id, ns) with the set of open components, the button and its state as parameters in order to update the set of open components. This function is presented below.

```
update_buttons(open_components, b_id, b_status) =
  if not(b_status) then union(open_components, {b_id})
  else diff(open_components, {b_id})
```

The behaviour of the other electrical components, however, is related to receiving energy from a wire and then sending it through another wire. A monostable relay, for instance, connected to the left and right wires, may receive energy from one of these wires and then pass it to the other. The monostable relay activation impacts their related contact states as its magnetic coil may change their positions. In this context, it is important to constantly check if the monostable relay is electrified or not. Evolving the relays and their respective contacts is one of the choices available in the PATH_MASTER process.

The function is_relay_active() identifies whether a relay id is electrified by searching whether there is a valid path between id to one of the members of the sets POSITIVES_IDS or NEGATIVES_IDS.

In this context, a path is electrified if it connects two energy sources with different poles. This function returns true if this path exists and false otherwise.

In our model, the function update_contacts is responsible for updating the list of open components every time a relay state is updated. A contact identified by an id is connected to neighbouring components on the left and right, and can allow or prevent the flow of electrical energy when its respective ENDPOINT is inserted or removed from the set OPEN_COMPONENTS. The synchronisation of its behaviour is due to the fact that the set OPEN_COMPONENTS is one of the parameters of the recursive PATH_MASTER process. In this context, the list of open components is updated in the process recursive call.

Electrical components physically require some time to reach their operating states. Thus the system safety check must be safeguarded by the specific time period for the exchange of signals on a luminous panel. In this context, one may use more complex structures in order to control the electricity flow in a timely manner: blocks. A block represents a complex structure that allows delaying the other components activation or deactivation. In this context, a block may be represented as a box with a thicker line on the top or bottom, for delaying the components activation and deactivation, respectively.

A block have five or six connections: two direct connections to the energy sources, two dependent connections and one or two independent connections. A block is activated when its independent connections are connected one to another, or when one of its independent connections is connected to an energy source. An activated block may provide energy to its dependent connections according to its timed behaviour: a timed activation block provides energy after a certain time of its activation, while a timed deactivation block provides energy right after its activation. However, this latter block remains providing energy after a certain time when it is no longer activated.

In this context, the EVOLVE_TIME() process in our approach has the function of uniformly synchronising the passage of time for components that need a certain period to be activated or deactivated. It is responsible for updating the state of every timed component at once. This process is invoked right after PATH_MASTER performs a tick event (that represents time passage) and it receives a list of components with timed behaviour as a parameter. Then, it updates the state of these timed components at the same time, providing a time synchronisation between all these components. For that, the EVOLVE_TIME() process updates the list of energy sources (as these components may also provide energy) and the time spent on each component state.

In addition to blocks, the other timed component is the capacitor. This component is special as it may charge when it is connected to the energy sources for a certain time and, once charged, it may provide energy to the system for another certain time. A capacitor has a dual timed behaviour and may act as an energy source. The state of this component is also updated in the EVOLVE_TIME()

process by updating the list of energy sources, the charges assumed by each side of the capacitor (positive or negative) and the time spent in the components states.

The last components that may be described are the outputs. The channel output_status executes the events related to outputs behaviour. Outputs are activated once they are electrified and deactivated when they are no longer electrified. Following the same logic applied to the other components, the function is_output_active() checks at all times whether the output is electrified, and if the hypothesis is confirmed it returns true, otherwise it returns false.

By using the model presented in this section, one may analyse many different properties of these systems. The next section is devoted to detailing some of these verifications. Nonetheless, in order to guarantee the correct definition of the system structure and behaviour, we embedded a short circuit analysis into the model. When there is a path between a positive and a negative energy source without any other component that consumes power, the system may overheat and break. So, we created an event short_circuit that is executed every time this configuration exists. Then, it is possible to create an assertion based on traces refinement to verify if this event is executed:

```
assert RUN(ALPHA_PATH_MASTER) [T= SYSTEM
```

The alphabet of a system without a short circuit is represented in ALPHA_PATH_MASTER. The FDR4 special function RUN() offers all the alphabet elements of PATH_MASTER recursively with the exception of the short_circuit event. However, when the system performs an event that is not part of this alphabet, the assertion fails because, in order to achieve the refinement in traces, the analysed processes need to be equivalent in the events performed.

5   Verification of Relay-Based RISs

It is important to note that, in the context of safety-critical systems, any unstable configuration can cause unwanted behaviour, or even, overheating and hardware failure due to the constant movements of the contacts, for example. The system safety proof presented by logical models can be invalidated if the system contains unstable states as the instability prevents the system to reach a reliable state (one single set of responses for a set of inputs). Thus, the verification of relay-based RISs regarding the Ringbell Effect is important in order to guarantee the system structural integrity, safety, availability, and reliability. We also specified other assertions to analyse some important safety properties of these systems. Besides, it is also possible to analyse the RISs regarding some standard properties of concurrent systems. For instance, it is possible to analyse their deadlock and livelock freedom as well as their determinism:

```
SYSTEM = PATH_MASTER
assert SYSTEM:[deadlock free]
assert SYSTEM:[divergence free]
assert SYSTEM:[deterministic[FD]]
```

These verifications are important to guarantee the system reliability and availability. The analysis proposed in this work can be extended. A more experienced user may define new assertions according to his needs.

5.1   Contacts Status Verification

The verification of safety of relay-based RISs is generally related to guaranteeing the absence of certain combinations of component states. For instance, one must logically prove that two green signals will never be activated at the same time in order to avoid two trains occupying the same track portion.

In CSP, we compose the original system with a monitor process, which monitors the states of the desired contacts related to the relays. When these components reach a certain combination of states, the monitoring process executes an **error** event, which is a special event that is not part of the alphabet of the original system. Then, using CSP's traces refinement, it is possible to verify if the modelled system combined with the monitor process will execute this **error** event. In a case where this event is detected, the refinement fails.

The monitor of contacts status receives as input a map of endpoints that must be tested. Each of these endpoints is associated with a Boolean value and the test consists of checking whether the state represented in this map can be reached in the instantiated system. For instance, it is possible to verify if, in the example enclosed in Fig. 1, the contacts "C1" and "C2" may be activated at the same time by using the following assertion:

```
assert STOP [T= SYSTEM_CONTACTS_STATUS((|C1_ENDPOINT_id => true,
                              C2_ENDPOINT_id => true|))
```

5.2   Ringbell Effect Verification

The CSP specification supports capturing system states that are not considered by related works. The Ringbell Effect seen in Fig. 1, for instance, a logical verification would consider that the precondition for the activation of R1 is that R2 is activated, which, in turn, requires R1 to be deactivated. A logical verification cannot detect this problem as the precondition for a component activation cannot be its own deactivation, so this state is generally not valid. Nevertheless, this is a dangerous configuration of a relay-based system, as one relay may activate and deactivate each other successfully, making the system overheat and break.

The analysis of the existence of such cycles of events can be made by examining if a component ever reaches a stable state given a set of inputs. In this context, it is possible to specify a monitor (MONITORED_SYSTEM_UNSTABLE_CONTACT) that produces another special event, switch, every time the monitored component state changes. Using this information, it is possible to identify the potential for this component to continue indefinitely unstable using the following assertion:

```
assert not MONITORED_SYSTEM_UNSTABLE_CONTACT(C1_ENDPOINT_id,
                              (| B1_id => true |))
    [T= RUN({switch})
```

Using the FDR4 trace refinement assertion to analyse the example presented in Fig. 1, for instance, it is possible to check if the endpoint of the contact C1, C1_ENDPOINT_id, stabilises when the button B1 is continuously pressed (set to true) in the monitored system. If this process refines the continuous execution of the switch event, it is possible to conclude that it does not stabilise. Thus, the negation at the beginning of the assertion makes it to return true if the refinement does not occur, indicating the absence of the Ringbell Effect.

5.3   Concomitant Active Lights Verification

In the context of safety-critical systems, any unstable configuration can potentially lead to undesirable outcomes. For instance, it is imperative to guarantee that the simultaneous activation of two light signals will never occur, as it could result in confusion and compromise the comprehension of crucial commands, such as a stop command.

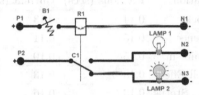

Fig. 2. Verification of Active Lamps Problem.

In the problem depicted in Fig. 2, only one light may be activated at each position of the relay contact. The verification consists of a parallel composition of the system to be checked with a monitor process SYSTEM_LAMPS_STATUS(), which monitors the states of the selected lamps. When these components reach a certain combination of states sent as a function parameter, the monitoring process executes an error event, which is a special event that is not part of the alphabet of the original system.

By employing CSP's traces refinement, it is possible to verify if the modelled system combined with the monitoring process executes the error event. In a case where this event is detected, the refinement fails, indicating that the system is not safe. The monitor of lamp status takes a map of lamp IDs as input, and each output lamp is associated with a Boolean value (l_status). The test involves verifying whether the state represented in this map can be reached in the instantiated System.

For instance, it is possible to verify if, in the example enclosed in Fig. 2, the lamps "LAMP 1" and "LAMP 2" may be activated at the same time, using the following assertion:

```
assert STOP [T= SYSTEM_LAMPS_STATUS( (| LAMP_1_id => true,
                                         LAMP_2_id => true|),
                         {B1_id, C1_ENDPOINT_UP_id})
```

The first parameter of the assertion is the map containing the combination of states whose existence is desired to be verified, and the second parameter is the set of open components. The logic behind this verification is to check if dangerous or undesirable combinations of lamps (associated with a specific combination of open components) occur in the instantiated system.

5.4   Runtime Measurements

Comparing the previous [4] version of the specification and the current version presented in this work, we noticed a subtle difference in the execution time of each assertion. Therefore, the time spent on each assertion was measured three times and the average was calculated and organised in Table 2.

Table 2. Runtime metrics comparison of diagram in Fig. 1.

Verification	Previous (secs)	Current (secs)
Deadlock	0.14	0.13
Divergence	0.15	0.11
Determinism	0.15	0.10
Ringbell Effect	0.13	0.13
Contact Status	0.13	0.16
Short Circuits	0.14	0.11

The verifications were performed using a Powershell in a computer with CPU AMD Ryzen 5600 six core and twelve threads, clock base 3.5 GHz cache L3 32mb, 16 GB RAM DDR4 3200 MHz (2 × 8 GB), and storage 1 × 1Tb NVMe SSD. As the previous version of our model could only handle small examples, the results presented in this paper demonstrate a considerable improvement.

6   Case Study

In order to evaluate our model, an industrial case study is used: an adaptation of a railway traffic light, as depicted in Fig. 3. The adaptation consisted in removing alternating current electrical circuits and AC/DC transformers. The diagram presented in this work is a simplified version of a scheme used by the SNCF, the French National Railway Company. A similar version of this diagram has already been published in an industrial work presented in [16]. In this section, we explain the case study as well as the functioning of a railway traffic light as detailed in [20].

In France, light signaling may by used in the railway context. In the signal panels, a green light (VL) indicates that normal traffic is allowed, in the absence of any restrictive signs. The red light (S) indicates "path closed".

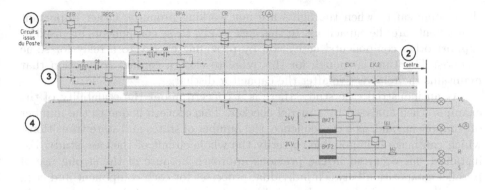

Fig. 3. Example of Luminous Panel used by SNCF.

A yellow light (A) sends an alert message, through which the train operator is alerted to stop before the next announced stop sign. A pair of yellow lights (R) indicates a speed limit of the respective part of the tracks, recommending a maximum speed equal to 30 km/h. In order to control a traffic light, an electrical circuit is used according to a relay-based logic. Our case study is an example of how a set of components receive the system inputs and work together in order to control a traffic light in a safe manner. In a relay diagram, the system inputs are generally represented as a sequence of lines containing relays. The electrification of these wires is controlled by a control panel or another system. The relays depicted in these lines control the position of contacts in our model.

To understand the behaviour of our case study model, it is possible to analyse the preconditions for each light to be activated (Fig. 3). The lights VL and A, for instance, are activated when they are connected to a positive energy source and the independent connection of a block (BKF1). Regarding VL, the precondition for its activation is that the relays RPCS, RPA, CR and C(A) are electrified so the contacts between this light and its energy sources are all closed. Similarly, the activation of A is also controlled by the states of RPCS and RPA, however, in this case, the activation of this light occurs when the former is electrified while the latter is not. This is an interesting behaviour as it indicates that VL (the green light) and A (the yellow light) are never activated at the same time. In this context, in order to guarantee that two lights will not be activated at the same time, some components states allow one light to be on while blocking the activation of other lights. For instance, RPA guarantees that A and R will never be activated at the same time and CR guarantees that same behaviour for VL and R. To conclude the lights studied in our case study, the light S (red) is activated when the relay RPCS is not electrified, being the only light that activates when RPCS is not electrified.

Furthermore, there are other components whose behaviours must be taken into consideration. The blocks BKF1 and BKF2 are responsible for delaying the deactivation of the relays EX1 and EX2. These relays are responsible for activating an emergency light when the blocks lose energy for a long time, guaranteeing the system safety when the lights are not working properly. Other important components are the capacitors. In this case study, these components are used to support other components' activation by providing energy to a relay for some seconds. This time is enough for this relay to close a contact connection that maintains the relay active after the capacitor discharge.

As an industrial case study, there is a concern about the scalability of the example when analysed by a model checker. This concern is due to the number of components and, as a consequence, the number of states and state transitions, which can make it impossible to verify the whole circuit of the case study. For instance, this occurred in the previous approach because of the strong use of parallel composition between individual processes for each component and each wire. Likewise, it also became impossible to model the flow of electrical current in both directions, a factor that prevented the specification of capacitors' behaviour. In order to diminish this problem, an optimisation strategy was implemented to enable the checking of larger diagrams: a trade-off was performed regarding the compositionality of the provided semantics versus the analysis effort, keeping parallelism only at the verification level.

7   Optimisation

In this work, we take advantage of the component-based nature of the system in order to provide faster verification. The strategy consists of verifying different parts of the specification separately instead of analysing the whole system at once. As the time spent on model checking such relay-based RISs grows exponentially as we add more components into the model, this proposed solution has the potential of reducing the time spent on verification as we reduce the number of components used in each analysis.

Given the circumstances, it is important to consider that this strategy is viable for our model as each component can be treated as an input or output of the system, allowing the communication/composition between different diagrams. For instance, as we divide a relay diagram, we may separate a relay from its related contacts. Nonetheless, the link between these components does not disappear. The relay can now be considered as an output in its sub-diagram, while its related contact can be treated as an input.

In our case study, we divide the model according to the four different circuits, of Fig. 3, that it contains: (1) the system inputs; (2) the circuit containing the first capacitor; (3) the circuit containing the second capacitor; and (4) the circuit containing the blocks and lamps. Then, we were able to perform the deadlock-freedom, divergence-freedom, deterministic and short circuit verification, as well as the Ringbell Effect Verification, the Contacts Status Verification and the Active Lights Verification in order to guarantee the stability of the model and certain configurations of components states are not achieved (red and green lights on at the same time, for instance).

The Ringbell Effect Verification of each part of the diagram is done in two steps. In the first step, for each part (1 to 4), we consider all possible statuses of relays of other sub-diagrams (external relays) that have influence in the sub-diagram under analysis. If the verification fails, we have the possibility of a contact in the sub-diagram under analysis not reaching a stable state. In these cases, we proceed to a second step of verification, considering the statuses of the external relays under which the verification failed. The intention of the second step of the verification is to confirm that this combination of statuses of the external relays is possible in the whole diagram. If this is the case, the Ringbell Effect is confirmed; otherwise, the Ringbell Effect found in the partitioned model is a false positive because the combination of statuses of the external relays that caused the problem is unachievable.

The verification of the sub-diagrams (1), (2), (3) and (4) took, on average, 63.57 s, 4.43 s, 4.40 s and 564.09 s, respectively. The runtime of all assertions in each sub-diagram was measured three times. The measurement was made in the same computational environment described in Sect. 5.4.

It is important to highlight that this optimisation methodology works for the case study because three fractions of the system behave as input and one of them behaves as output. There is no cycle of dependency where one part of the system is fully functioning only according to the output of another part of the circuit. In addition, it is necessary to develop a different approach to perform deadlock, livelock and determinism analysis as a problem regarding these properties may still arise when the model fragments are composed. We aim to address this problem in future work.

8   Conclusion

This work proposes a formal methodology using CSP for analysing relay-based Railway Interlocking Systems. CSP allows analysis of system state transition and transient states between input and reaction, crucial for electrical RIS analysis. In our approach, the behaviour of each component is invariable. This allows easy system modelling through component instantiation and composition, simplifying the process without compromising transparency for end-users.

The system specification is based on a single process for the system state evolution, using sub-processes and functions for each component. The work proposes assertions to analyse properties like deadlock-freedom, Ringbell Effect, and safety issues. The model allows further verification with user-defined assertions.

Our model is evaluated using an industrial case study: a signal control logic example. The details of the study and proposed specification are presented. An analysis optimisation methodology is discussed, leveraging the component-based division of the model into smaller parts for efficiency in the model checker. The model is validated based on the specification of several different examples[2], modelling all possible components. These examples were all analysed through model checking and animations.

---

[2] https://www.dimap.ufrn.br/~marcel/research/RIS/SBMF2023.

Future work includes extending the model for alternate current use, accommodating special components like lamp bulbs. This requires modelling new energy sources, block adaptation, and adding components. Sequencing system inputs and outputs aims to reduce state count and analysis time for systems with numerous components. Additionally, we aim at providing a tool that automates the generation of the model, integrates with the FDR4 API to accomplish the model verification and returns to the end-user the results on a friendly interface. Such transparency fosters the use of the approach as end-users will need no knowledge on Formal Methods (CSP).

References

1. de Almeida Pereira, D.I.: Analysis and formal specification of relay-based railway interlocking systems. Ph.D. thesis, Centrale Lille Institut (2020)
2. de Almeida Pereira, D.I., Debbech, S., Perin, M., Bon, P., Collart-Dutilleul, S.: Formal specification of environmental aspects of a railway interlocking system based on a conceptual model. In: International Conference on Conceptual Modeling. pp. 338–351. Springer (2019)
3. de Almeida Pereira, D.I., Deharbe, D., Perin, M., Bon, P.: B-specification of relay-based railway interlocking systems based on the propositional logic of the system state evolution. In: International Conference on Reliability, Safety, and Security of Railway Systems. pp. 242–258. Springer (2019)
4. de Almeida Pereira, D.I., Oliveira, M.V.M., Bezerra, P.E.R., Bon, P., Collart-Dutilleul, S.: Csp specification and verification of relay-based railway interlocking systems. In: Proceedings of the 37th ACM/SIGAPP Symposium on Applied Computing. pp. 97–106 (2022)
5. de Almeida Pereira, D.I., Oliveira, M.V.M., Conserva Filho, M.S., Da Rocha Silva, S.R.: Bts: A tool for formal component-based development. In: International Conference on Integrated Formal Methods. pp. 211–226. Springer (2017)
6. Amendola, A., et al.: NORMA: a tool for the analysis of relay-based railway interlocking systems. In: TACAS 2022. LNCS, vol. 13243, pp. 125–142. Springer, Cham (2022). https://doi.org/10.1007/978-3-030-99524-9_7
7. Bezerra, P.E.R.: CSP Specification and Verification of a Relay-Based Rail Interlocking System. Master's thesis, Universidade Federal do Rio Grande do Norte (2023)
8. Cavada, R., Cimatti, A., Mover, S., Sessa, M., Cadavero, G., Scaglione, G.: Analysis of relay interlocking systems via smt-based model checking of switched multi-domain kirchhoff networks. In: 2018 Formal Methods in Computer Aided Design (FMCAD). pp. 1–9. IEEE (2018)
9. Cenelec, E.: 50128-railway applications-communication, signalling and processing systems-software for railway control and protection systems. Book EN 50128 (2012)
10. Ghosh, S., Das, A., Basak, N., Dasgupta, P., Katiyar, A.: Formal methods for validation and test point prioritization in railway signaling logic. IEEE Trans. Intell. Transp. Syst. **18**(3), 678–689 (2016)
11. Hansen, K.M.: Formalising railway interlocking systems. In: Nordic Seminar on Dependable Computing Systems. pp. 83–94. Citeseer (1998)

12. Haxthausen, A.E., Kjær, A.A., Le Bliguet, M.: Formal development of a tool for automated modelling and verification of relay interlocking systems. In: FM 2011: Formal Methods: 17th International Symposium on Formal Methods, Limerick, Ireland, June 20–24, 2011. Proceedings 17. pp. 118–132. Springer (2011)

13. Haxthausen, A.E., Le Bliguet, M., Kjær, A.A.: Modelling and verification of relay interlocking systems. In: Monterey Workshop. pp. 141–153. Springer (2008)

14. Hoare, C.A.R.: Communicating sequential processes. Commun. ACM **21**(8), 666–677 (1978)

15. James, P., et al.: Verification of solid state interlocking programs. In: Counsell, S., Núñez, M. (eds.) SEFM 2013. LNCS, vol. 8368, pp. 253–268. Springer, Cham (2014). https://doi.org/10.1007/978-3-319-05032-4_19

16. Lecomte, T., et al.: Low cost high integrity platform. arXiv preprint: arXiv:2005.07191 (2020)

17. Mirabadi, A., Yazdi, M.: Automatic generation and verification of railway interlocking control tables using fsm and nusmv. Transport Problems **4**, 103–110 (2009)

18. Oliveira, M.V.M., Sampaio, A.C.A., Antonino, P.R.G., Ramos, R.T., Cavancalti, A.L.C., Woodcock, J.C.P.: Compositional Analysis and Design of CML Models. Tech. Rep. D24.1, COMPASS Deliverable (2013), http://www.compass-research.eu/

19. Pasquale, T., Rosaria, E., Pietro, M., Antonio, O., Ferroviario, A.S.: Hazard analysis of complex distributed railway systems. In: 22nd International Symposium on Reliable Distributed Systems, 2003. Proceedings. pp. 283–292. IEEE (2003)

20. Rétiveau, R.: La signalisation ferroviaire. Presse de l'école nationale des Ponts et Chaussées (1987)

21. Roscoe, A.W.: Understanding concurrent systems. Springer Science & Business Media (2010)

22. Scattergood, B., Armstrong, P.: Cspm: A reference manual. Tech, Rep (2011)

23. Schneider, S.: Concurrent and Real Time Systems: the CSP approach, vol. 1. Wiley-Interscience (1999)

24. Schon, W., Larraufie, G., Moens, G., Pore, J.: Railway signalling and automation volume 3 (2014)

25. She, X., Sha, Y., Chen, Q., Yang, J.: The application of graphic theory on railway yard interlocking control system. In: 2007 IEEE Intelligent Vehicles Symposium. pp. 883–887. IEEE (2007)

26. Sun, P., Collart-Dutilleul, S., Bon, P.: A model pattern of railway interlocking system by petri nets. In: 2015 International Conference on Models and Technologies for Intelligent Transportation Systems (MT-ITS). pp. 442–449. IEEE (2015)

27. Theeg, G.: Railway signalling & interlocking international compendium. PMC Media House GmbH, BingenHamburg (2017)

28. Theeg, G., Vlasenko, S.: Railway signalling & interlocking. In: International Compendium, vol. 448. Eurail-press Publ Hamburg (2009)

29. Thomas Gibson-Robinson, Philip Armstrong, A.R.: Failures Divergences Refinement (FDR) Version 3 (2013), https://www.cs.ox.ac.uk/projects/fdr/

30. Van Eijk, P.: Verifying relay circuits using state machines. Logic Group Preprint Series 173 (1997)

31. Wang, J., Wang, J., Roberts, C., Chen, L.: Parallel monitoring for the next generation of train control systems. IEEE Trans. Intell. Transp. Syst. **16**(1), 330–338 (2014)

32. Winter, K.: Model checking railway interlocking systems. Australian Computer Science Communications **24**(1), 303–310 (2002)
33. Xiangxian, C., Yulin, H., et al.: A component-based topology model for railway interlocking systems. Mathematics and Computers in Simulation **81**(9), 1892–1900 (2011)

ULKB Logic: A HOL-Based Framework for Reasoning over Knowledge Graphs

Guilherme Lima[1]([⊠]), Alexandre Rademaker[1,2], and Rosario Uceda-Sosa[3]

[1] IBM Research Brazil, Rio de Janeiro, Brazil
guilherme.lima@ibm.com, alexrad@br.ibm.com
[2] Getulio Vargas Foundation, School of Applied Mathematics, Rio de Janeiro, Brazil
[3] IBM TJ Watson Research Center, Yorktown Heights, NY, USA
rosariou@us.ibm.com

Abstract. ULKB Logic is an open-source framework written in Python for reasoning over knowledge graphs. It provides an interactive theorem prover-like environment equipped with a higher-order language similar to the one used by HOL Light. The main goal of ULKB Logic is to ease the construction of applications that combine state-of-the-art computational logic tools with the knowledge available in knowledge graphs, such as Wikidata. To this end, the framework provides APIs for fetching statements from SPARQL endpoints and operating over the constructed theories using automated theorem provers and SMT solvers (such as the E prover and Z3). In this paper, we describe the design and implementation of ULKB Logic, its interfaces for querying knowledge graphs and calling external provers, and plans for further development.

Keywords: HOL · Python · SPARQL · Wikidata

1 Introduction

ULKB Logic is a higher-order logic-based framework for reasoning over knowledge graphs. It is written in Python and released under the open-source Apache 2.0 license.[1] ULKB Logic is a component of a larger system called ULKB (short for Universal Logic Knowledge Base). Another component of the ULKB system is the ULKB Graph, a core knowledge graph augmented by a federation of commonsense and linguistic knowledge bases consolidated from Wikidata [30], ConceptNet [26], VerbNet [24], and WordNet [18].

In this paper, we present the logical foundations and implementation of ULKB Logic, and also its interfaces for fetching statements from knowledge graphs and calling external provers. These interfaces are key for achieving ULKB Logic's main goal, which is twofold:

(i) provide a common language and interactive theorem prover-like environment for representing commonsense and linguistic knowledge; and

---

[1] https://github.com/IBM/ULKB.

H. Barbosa and Y. Zohar (Eds.): SBMF 2023, LNCS 14414, pp. 55–71, 2024.
https://doi.org/10.1007/978-3-031-49342-3_4

(ii) ease the use of state-of-the-art computational logic tools to reason over the knowledge available in knowledge graphs.

ULKB Logic achieves (i) by adopting a dialect of higher-order logic similar to that used by the HOL family [9] of provers, especially the HOL Light [12] prover. We argue that this language (hereinafter referred to simply as HOL) is expressive and practical enough to be used in domains other than the formalization of mathematics and software verification. ULKB Logic can be seen as an attempt to use HOL as a lingua franca for representing commonsense and linguistic knowledge.

This brings us to (ii). Large quantities of commonsense and linguistic knowledge are available in public knowledge graphs like Wikidata [30] and Word-Net [18].[2] It is unrealistic to expect that all this knowledge put together could form a consistent, workable logical theory. But it is reasonable to think that selected parts of Wikidata and WordNet could be used in a particular application. Enabling this kind of application is the motivation behind ULKB Logic's interface for querying knowledge graphs. This interface is built on top of SPARQL [32], the standard query language of the Semantic Web, and allows logic formulas to be used as queries.

Another observation related to (ii) concerns the form of the statements stored in popular commonsense and linguistic knowledge graphs. These are usually flat, first-order statements which may involve numbers but rarely involve complex data structures or even function applications. The restricted form of statements means that robust computational logic tools, like the E prover [25] and the Z3 SMT solver [19], can be readily used to reason over theories constructed from these graphs. Enabling the use of such tools within an interactive HOL environment is the motivation behind ULKB Logic's external prover interface.

The rest of the paper is organized as follows. Section 2 presents the logical foundations and implementation of ULKB Logic. Section 3 describes ULKB Logic's interfaces for querying knowledge graphs and calling external provers. Section 4 discusses some related work. Section 5 presents our conclusions and future work.

2   Logical Foundations and Implementation

ULKB Logic is in essence a Python library, called `ulkb`, for constructing expressions in typed, (classical) higher-order logic (HOL). This logic is the same variant of simple type theory [1,7] with polymorphic type variables used by HOL Light [12,13]. In HOL, the logical connectives and quantifiers are defined in terms of a more basic *core language* which we describe next.

---

[2] Wikidata is a sister project of Wikipedia and one of the largest publicly available knowledge graphs. WordNet is a comprehensive semantic lexicon for the English language.

2.1   Types

The *types* of ULKB Logic's core language are defined as follows (the corresponding Python functions are shown on the right):

$$
\begin{array}{ll}
\tau ::= \alpha & \text{TypeVariable}(\alpha) \\
\quad | \text{ bool} & \text{BoolType}() \\
\quad | \ (\tau_1 \ \text{->} \ \tau_2) & \text{FunctionType}(\tau_1, \ \tau_2) \\
\quad | \ (\kappa \ \tau_1 \ \tau_2 \ ... \ \tau_n) & \text{TypeApplication}(\kappa, \ \tau_1, \ \tau_2, \ ..., \ \tau_n)
\end{array}
$$

A type τ is either a type variable α ranging over types; the boolean type bool of logical propositions; a function type $(\tau_1 \ \text{->} \ \tau_2)$ of functions from τ_1 to τ_2; or a type application $(\kappa \ \tau_1 \ ... \ \tau_n)$ where κ is an n-ary type constructor.

Type constructors are the basic building blocks of types. They are created in Python by the function $\text{TypeConstructor}(\kappa, \ n)$ where κ is a name identifying the type constructor and n is its arity. A type application builds a type by applying a given type constructor to the required number of arguments (other types). For example, the type int of integers can be defined as the type obtained by applying the 0-ary type constructor int to zero arguments (line 3 below):[3]

```
1 >>> from ulkb import *             # import ULKB Logic namespace
2 >>> int_tc = TypeConstructor('int', 0)  # create the int type constr.
3 >>> int_ty = TypeApplication(int_tc)     # create the int type
4 >>> print(int_ty)                   # ": *" means "is a type"
5 int : *
```

As another example, the type of lists of integers (list int) can be defined as the type obtained by applying the unary type constructor list to the previously constructed type int:

```
1 >>> list_tc = TypeConstructor('list', 1) # create the list type constr.
2 >>> list_int_ty = list_tc(int_ty)        # create the (list int) type
3 >>> print(list_int_ty)
4 list int : *
```

At line 2, list_tc(int_ty) is a more compact way of writing the type application TypeApplication(list_tc, int_ty).

Internally, the boolean type bool and the function type $(\tau_1 \ \text{->} \ \tau_2)$ are defined as type applications of the builtin type constructors bool and fun whose arities are zero and two, respectively. The syntax of type expressions is thus reduced to two syntactic categories: type variables and type applications.

---

[3] Type int is actually part of ULKB Logic's standard prelude, which also includes real and str.

2.2   Terms

There are four different kinds of *terms* in ULKB Logic's core language:

$$
\begin{aligned}
t ::=\ & x & & \texttt{Variable}(x,\ \tau)\\
\mid\ & c & & \texttt{Constant}(c,\ \tau)\\
\mid\ & (t_1\ t_2) & & \texttt{Application}(t_1,\ t_2)\\
\mid\ & (\texttt{fun}\ x\ \texttt{=>}\ t_1) & & \texttt{Abstraction}(x,\ t_1)
\end{aligned}
$$

A term t is either a variable x, a constant c, the application of a term t_1 to a term t_2, or the abstraction of a variable x over a term t_1.

Constants and variables are simply names with associated types. What distinguishes them is that only variables can be bound by (λ-)abstractions. An application $(t_1\ t_2)$ stands for the application of function t_1 to argument t_2. An abstraction ($\texttt{fun}\ x\ \texttt{=>}\ t$) stands for the anonymous function mapping x (the function argument) to expression t (the function body).

Every term is associated with a single type, but a constant of a polymorphic type gives rise to an infinite family of constant terms.[4] We write "$t\ :\ \tau$" to mean that term t has type τ. The usual *typing rules* govern the association of terms to types:

$$
\frac{t_1\ :\ \tau_1\ \texttt{->}\ \tau_2 \qquad t_2\ :\ \tau_1}{(t_1\ t_2)\ :\ \tau_2}\ \text{app}
\qquad\qquad
\frac{t\ :\ \tau_2}{(\texttt{fun}\ x\ :\ \tau_1\ \texttt{=>}\ t)\ :\ \tau_1\ \texttt{->}\ \tau_2}\ \text{abs}
$$

These rules are applied automatically by ULKB Logic at term construction time. For example:

```
1 >>> a = TypeVariable('a')          # create the type (a : *)
2 >>> k = Constant('k', a)           # create the term (k : a)
3 >>> x = Variable('x', a)           # create the term (x : a)
4 >>> id_ = Abstraction(x, x)        # create the identity function
5 >>> print(id_)
6 (fun x => x) : a -> a
7 >>> print(Application(id_, k))     # create the app. of id_ to k
8 (fun x => x) k : a
```

At line 7, the application of the identity function ($\texttt{fun}\ x\ \texttt{=>}\ x$) of type ($\texttt{a}\ \texttt{->}\ \texttt{a}$) to the constant ($\texttt{k}\ :\ \texttt{a}$) produces the term (($\texttt{fun}\ x\ \texttt{=>}\ x$) $\texttt{k}$) of type $\texttt{a}$.

There is a more compact way of writing abstractions and applications in ULKB Logic. For example, instead of $\texttt{Abstraction(x, x)}$ we can write:

---

[4] The support for type variables distinguishes the variant of simple type theory adopted here from Church's original formulation [7]. The idea of type variables can be traced back to LCF [10] and provides, within the object language, some of the informal meta-theoretic notations used by Church.

```
>>> id_ = (x >> x)
>>> print(id_)
(fun x => x) : a -> a
```

This works because ULKB Logic overrides Python's right shift operator $(x >> t)$ to mean `Abstraction(x, t)` when x is a variable and t is a term. Moreover, instead of writing `Application(id_, k)` for the application of `id_` to `k`, we can apply `id_` directly to `k`, as if it were a Python function:

```
>>> print(id_(k))
(fun x => x) k : a
```

2.3 Deductive System

The term obtained at the end of the last section (`(fun x => x) k`) is a *redex*, i.e., a term that can be simplified by the β-reduction rule of the λ-calculus. In ULKB Logic, β-reduction is embodied by the following *inference rule*:

$$\frac{}{\vdash ((\text{fun } x \Rightarrow t_1)\ t_2) = t_1[x := t_2]}\ \text{BetaConv}$$

where $t_1[x := t_2]$ stands for the term obtained by substituting the free occurrences of variable x in t_1 by the term t_2.

If we apply rule `BetaConv` to the redex (`(fun x => x) k`) we get:

```
>>> print(BetaConv(id_(k)))
|- (fun x => x) k = k
```

The resulting object is a *sequent*, i.e., a theorem of the logic. This particular theorem asserts that the application (`(fun x => x) k`) is equal "=" to the constant `k`, which is the result of substituting the free occurrences of `x` by `k` in the body of (`fun x => x`).

In HOL-based provers, an inference rule is a function (in the metalanguage) that builds a theorem from a given input. (`BetaConv` above takes a redex as input and constructs a theorem stating that this redex equals the term obtained by β-reducing it.) Soundness is enforced by adopting the so-called "LCF approach" [10]: the privilege of creating theorems is reserved to a small set of primitive rules which form the logical kernel of the system—everything else is defined in terms of this kernel. As it happens, `BetaConv` is *not* a primitive rule of ULKB Logic, but it is derived from them.

The *primitive rules* of ULKB Logic are shown in Fig. 1. These are essentially the same primitive rules adopted by HOL Light [12], and are similar to those for the internal logic of a topos [16]. These ten rules govern the deducibility of sequents of the form $\Gamma \vdash p$ where p is a term of type `bool` and Γ is a (possibly empty) set of terms of type `bool`.

Rule Assume	$t : \mathtt{bool} \vdash t : \mathtt{bool}$	Rule Refl	$\vdash t = t$
Rule Trans	$\dfrac{\Gamma_1 \vdash t_1 = t_2 \quad \Gamma_2 \vdash t_2 = t_3}{\Gamma_1 \cup \Gamma_2 \vdash t_1 = t_3}$	Rule MkComb	$\dfrac{\Gamma_1 \vdash f = g \quad \Gamma_2 \vdash t_1 = t_2}{\Gamma_1 \cup \Gamma_2 \vdash (f\ t_1) = (g\ t_2)}$
Rule Abs	$\dfrac{\Gamma \vdash t_1 = t_2}{\Gamma \vdash (\mathtt{fun}\ x \Rightarrow t_1) = (\mathtt{fun}\ x \Rightarrow t_2)}$	Rule Beta	$\vdash (\mathtt{fun}\ x \Rightarrow t)\ x = t$
Rule EqMP	$\dfrac{\Gamma_1 \vdash t_1 = t_2 \quad \Gamma_2 \vdash t_1 : \mathtt{bool}}{\Gamma_1 \cup \Gamma_2 \vdash t_2 : \mathtt{bool}}$	Rule Deduct Antisym	$\dfrac{\Gamma_1 \vdash t_1 : \mathtt{bool} \quad \Gamma_2 \vdash t_2 : \mathtt{bool}}{(\Gamma_1 - \{t_2\}) \cup (\Gamma_2 - \{t_1\}) \vdash t_1 = t_2}$
Rule Inst Type	$\dfrac{\Gamma \vdash t : \mathtt{bool}}{\Gamma[\alpha := \tau] \vdash t[\alpha := \tau] : \mathtt{bool}}$	Rule Inst	$\dfrac{\Gamma \vdash t_1 : \mathtt{bool}}{\Gamma[x := t_2] \vdash t_1[x := t_2] : \mathtt{bool}}$

Fig. 1. Deductive system of ULKB Logic. In `RuleAbs`, x must not occur free in Γ.

One difference between ULKB Logic and HOL Light is that, in ULKB Logic, α-conversion (renaming of bound variables) coincides with syntactical equality. This is because ULKB Logic uses a *locally nameless* representation of terms [4, 17], i.e., one in which bound variables are represented by de Bruijn indices and free variables are represented by names. As a consequence, in the metalanguage, α-convertible terms are equal (no explicit conversion is needed):

```
>>> x, y = Variables('x', 'y', a)
>>> print((x >> x) == (y >> y))
True
```

2.4 Logical Constants

We now present the logical constants of ULKB Logic. We start with *equality*, which occurs in most of the rules of Fig. 1. Equality is represented by the primitive (undefined) constant (`equal` : α `->` α `->` `bool`), which is associated with the infix notation "=".[5] Type variable α in the type of `equal` is instantiated by ULKB Logic at the moment the constant is applied to some argument:

```
>>> print(equal(id_))
equal (fun x => x) : (a -> a) -> bool
```

---

[5] The type of `equal` is actually (α `->` (α `->` `bool`)). ULKB Logic follows the standard practice of assuming "->" associates to the right and omits redundant parentheses accordingly. Similarly, application is assumed to associate to the left, i.e., ($t_1\ t_2\ t_3$) means (($t_1\ t_2$) t_3).

That is, when we apply (equal : α -> α -> bool) to the identity function
(fun x => x : a -> a), the occurrences of α in the type of equal are instantiated as (a -> a) and we get as a result of the application a term of type
(a -> a) -> bool. This term is the unary predicate that expects a function
from a to a as argument and asserts that it is equal to (fun x => x).

The next logical constant is (true : bool) which represents the true proposition. Different from equal, the constant true is not a primitive one. It is
introduced by the following definition:

```
>>> show_definitions(offset=0, id='true')
4  definition (true : bool) := (fun p => p) = (fun p => p)
```

The call to show_definitions() lists the definitions installed in the current
theory matching the given criteria. The definition listed above introduces two
things: a new constant true of type bool and a new (non-creative) axiom

$$\vdash \text{true} = ((\text{fun p => p}) = (\text{fun p => p}))$$

which allows us to eliminate the constant true. No less important is the fact
that this definition works, i.e., we can use it to prove true:

```
>>> def_true = lookup_definition('true')
>>> print(def_true)
|- true <-> (fun p => p) = (fun p => p)
>>> x = Variable('x', BoolType())
>>> print(RuleEqMP(RuleSym(def_true), RuleRefl(x >> x)))
|- true
```

(RuleSym is a derived rule that infers $\Gamma \vdash t_2 = t_1$ from $\Gamma \vdash t_1 = t_2$.)

The remaining logical connectives are introduced by similar definitions
accompanied by corresponding introduction and elimination theorems. We won't
show the definitions here, but Table 1 gives an overview of the constants they
introduce.

The last column of Table 1 (Macro) lists Python functions that make the
application of the logical constants more convenient. Using these functions, for
example, instead of writing:

```
>>> x, y = Variables('x', 'y', a)
>>> print(forall(Abstraction(x, forall(Abstraction(y, equal(x, y))))))
(forall x y, x = y) : bool
```

We can write:

```
>>> x, y = Variables('x', 'y', a)
>>> print(Forall(x, y, Equal(x, y)))
(forall x y, x = y) : bool
```

Table 1. Logical constants of ULKB Logic.

	Notation	Constant		Macro
Equality	t_1 = t_2	(equal	: a -> a -> bool)	Equal(t_1, t_2)
Truth	true	(true	: bool)	Truth()
Falsity	false	(false	: bool)	Falsity()
Negation	not t	(not	: bool -> bool)	Not(t)
Conjunction	t_1 and t_2	(and	: bool -> bool -> bool)	And(t_1, t_2)
Disjunction	t_1 or t_2	(or	: bool -> bool -> bool)	Or(t_1, t_2)
Implication	t_1 -> t_2	(implies	: bool -> bool -> bool)	Implies(t_1, t_2)
Equivalence	t_1 <-> t_2	(equal	: bool -> bool -> bool)	Iff(t_1, t_2)
Existential	exists x, t	(exists	: (a -> bool) -> bool)	Exists(x, t)
Unique	exists1 x, t	(exists1	: (a -> bool) -> bool)	Exists1(x, t)
Universal	forall x, t	(forall	: (a -> bool) -> bool)	Forall(x, t)

2.5 Theories

In ULKB Logic, constant declarations, definitions, axioms, theorems, etc., are kept in an object called *theory*. Multiple theories can coexist but at any given time only one of them, called *top*, is active. By default, commands such as `show_definitions()` and `lookup_definition()`, whose usage was illustrated in the previous section, operate on the top theory.

Internally, a theory keeps a list of *extensions*, which can be of three kinds:

1. *Assumptions*, introducing new type constructors, constants, or axioms.
2. *Assertions*, introducing new definitions or theorems.
3. *Notations*, introducing new notations.

There are Python functions to install extensions of each kind into the top theory. For example, `new_constant()` installs an undefined constant; `new_definition()` installs a definition; `new_axiom()` installs an unproven theorem; `new_theorem()` install a (proven) theorem; etc.

A *theory file* is any Python script that modifies the top theory. By default, the `ulkb` library loads a theory file containing the *standard prelude*, which installs several basic extensions, such as the declarations of `bool`, `fun`, and `equal`, the definitions of the logical constants, etc. The list of all extensions of the top theory can be displayed using `show_extensions()`.

3 Graph API and External Provers

ULKB Logic comes with a Graph API for querying knowledge graphs using logic formulas. This API is implemented by the `graph` module of the `ulkb` library. In this section, we use the Wikidata [30] knowledge graph to build an example illustrating some of the functions of the `graph` module. Later, we expand the example to illustrate ULKB Logic's support for calling external provers.

3.1   Graph API

The interface of ULKB Logic's `graph` module consists of four main functions:

1. `graph.ask`(q), evaluates an *ask* query.
2. `graph.select`(q), evaluates a *select* query.
3. `graph.construct`(p, q), evaluates a *construct* query.
4. `graph.paths`(c_1, c_2), evaluates a *path* query.

In (1), (2), and (3), the parameters p and q are formulas (terms of type `bool`) usually containing free variables. An *ask* query tests whether some instantiation of q occurs in the knowledge graph, while a *select* query retrieves all such instantiations. A *construct* query is similar to a select query but takes an extra formula p as an argument. This formula p functions as a template to construct a new formula for each instantiation of q occurring in the graph. (We will illustrate the use of construct queries and discuss syntactical restrictions for p and q in a moment.) Finally, a *path* query searches for paths in the graph connecting the constants c_1 and c_2.

Moving to our example, we start by configuring the `graph` module to use Wikidata's public SPARQL endpoint:

```
>>> settings.graph.uri = 'https://query.wikidata.org/sparql'
>>> settings.graph.namespaces = { # Wikidata SPARQL prefixes
...      'wd': 'http://www.wikidata.org/entity/',
...      'wdt': 'http://www.wikidata.org/prop/direct/'}
```

Variable `settings.graph.uri` holds the address of the endpoint and variable `settings.graph.namespaces` holds the prefix table which is used by `graph` module to expand prefixes such as "`wd:`" and "`wdt:`" into full URLs.

We next declare our nonlogical vocabulary:

```
>>> # individuals (nodes)
>>> a            = TypeVariable('a') # a : *
>>> actor        = new_constant('wd:Q33999', a, label='actor')
>>> blond_hair   = new_constant('wd:Q202466', a, label='blond hair')
>>> female       = new_constant('wd:Q6581072', a, label='female')
>>> Porto_Alegre = new_constant('wd:Q40269', a, label='Porto Alegre')
>>> singer       = new_constant('wd:Q177220', a, label='singer')
>>> # binary relations (edges)
>>> aab          = FunctionType(a, a, BoolType()) # a -> a -> bool : *
>>> date_of_death = new_constant('wdt:P570', aab, label='date of death')
>>> gender       = new_constant('wdt:P21', aab, label='gender')
>>> hair_color   = new_constant('wdt:P1884', aab, label='hair color')
>>> occupation   = new_constant('wdt:P106', aab, label='occupation')
>>> place_of_birth= new_constant('wdt:P19', aab, label='place of birth')
```

Each `new_constant()` call installs into the top theory a new constant with the given type. Here constants of type a represent individuals (nodes), while those of type (a -> a -> bool) represent binary relations (edges) on individuals. The label argument specifies a label to be used when displaying the constant.

With the vocabulary defined, we can now write a query as a logic formula:

```
1 >>> x, y = Variables('x', 'y', a)
2 >>> q = And(gender(x, female), place_of_birth(x, Porto_Alegre), # (i)
3 ...         Or(occupation(x, singer), occupation(x, actor)),     # (ii)
4 ...         Not(hair_color(x, blond_hair)),                      # (iii)
5 ...         Exists(y, date_of_death(x, y)))                      # (iv)
6 >>> print(q)
7 <gender> x <female> and <place of birth> x <Porto Alegre> and
  ↪  (<occupation> x <singer> or <occupation> x <actor>) and not <hair
  ↪  color> x <blond hair> and (exists y, <date of death> x y) : bool
```

This query matches the x's such that (i) x is a female born in Porto Alegre (ii) who is a singer or actress, (iii) has non-blond hair, and (iv) is no longer alive. The "<" and ">" in the output (line 7) indicate that the constants' labels are being displayed (not their ids).

The code below uses graph.construct() to find ten instances of query q in Wikidata and installs them into the theory as new axioms:

```
>>> for f in graph.construct(q, q, limit=10):
...     new_axiom(f)
```

The call graph.construct() selects entities in the graph that satisfy the free variables in its second argument (q) and substitutes these entities for the corresponding free variables in its first argument (here also q). The result is an iterator of (grounded) formulas which is consumed by the for-loop.

Internally, graph.construct() translates the formula q into a SPARQL CONSTRUCT [32] query, sends it to the SPARQL endpoint, and translates each resulting graph back to a ULKB Logic formula, possibly creating new constants in the process. At its core, SPARQL has the same expressive power as non-recursive safe Datalog with negation [2]. ULKB Logic's translation algorithm borrows some ideas from Polleres and Wallner's [21] and currently supports a subset of the AND-UNION-OPT-FILTER fragment of SPARQL [22].

Back to our example, after running the for-loop, if we ask ULKB Logic to list the axioms in the top theory:

```
>>> show_axioms()
```

one of the many axioms it outputs is the following:

```
32  axiom <gender> <Elis Regina> <female> and <place of birth> <Elis
 ↪  Regina> <Porto Alegre> and (<occupation> <Elis Regina> <singer> or
 ↪  <occupation> <Elis Regina> <actor>) and not <hair color> <Elis
 ↪  Regina> <blond hair> and (exists y, <date of death> <Elis Regina> y)
```

There are a couple of things to note here. First, because we didn't pass a name to the `new_axiom()` call in the for-loop, ULKB Logic creates an anonymous axiom—internally, a new unique name (derived from the formula) is generated for the axiom. Second, the Graph API automatically fetched and set the label "Elis Regina" to the constant introduced by the instantiated query. It does so by searching for standard labeling predicates, such as `rdfs:label`.[6]

3.2 External Provers

So far, we have used the Graph API to build a "theory" about female singers and actresses of the past. We will now use external provers to derive theorems from this theory. Note that external provers are not necessarily required for this task: we could use ULKB Logic's deductive system directly. For example, we could apply the and-elimination rule to the axiom shown at the end of the previous section to obtain a theorem stating that "Elis Regina's place of birth is Porto Alegre". But our goal here is to illustrate the use of external provers.

The code below shows how we can use the Z3 SMT solver [19] to derive the same fact:

```
>>> Elis_Regina = Constant('wd:Q465877', a, label='Elis Regina')
>>> print(RuleZ3(place_of_birth(Elis_Regina, Porto_Alegre)))
|- <place of birth> <Elis Regina> <Porto Alegre>
```

`RuleZ3` is a special kind of inference rule. It takes as input a first-order formula p and tries to use Z3 to prove the sequent $\Gamma \vdash p$ where Γ is the set of all (first-order) axioms and theorems in the top theory. If Z3 is successful, as in the case above, `RuleZ3` returns a new theorem $\vdash p$. Otherwise, if Z3 fails to prove $\Gamma \vdash p$, `RuleZ3` raises an exception.

Here is what happens when we try to prove that Elis Regina was born in Brazil (the country in which the city of Porto Alegre is located):

```
>>> Brazil = Constant('wd:Q155', a, label='Brazil')
>>> try:
...     print(RuleZ3(place_of_birth(Elis_Regina, Brazil)))
... except RuleError as err:
...     print(err)
RuleZ3: failed to prove '<place of birth> <Elis Regina> <Brazil> : bool'
```

`RuleZ3` fails because there is no axiom linking the city of Porto Alegre to Brazil in the top theory.

---

[6] Predicate `rdfs:label` is part of the RDF Schema vocabulary (https://www.w3.org/TR/rdf12-schema/); it is used to provide a human-readable name for a resource.

One way to obtain the missing link between Porto Alegre and Brazil is by loading statements about Porto Alegre from Wikidata:

```
>>> for f in graph.paths(Porto_Alegre, x, length=1, limit=200):
...      new_axiom(f)
```

The call to `graph.paths()` selects at most 200 paths of length 1 connecting the entity `Porto_Alegre` to some other entity (represented by the variable `x`). These are some of the axioms we obtain (the 165th axiom is the one we are after):

```
>>> show_axioms(offset=163, limit=3)
163  axiom <shares border with> <Porto Alegre> <Viamo>
164  axiom <instance of> <Porto Alegre> <million city>
165  axiom <country> <Porto Alegre> <Brazil>
```

Let us now install an axiom relating the predicates `place_of_birth` and `country`:

```
>>> country = Constant('wdt:P17', aab, label='country')
>>> x, y, z = Variables('x', 'y', 'z', a)
>>> ax = new_axiom(Forall(x, y, z, Implies(
...      place_of_birth(x, y), country(y, z), place_of_birth(x, z))))
>>> print(ax)
|- forall x y z, <place of birth> x y -> <country> y z -> <place of
↪  birth> x z
```

This axiom states that if x was born in y and y's country is z, then x was born in z. Using this axiom and the 165th one shown in the previous block, `RuleZ3` is now able to prove that Elis Regina was born in Brazil:

```
>>> thm = RuleZ3(place_of_birth(Elis_Regina, Brazil))
>>> print(new_theorem(thm))
|- <place of birth> <Elis Regina> <Brazil>
```

We use the `new_theorem()` call above to install the theorem produced by `RuleZ3` into the top theory. This way, subsequent calls to `RuleZ3` can reuse this fact, instead of having to prove it again from scratch:

```
>>> show_theorems()
216  theorem <place of birth> <Elis Regina> <Brazil>
```

Besides `RuleZ3`, ULKB Logic also provides a `RuleE` which tries to use the automated theorem prover E [25] to prove a given first-order formula from the top theory. Currently, both `RuleZ3` and `RuleE` are unsafe in the sense that they are implemented as privileged rules which create theorems directly. We are working on re-implementing these rules as derived rules which use Z3 and E as "hammers" to guide proof construction using ULKB Logic's deductive system.

3.3   Encoders and Decoders

We conclude this section with a brief discussion of ULKB Logic's *codec* subsystem, which is used by both the Graph API and the subsystem responsible for calling external provers. In ULKB Logic, the objects that comprise a logical theory (types, terms, definitions, axioms, theorems, etc.), including the theory itself, are instances of a Python class called *syntactical object*. The codec subsystem implements a plugin architecture that deals with encoding and decoding syntactical objects, i.e., converting them to and from various logical formats.

Table 2 shows the main formats currently supported by ULKB Logic. The Graph API uses the `sparql` codec to convert formulas (terms of type `bool`) to SPARQL queries; `RuleZ3` uses the `z3` codec to interface with the Z3 prover; and `RuleE` uses the TPTP [27] codec to interface with the E prover. TPTP, short for Thousands of Problems for Theorem Provers, is a popular library of problems written in a well-defined family of logical languages. This family of languages is supported by many automated theorem proving systems, including E [25] and Vampire [23].

Table 2. Codecs currently available in ULKB Logic.

Format	Encoder	Decoder	Description
ast	*obj*.to_ast()	*cls*.from_ast(*data*)	abstract syntax tree
json	*obj*.to_json()	*cls*.from_json(*data*)	JSON
ofn	-	*cls*.from_ofn(*data*)	OWL functional notation
sparql	*obj*.to_sparql()	*cls*.from_sparql(*data*)	SPARQL query
tptp	*obj*.to_tptp()	-	TPTP theory
z3	*obj*.to_z3()	*cls*.from_z3(*data*)	Z3 Python object

4   Related Work

There are three classes of work related to ULKB Logic. First, there are general-purpose, interactive theorem provers based on HOL. The most successful of these in modern times are Isabelle/HOL [20] and HOL Light [12]. Both are industrial-grade tools which have been used extensively for software verification and formalization of mathematics. For instance, a combination of Isabelle/HOL and HOL Light was used by Thomas Hales to formalize the proof of the Kepler conjecture [11].

Isabelle/HOL and HOL Light are obviously in a different league than ULKB Logic, but their success indicates we are building on solid ground. More modest implementations of HOL are HolPy [33] (Python) and HaskHOL [3] (Haskell). These are general purpose clones of HOL Light—the former comes with a library of mathematics which is something ULKB Logic currently lacks.

The second class of work related to ULKB Logic consists of applications of logic to knowledge graphs. The vast majority of these are automated reasoners for Semantic Web technologies. For example, description logics-based reasoners for OWL [31] and Prolog-like engines for rule languages like SWRL [14]. As we discussed at the end of the last section (in Table 2), ULKB Logic has support for importing OWL documents—it does so by using a first-order translation of OWL. We have plans to extend this support to SWRL documents and to integrate rule engines as external reasoners.

The third class of related work is the smallest one. It concerns those works that, like ULKB Logic, try to combine the world of higher order logic-based *interactive* theorem provers and the world of knowledge graphs. There are very few such works. For example, Tang et al. [28] discuss is an early attempt to use Isabelle/HOL to formalize an ontology (DAML+OIL). And Dapoigny and Barlatier [8] and Lai et al. [15] discuss the use of the Coq [29] proof assistant to represent and query (dependently typed) knowledge graphs. None of these works try to interface with actual knowledge graphs.

When we set out to implement the ULKB Logic, back in 2022, instead of building a Python-based HOL prover from scratch, we considered the possibility of reusing HOL Light or its Python clone HolPy. Some reasons led us to give up on the idea though. Regarding HOL Light, although it has a simple code base compared to other industrial-grade provers it is still pretty complex and, more importantly, was designed with interactive proving and formalization of mathematics in mind. There is no easy way to call or reuse the result of external provers, let alone to query external knowledge graphs. Implementing such functionalities directly in OCaml, the language in which HOL Light is written, would be no simple task.

Regarding HolPy, at the time we considered using it, its code base did not seem mature enough. There is still not much documentation about it (besides a short report on arXiv.org [33]) and the project does not seem to be very active (the last commit was on February 2023). Also, although HolPy is similar to HOL Light, it adopts a different set of primitive rules and a slightly different grammar for type expressions. It is unclear how these differences would impact an eventual integration with HOL Light, which is in our plans. (One possibility for such integration is to call OCaml directly from Python or to establish some form of communication between the two sides, along the lines of [6].)

5   Conclusion

This paper presented ULKB Logic, an open-source HOL-based framework for reasoning over knowledge graphs. We stated at the beginning that the goal of ULKB Logic was to provide a common language and environment to enable the use of state-of-the-art computational logic tools to reason over knowledge graphs. Ultimately, we envision a system that combines the power and robustness of modern higher-order logic-based proof assistants with the comprehensiveness and flexibility of knowledge graphs, creating thus opportunities for advancements in various domains, such as artificial intelligence, natural language processing, and formal verification.

Before we get there, however, there is plenty of work to be done. For example, many derived rules which are common in HOL systems are still not implemented in ULKB Logic. (So far, we have been focused on interfacing with knowledge graphs and external reasoners.) Another thing we need to improve is ULKB Logic's support for Semantic Web technologies. As mentioned in Sect. 4, we intend to add support for importing SWRL [14] documents and for interfacing with rule- and description logics-based reasoners [5].

Related to that, we are currently working on enhancing the interaction between ULKB Logic and provers that accept TPTP [27] as input. In particular, we are adding support for TPTP THF which will enable the integration of automated provers which deal with HOL natively. We are also investigating the possibility of interfacing directly with HOL Light, along the lines of [6].

Finally, improving ULKB Logic's ability to deal with large theories is also on our roadmap. One possibility is using a database or some other kind of specialized storage system to maintain the extensions of a theory.

References

1. Andrews, P.B.: An Introduction to Mathematical Logic and Type Theory: To Truth Through Proof, 2nd edn. Kluwer, Dordrecht (2002). https://doi.org/10.1007/978-94-015-9934-4
2. Angles, R., Gutierrez, C.: The expressive power of SPARQL. In: Sheth, A., et al. (eds.) ISWC 2008. LNCS, vol. 5318, pp. 114–129. Springer, Heidelberg (2008). https://doi.org/10.1007/978-3-540-88564-1_8
3. Austin, E.C.: HaskHOL: a Haskell hosted domain specific language for higher-order logic theorem proving. Master's thesis, Electrical Engineering and Computer Science Faculty, University of Kansas (2011)
4. Aydemir, B., Charguéraud, A., Pierce, B.C., Pollack, R., Weirich, S.: Engineering formal metatheory. In: Proceedings of 35th Annual ACM SIGPLAN-SIGACT Symposium on Principles of Programming Languages. POPL '08, pp. 3–15. ACM, New York (2008). https://doi.org/10.1145/1328438.1328443
5. Baader, F., Calvanese, D., McGuinness, D.L., Nardi, D., Patel-Schneider, P.F. (eds.): The Description Logic Handbook: Theory, Implementation and Applications, 2nd edn. Cambridge University Press, Cambridge (2007)
6. Bansal, K., Loos, S., Rabe, M., Szegedy, C., Wilcox, S.: HOList: an environment for machine learning of higher-order theorem proving. In: Proceedings of 36th International Conference on Machine Learning, Long Beach, California, USA. PMLR (2019)
7. Church, A.: A formulation of the simple theory of types. J. Symb. Logic 5(2), 56–68 (1940). https://doi.org/10.2307/2266170
8. Dapoigny, R., Barlatier, P.: Modeling ontological structures with type classes in Coq. In: Pfeiffer, H.D., Ignatov, D.I., Poelmans, J., Gadiraju, N. (eds.) ICCS-ConceptStruct 2013. LNCS (LNAI), vol. 7735, pp. 135–152. Springer, Heidelberg (2013). https://doi.org/10.1007/978-3-642-35786-2_11
9. Gordon, M.J.C., Melham, T.F. (eds.): Introduction to HOL: A Theorem Proving Environment for Higher Order Logic. Cambridge University Press, Cambridge (1993)

10. Gordon, M.J.C., Milner, A.J., Wadsworth, C.P.: Edinburgh LCF: A Mechanised Logic of Computation. Springer, Berlin (1979). https://doi.org/10.1007/3-540-09724-4
11. Hales, T., et al.: A formal proof of the Kepler conjecture. Forum Math. Pi **5**, 1–29 (2017). https://doi.org/10.1017/fmp.2017.1
12. Harrison, J.: HOL Light: an overview. In: Berghofer, S., Nipkow, T., Urban, C., Wenzel, M. (eds.) TPHOLs 2009. LNCS, vol. 5674, pp. 60–66. Springer, Heidelberg (2009). https://doi.org/10.1007/978-3-642-03359-9_4
13. Harrison, J.: HOL Light tutorial (2017). https://www.cl.cam.ac.uk/~jrh13/hol-light/tutorial.pdf
14. Horrocks, I., Patel-Schneider, P.F., Boley, H., Tabet, S., Grosof, B., Dean, M.: SWRL: a semantic web rule language combining OWL and RuleML. W3C member submission, W3C, May 2004. https://www.w3.org/Submission/SWRL/
15. Lai, Z., Ng, A.B., Wong, L.Z., See, S., Lin, S.: Dependently typed knowledge graphs. Technical report. arXiv:2003.03785, arXiv.org (2020)
16. Lambek, J., Scott, P.J.: Introduction to Higher Order Categorical Logic. Cambridge University Press, Cambridge (1986)
17. McBride, C., McKinna, J.: Functional pearl: I am not a number-I am a free variable. In: Proceedings of 2004 ACM SIGPLAN Workshop on Haskell. Haskell '04, pp. 1–9. ACM, New York (2004). https://doi.org/10.1145/1017472.1017477
18. Miller, G.A.: WordNet: a lexical database for English. Commun. ACM **38**(11), 39–41 (1995). https://doi.org/10.1145/219717.219748
19. de Moura, L., Bjørner, N.: Z3: an efficient SMT solver. In: Ramakrishnan, C.R., Rehof, J. (eds.) TACAS 2008. LNCS, vol. 4963, pp. 337–340. Springer, Heidelberg (2008). https://doi.org/10.1007/978-3-540-78800-3_24
20. Nipkow, T., Paulson, L.C., Wenzel, M.: Isabelle/HOL: A Proof Assistant for Higher-Order Logic. Springer, Heidelberg (2002). https://doi.org/10.1007/3-540-45949-9
21. Polleres, A., Wallner, J.P.: On the relation between SPARQL 1.1 and answer set programming. J. Appl. Non-Classical Logics **23**(1–2), 159–212 (2013). https://doi.org/10.1080/11663081.2013.798992
22. Pérez, J., Arenas, M., Gutierrez, C.: Semantics and complexity of SPARQL. ACM Trans. Database Syst. **34**(3), 16:1–16:45 (2009). https://doi.org/10.1145/1567274.1567278
23. Riazanov, A., Voronkov, A.: The design and implementation of VAMPIRE. AI Commun. **15**(2–3), 91–110 (2002)
24. Schuler, K.K.: VerbNet: a broad-coverage, comprehensive verb lexicon. Ph.D. thesis, University of Pennsylvania, Philadelphia, PA, USA (2005)
25. Schulz, S., Cruanes, S., Vukmirović, P.: Faster, higher, stronger: E 2.3. In: Fontaine, P. (ed.) CADE 2019. LNCS (LNAI), vol. 11716, pp. 495–507. Springer, Cham (2019). https://doi.org/10.1007/978-3-030-29436-6_29
26. Speer, R., Chin, J., Havasi, C.: ConceptNet 5.5: an open multilingual graph of general knowledge. In: Proceedings of 31st AAAI Conference on Artificial Intelligence (AAAI-17), San Francisco, California, USA, 4–9 February 2017, pp. 4444–4451. AAAI (2017)
27. Sutcliffe, G.: The TPTP problem library and associated infrastructure. J. Automat. Reason. **59**(4), 483–502 (2017). https://doi.org/10.1007/s10817-017-9407-7
28. Tang, Y., Sun, J., Dong, J.S., Mahony, B.: Reasoning about semantic web in Isabelle/HOL. In: Proceedings of 11th Asia-Pacific Software Engineering Conference, pp. 46–53 (2004). https://doi.org/10.1109/APSEC.2004.82

29. The Coq Development Team: The Coq Reference Manual: Release 8.14.0, October 2021
30. Vrandečić, D., Krötzsch, M.: Wikidata: a free collaborative knowledgebase. Commun. ACM **57**(10), 78–85 (2014). https://doi.org/10.1145/2629489
31. W3C-OWL-WG-2012: OWL 2 web ontology language document overview (second edition). W3C recommendation, W3C, December 2012. http://www.w3.org/TR/2012/REC-owl2-overview-20121211/
32. W3C SPARQL Working Group: SPARQL 1.1 overview. W3C recommendation, W3C (2013). http://www.w3.org/TR/2013/REC-sparql11-overview-20130321/
33. Zhan, B.: HolPy: interactive theorem proving in Python. Technical report. arXiv:1905.05970, arXiv.org (2020)

Testing

Language-Based Testing for Pushdown Reactive Systems

Adilson Luiz Bonifacio[✉][iD]

Computing Department, University of Londrina, Londrina, Brazil
bonifacio@uel.br

Abstract. Testing reactive systems is important to guarantee a precise and robust software development process. Pushdown reactive systems are complex applications where the interaction with the environment is regulated by a pushdown memory and, in general, can be specified by the formalism of Input/Output Visibly Pushdown Labeled Transition System (IOVPTS). A conformance checking can then be applied to verify whether an implementation is in compliance to a specification using an appropriate conformance relation. In this work, we establish a conformance relation based on Visibly Pushdown Languages (VPLs) to model sets of desirable and undesirable behaviors of systems. Further, we show that test suites with a complete fault coverage can be generated using this new conformance relation for pushdown reactive systems.

Keywords: Pushdown reactive systems · Visibly Pushdown Languages · Visual conformance checking

1 Introduction

Real-world systems, such as communication protocols, vehicle and aircraft control systems, and most of industrial control systems, are indeed reactive systems, where the behavior is dictated by the interaction with the environment [9]. Reactive hardware and software systems, in general, are critical applications that require a precise and robust development process, particularly in the testing activity, where high costs are associated to maintenance when the testing step is poorly conducted during the system development process [12]. Model-based testing [5,11] meets such requirement relying on formal methods, supporting several models and testing approaches for reactive systems.

Reactive behaviors can be properly specified by the formalism of Input/Output Labeled Transition Systems (IOLTSs) [8], and so a conformance checking can be applied to verify whether an implementation is in compliance to its respective specification [3,14]. In a more general setting, pushdown reactive systems are complex applications where the interaction with the environment is regulated by a pushdown memory through the communication channel. Therefore aspects of conformance testing and test suite generation have been studied using more expressive formalisms [6,7]. A more recent work has proposed a new

H. Barbosa and Y. Zohar (Eds.): SBMF 2023, LNCS 14414, pp. 75–91, 2024.
https://doi.org/10.1007/978-3-031-49342-3_5

conformance relation [4] for the Input/Output Visibly Pushdown Labeled Transition Systems (IOVPTSs), an extension of the IOLTS models, in the same spirit of the classical **ioco** relation [13]. It is easy to see that these approaches can deal with a more wide range of systems, where a stack memory is present.

However, conformance relations are specifically designed to capture faulty behaviors when checking implementations against their respective specifications. In this work we go further and address this problem using formal languages, where particular sets of desirable and undesirable behaviors can be specified by Visibly Pushdown Languages (VPLs) [1]. Hence, besides the classical conformance testing, we can now test whether or not specific behaviors and properties are present in the systems. Notice that such behaviors or properties are not necessarily detected by using conformance **ioco-like** relations. Also, note that the class of VPLs is strictly more powerful than the classical regular languages treated by **ioco** relation and some extensions. Therefore we gain a wider range of possibilities when specifying and testing pushdown reactive systems.

We then propose and prove the correctness of an efficient process that can check conformance on a white-box testing scenario, where the tester previously knows the structure of implementations under test (IUTs), and the participating models have an auxiliary stack memory, using a language-based approach, instead of a specific conformance relation. That is we give a more general conformance relation based on VPLs, extending the previous approach [4], where test suites with a complete fault coverage can be generated using a visual conformance relation that can specify desirable and undesirable behaviors of pushdown reactive systems.

The remainder of this paper is organized as follows. Section 2 presents VPTS and IOVPTS models, the useful notion of contracted VPTSs, and their relationship to VPAs. In Sect. 3 we define a visual conformance relation, give a fault model over VPLs, and show how to obtain complete test suites, of polynomial complexity, for checking this class of models. Section 4 gives concluding remarks.

2   Reactive Pushdown Models

In this section we introduce the formalism of Visibly Pushdown Labeled Transition System (VPTS), and its variation Input/Output VPTS, both models that can properly specify pushdown reactive systems. We also discuss the notion of contracted VPTSs, an important property that allows the model-based testing process in this setting. But first, we start with some notation to ease the reference when testing complex reactive systems.

2.1   Notation

Here we establish some basic notation. Let X and Y be sets we indicate by $X - Y = \{z \mid z \in X \text{ and } z \notin Y\}$ the set difference. Also, we assume that $X_Y = X \cup Y$ and when $Y = \{y\}$ is a singleton we may write X_y for $X_{\{y\}}$. If X is a finite set, the size of X will be indicated by $|X|$.

An alphabet is any non-empty set of symbols. Let A be an alphabet, a word over A is any finite sequence $\sigma = x_1 \ldots x_n$ of symbols in A, that is, $n \geq 0$ and $x_i \in A$, for all $i = 1, 2, \ldots, n$. When $n = 0$, σ is the empty sequence, also indicated by ε. The set of all finite sequences, or words, over A is denoted by $A^\star$, and the set of all nonempty finite words over A is indicated by A^+. When we write $x_1 x_2 \ldots x_n \in A^\star$, it is implicitly assumed that $n \geq 0$ and that $x_i \in A$, $1 \leq i \leq n$, unless explicitly noted otherwise. The length of a word α over A is indicated by $|\alpha|$. Hence, $|\varepsilon| = 0$.

Further, let $\sigma = \sigma_1 \ldots \sigma_n$ and $\rho = \rho_1 \ldots \rho_m$ be two words over A. The concatenation of σ and ρ, indicated by $\sigma\rho$, is the word $\sigma_1 \ldots \sigma_n \rho_1 \ldots \rho_m$. Clearly, $|\sigma\rho| = |\sigma| + |\rho|$. A language G over A is any set $G \subseteq A^\star$ of words over A. Also let G_1, $G_2 \subseteq A^\star$ be languages over A. The product of G_1 and G_2, indicated by $G_1 G_2$, is the language $\{\sigma\rho \,|\, \sigma \in G_1, \rho \in G_2\}$. If $G \subseteq A^\star$ is a language over A, then its complement is the language $\overline{G} = A^\star - G$.

We also use the notion of morphism to treat alphabets. So let A, B be alphabets. A *homomorphism*, or just a *morphism*, from A to B is any function $h : A \to B^\star$. A morphism $h : A \to B^\star$ can be extended in a natural way to a function $\widehat{h} : A^\star \to B^\star$, thus either $\widehat{h}(\sigma) = \varepsilon$ if $\sigma = \varepsilon$ or $\widehat{h}(\sigma) = h(a)\widehat{h}(\rho)$ if $\sigma = a\rho$ with $a \in A$. In order to avoid cluttering the notation, we may write h instead of $\widehat{h}$, when no confusion can arise. When $a \in A$, we define the simple morphism $h_a : A \to A - \{a\}$ by letting $h_a(a) = \varepsilon$, and $h_a(x) = x$ when $x \neq a$. Hence, $h_a(\sigma)$ erases all occurrences of a in the word σ.

2.2   The Formalism of VPTS

Visibly Pushdown Labeled Transition System (VPTS) is an appropriate formalism with a potentially infinite memory that allow us to model pushdown reactive systems. VPTS models can specify the asynchronous exchange of messages between a system and the environment, where the outputs do not have to occur synchronously with inputs, *i.e.*, output messages are generated as separated events. Next we formally define VPTS models.

Definition 1. *A* Visibly Pushdown Labeled Transition System *(VPTS) over an input alphabet L is a tuple* $\mathcal{S} = \langle S, S_{in}, L, \Gamma, T \rangle$, *where:*

- *S is a finite set of* states *or* locations;
- *$S_{in} \subseteq S$ is the set of* initial states;
- *There is a special symbol $\varsigma \notin L$, the* internal action symbol;
- *Γ is a set of* stack symbols. *There is a special symbol $\bot \notin \Gamma$, the* bottom-of-stack symbol;
- *$T = T_c \cup T_r \cup T_i$, where $T_c \subseteq S \times L_c \times \Gamma \times S$, $T_r \subseteq S \times L_r \times \Gamma_\bot \times S$, and $T_i \subseteq S \times (L_i \cup \{\varsigma\}) \times \{\sharp\} \times S$, where $\sharp \notin \Gamma_\bot$ is a place-holder symbol.*

Assume that $t = (p, x, Z, q)$ is a transition of T. We call by *push-transition* when $t \in T_c$ and the meaning is reading an input x when moving from the state p to q in $\mathcal{S}$, and pushes Z onto the stack. We also call *pop-transition* if $t \in T_r$, and in this case, the intended meaning is that, changing $\mathcal{S}$ from p to q, $x \in L_r$ is read in $\mathcal{S}$, and pops Z from the stack. Notice that a pop move can be taken when the stack is empty, leaving the stack unchanged, if the pop symbol is $\perp$. Finally, we call by a *simple-transition* when $t \in T_i$ and $x \in L_i$, and by an *internal-transition* when $t \in T_i$ and $x = \varsigma$. A simple-transition t that reads x when moving from p to q does not change the stack. Likewise an internal-transition does not change the stack, but further does not read any symbol from the input.

Next we give the notion of configurations and precisely define elementary moves in VPTS models.

Definition 2. *Let* $\mathcal{S} = \langle S, S_{in}, L, \Gamma, T \rangle$ *be a VPTS. A* configuration *of* $\mathcal{S}$ *is a pair* $(p, \alpha) \in S \times (\Gamma^*\{\perp\})$. *When* $p \in S_{in}$ *and* $\alpha = \perp$, *we say that* (p, α) *is an* initial configuration *of* $\mathcal{S}$. *The set of all configurations of* $\mathcal{S}$ *is indicated by* $\mathcal{C}_{\mathcal{S}}$. *Let* $(q, \alpha) \in \mathcal{C}_{\mathcal{S}}$, *and let* $\ell \in L_\varsigma$. *Then we write* $(p, \alpha) \xrightarrow{\ell} (q, \beta)$ *if there is a transition* $(p, \ell, Z, q) \in T$, *and either:*

1. $\ell \in L_c$, *and* $\beta = Z\alpha$;
2. $\ell \in L_r$, *and either (i)* $Z \neq \perp$ *and* $\alpha = Z\beta$, *or (ii)* $Z = \alpha = \beta = \perp$;
3. $\ell \in L_i \cup \{\varsigma\}$ *and* $\alpha = \beta$.

Then an elementary move *of* $\mathcal{S}$ *is represented by* $(p, \alpha) \xrightarrow{\ell} (q, \beta)$ *when the transition* $(p, \ell, Z, q) \in T$ *is used in this move. Further, after any elementary move* $(p, \alpha) \xrightarrow{\ell} (q, \beta)$, $(q, \beta) \in \mathcal{C}_{\mathcal{S}}$ *is also a configuration of* $\mathcal{S}$.

From now on, when graphically depicting VPTSs, we will represent a push-transition (s, x, Z, q) by x/Z_+ next to the corresponding arc from s to q in the figure. Similarly, a pop-transition (s, x, Z, q) will be indicated by the label x/Z_- next to the arc from s to q. Simple- or internal-transitions over $(s, x, \natural, q)$ will be indicated by the label x next to the corresponding arc.

Example 3. *Figure 1 represents a VPTS* $\mathcal{S}_1$ *where the set of states is* $S = \{s_0, s_1\}$, $S_{in} = \{s_0\}$. *Also, we have* $L_c = \{b\}$, $L_r = \{c, t\}$, $L_i = \{\}$, *and* $\Gamma = \{Z\}$. *We have a push-transition* (s_0, b, Z, s_0), *the pop-transitions* (s_0, c, Z, s_1), (s_0, t, Z, s_1), (s_1, c, Z, s_1), (s_1, t, Z, s_1), *and the internal-transition* $(s_1, \varsigma, \natural, s_0)$. *Intuitively, the behavior of* $\mathcal{S}$ *says that we can have the symbol* b *as many as we want, while pushing the symbol* Z *on the stack. Next at least one corresponding* c *or* t *must occur, and then one symbol* Z *must be popped from the stack,*

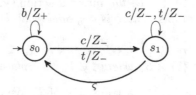

Fig. 1. A VPTS $\mathcal{S}_1$, with $L_c = \{b\}$, $L_r = \{c, t\}$, $L_i = \emptyset$.

or several symbols c and t can occur while the stack memory is not empty. After that, this process can be restarted moving S back to state s_0, over the internal label ς.

When a sequence of events is induced over a VPTS model we can observe its behavior. That is, we can obtain the semantics of a VPTS by its traces, or behaviors.

Definition 4. *Let $S = \langle S, S_{in}, L, \Gamma, T \rangle$ be a VPTS and let $(p, \alpha), (q, \beta) \in \mathcal{C}_S$.*

1. *Let $\sigma = l_1, \ldots, l_n$ be a word in $L_\varsigma^\star$. We say that σ is a trace from (p, α) to (q, β) if there are configurations $(r_i, \alpha_i) \in \mathcal{C}_S$, $0 \leq i \leq n$, such that $(r_{i-1}, \alpha_{i-1}) \xrightarrow{l_i} (r_i, \alpha_i)$, $1 \leq i \leq n$, with $(r_0, \alpha_0) = (p, \alpha)$ and $(r_n, \alpha_n) = (q, \beta)$.*
2. *Let $\sigma \in L^\star$. We say that σ is an observable trace from (p, α) to (q, β) in S if there is a trace μ from (p, α) to (q, β) in S such that $\sigma = h_\varsigma(\mu)$.*

In both cases we also say that the trace starts at (p, α) and ends at (q, β), and we say that the configuration (q, β) is reachable from (p, α). We also say that (q, β) is reachable in S if it is reachable from an initial configuration of S.

Note that moves with internal symbol ς can occur in a trace, but when ς-labels are removed we just say that it is an observable trace. If σ is a trace from (p, α) to (q, β), we can also write $(p, \alpha) \xrightarrow{\sigma} (q, \beta)$. We may also write $(p, \alpha) \xrightarrow{\sigma}$, $(p, \alpha) \rightarrow (q, \beta)$, and $(p, \alpha) \rightarrow$ when $(q, \beta) \in \mathcal{C}_S$, $\sigma \in L_\varsigma^\star$, or both, respectively, are not important. Also we write $(p, \alpha) \xrightarrow[S]{\sigma} (q, \beta)$ to emphasize that the underlying VPTS is S. If σ is an observable trace from (p, α) to (q, β), we may also write $(p, \alpha) \xRightarrow{\sigma} (q, \beta)$, with similar shorthand notation also carrying over to the $\Rightarrow$ relation.

We call the traces of (p, α), or the traces starting at (p, α), for all traces starting at a given configuration (p, α). Now we can define the semantics of a VPTS by all traces starting at an initial configuration.

Definition 5. *Let $S = \langle S, S_{in}, L, \Gamma, T \rangle$ be a VPTS and let $(p, \alpha) \in \mathcal{C}_S$.*

1. *The set of traces of (p, α) is $tr(p, \alpha) = \{\sigma \mid (p, \alpha) \xrightarrow{\sigma}\}$. The set of observable traces of (p, α) is $otr(p, \alpha) = \{\sigma \mid (p, \alpha) \xRightarrow{\sigma}\}$.*
2. *The semantics of S is $\bigcup_{q \in S_{in}} tr(q, \perp)$, and the observable semantics of S is $\bigcup_{q \in S_{in}} otr(q, \perp)$.*

We will also indicate the semantics and, respectively, the observable semantics, of S by $tr(S)$ and $otr(S)$. If $(s, \alpha) \Rightarrow (p, \beta)$ then we also have $(s, \alpha) \rightarrow (p, \beta)$ in S, for all $(s, \alpha), (p, \beta) \in \mathcal{C}_S$. Moreover, $otr(S) = h_\varsigma(tr(S))$ and when S has no internal transitions we already have $otr(S) = tr(S)$.

We also note that ς-labeled self-loops can also be eliminated in a VPTS since they play no role when considering any system behaviors. So given a VPTS $S = \langle S, S_{in}, L, \Gamma, T \rangle$, for any $s \in S$ we postulate that $(s_0, \perp) \xrightarrow{\sigma} (s, \alpha\perp)$, for some

$\alpha \in \Gamma^*$, $\sigma \in L_\varsigma^*$, and $s_0 \in S_{in}$. Further, if $(s, \varsigma, \sharp, q) \in T$ then $s \neq q$. In general, ς-moves indicate that a VPTS can autonomously move along ς-transitions, without consuming any input symbol. But in some cases such moves may be undesirable, or simply we might want no observable behavior leading to two distinct states. Then we need the notion of determinism in VPTS models.

Definition 6. *Let* $\mathcal{S} = \langle S, S_{in}, L, \Gamma, T \rangle$ *be a VPTS. We say that* $\mathcal{S}$ *is deterministic if, for all* s, $p \in S_{in}$, s_1, $s_2 \in S$, $\beta_1, \beta_2 \in \Gamma^*$, *and* $\sigma \in L^*$, *we have that* $(s, \perp) \overset{\sigma}{\Rightarrow} (s_1, \beta_1 \perp)$ *and* $(p, \perp) \overset{\sigma}{\Rightarrow} (s_2, \beta_2 \perp)$ *imply* $s_1 = s_2$ *and* $\beta_1 = \beta_2$.

2.3   Contracted VPTSs

The syntactic description of VPTSs can also be reduced, without losing any semantic capability, by removing states that are not reachable from any initial state. Moreover, we can remove transitions in a VPTS model that cannot be exercised by some trace. Since every transition, except possibly for pop transitions, can always be taken, we concentrate on the pop transitions.

Definition 7. *We say that a VPTS* $\mathcal{S} = \langle S, S_{in}, L, \Gamma, T \rangle$ *is contracted if for every transition* $(p, b, Z, r) \in T$ *with* $b \in L_r$, *there are some* $s_0 \in S_{in}$, $\alpha \in \Gamma^*$ *and* $\sigma \in L^*$ *such that* $(s_0, \perp) \overset{\sigma}{\Rightarrow} (p, \alpha \perp)$, *where either (i)* $\alpha = Z\beta$ *for some* $\beta \in \Gamma^*$, *or (ii)* $\alpha = \varepsilon$ *and* $Z = \perp$.

Given a VPTS, Proposition 8 can then obtain a contracted VPTS. The idea is to construct a context free grammar (CFG) based on the given VPTS, in such a way that the CFG generates strings where terminals represent VPTS transitions. The productions of the CFG will indicate the set of transitions that can be effectively used in a trace over the VPTS.

Proposition 8. *Let* $\mathcal{S} = \langle S, S_{in}, L, \Gamma, T \rangle$ *be a VPTS. We can effectively construct a contracted VPTS* $\mathcal{Q} = \langle Q, Q_{in}, L, \Gamma, R \rangle$ *with* $|Q| \leq |S|$, *and such that* $tr(\mathcal{S}) = tr(\mathcal{Q})$. *Moreover, if* $\mathcal{S}$ *is deterministic, then* $\mathcal{Q}$ *is also deterministic.*

Proof. First we construct a context-free grammar G whose terminals represent transitions of $\mathcal{S}$. Non-terminals are of the form $[s, Z, p]$ where $s, p \in S$ are states of $\mathcal{S}$ and $Z \in \Gamma_\perp$ is a stack symbol. The main idea can be grasped as follows. Let $t_i = [s_i, a_i, Z_i, p_i]$, $1 \leq i \leq n$ be transitions of $\mathcal{S}$ and let $\sigma = a_1 a_2 \cdots a_n$ be an input string. If G has a leftmost derivation it must be the case that $\mathcal{S}$, starting at the initial configuration $(s_0, \perp)$, can move along the transitions $t_1, \ldots, t_n$, in that order, to reach the configuration $(r_1, W_1 W_2 \cdots W_m \perp)$. That is, $(s_0, \perp) \overset{\sigma}{\rightarrow} (r_1, W_1 W_2 \cdots W_m \perp)$, where $\sigma = a_1 a_2 \cdots a_n$. And vice-versa. We then show that leftmost derivations of G faithfully simulate traces of $\mathcal{S}$ and, conversely, that any trace of $\mathcal{S}$ can be simulated by a leftmost derivation of G. That done, we can easily extract from G a contracted VPTS $\mathcal{Q}$. A simple argument then proves that $L(\mathcal{Q}) = tr(\mathcal{S})$.

$$[s_0, \perp, -] \overset{*}{\hookrightarrow} t_1 \cdots t_n [r_1, W_1, r_2][r_2, W_2, r_3] \cdots [r_m, W_m, r_{m+1}][r_{m+1}, \perp, -]$$

The complete construction and the detailed proof can be found in [2].

2.4   Relating VPTS and VPA Models

Our testing approach is defined for VPTS models, but using their associated VPAs. A Visibly Pushdown Automaton (VPA) [1] is, basically, a Pushdown Automaton (PDA) [10], with a transition relation over an alphabet and a push-down stack (or just a stack, for short) associated to it. Any alphabet L is always partitioned into three disjoint subsets $L = L_c \cup L_r \cup L_i$. Elements in the set L_c are "call symbols", or "push symbols", and specify push actions on the stack. Elements in L_r are "return symbols", or "pop symbols", and indicate pop actions, and in L_i we find "simple symbols", that do not change the stack.

The next definition is a slight extension of the similar notion appearing in [1].

Definition 9. *A Visibly Pushdown Automaton (VPA) [1] over a finite input alphabet A is a tuple $\mathcal{A} = \langle S, S_{in}, A, \Gamma, \rho, F \rangle$, where:*

- *$A = A_c \cup A_r \cup A_i$ and A_c, A_r, A_i are pairwise disjoint;*
- *S is a finite set of* states;
- *$S_{in} \subseteq S$ is set of* initial states;
- *Γ is a finite stack alphabet, with $\perp \notin \Gamma$ the* initial stack symbol;
- *The* transition relation *is $\rho = \rho_c \cup \rho_r \cup \rho_i$, where $\rho_c \subseteq S \times A_c \times \Gamma \times S$, $\rho_r \subseteq S \times A_r \times \Gamma_\perp \times S$, and $\rho_i \subseteq S \times (A_i \cup \{\varepsilon\}) \times \{\natural\} \times S$, where $\natural \notin \Gamma_\perp$ is a place-holder symbol;*
- *$F \subseteq S$ is the set of* final states.

A transition $(p, \varepsilon, \natural, q) \in \rho_i$ is called an ε-move of $\mathcal{A}$. A configuration of $\mathcal{A}$ is any triple $(p, \sigma, \alpha) \in S \times A^* \times (\Gamma^* \{\perp\})$, and the set of all configurations of $\mathcal{A}$ it is indicated by $\mathcal{C}_\mathcal{A}$.

The semantics of a VPA is the language comprised by all input strings it accepts, and such language is said to be a *Visibly Pushdown Language (VPL)* [2]. That is, let A be an alphabet and let $G \subseteq A^*$ be a language over A, then G is a *Visibly Pushdown Language* if there is a VPA $\mathcal{A}$ such that $L(\mathcal{A}) = G$.

In the context of this work, we need the notion of non-blocking VPAs and also the notion of determinism for VPAs. Similarly to VPTS models, we say that a VPA is *deterministic* if there is at most one computation for a given input string [1,2]. Further, a *non-blocking* VPA can always read any string of input symbols when started at any state and with any stack configuration.

Next we show that any VPTS $\mathcal{S}$ gives rise to an associated VPA $\mathcal{S}_A$ in a natural way. We convert any ς-transition of $\mathcal{S}$ into a ε-transition of $\mathcal{S}_A$. The set of final states of $\mathcal{S}_A$ is just the set of all locations of $\mathcal{S}$. Conversely, we can associate a VPA to any given VPTS, provided that all states in the given VPA are final states.

Definition 10. *We have the following two associations:*

1. *Let $\mathcal{S} = \langle S, S_{in}, L, \Gamma, T \rangle$ be a VPTS. The VPA induced by $\mathcal{S}$ is $\mathcal{A}_\mathcal{S} = \langle S, S_{in}, L, \Gamma, \rho, S \rangle$ where, for all p, $q \in S$, $Z \in \Gamma$, $\ell \in L$, we have:*
   (a) *$(p, \ell, Z, q) \in \rho$ if and only if $(p, \ell, Z, q) \in T$;*
   (b) *$(p, \varepsilon, \natural, q) \in \rho$ if and only if $(p, \varsigma, \natural, q) \in T$.*

2. Let $\mathcal{A} = \langle S, S_{in}, L, \Gamma, \rho, S \rangle$ be a VPA. The VPTS induced by $\mathcal{A}$ is $\mathcal{S}_A = \langle S, S_{in}, L, \Gamma, T \rangle$ where:
   (a) $(p, \ell, Z, q) \in T$ if and only if $(p, \ell, Z, q) \in \rho$;
   (b) $(p, \varsigma, \natural, q) \in T$ if and only if $(p, \varepsilon, \natural, q) \in \rho$.

The relationship of a VPTS and its associated VPA is precisely given in [2].

Proposition 11 then establishes that the observable semantics of a VPTS S is just the language accepted by its associated VPA A_S. Further, it also says that $otr(\mathcal{S})$ is a visibly pushdown language, and that for any given VPTS $\mathcal{S}$, we can easily construct a VPA $\mathcal{A}$ with $L(\mathcal{A}) = otr(\mathcal{S})$.

Proposition 11. *Let $\mathcal{S}$ be a VPTS and A_S the VPA induced by $\mathcal{S}$. Then $otr(\mathcal{S}) = L(A_S)$ and, further, if $\mathcal{S}$ is deterministic and contracted then A_S is also deterministic. Conversely, let A be a VPA and $\mathcal{S}_A$ the VPTS induced by A. Then $L(\mathcal{A}) = otr(\mathcal{S}_A)$ and, also, if A is deterministic and has no ε-moves, then $\mathcal{S}_A$ is deterministic.*

Proof. The detailed proof can be found in [2].

Now we look at some closure properties involving VPLs [1,2]. The next proposition establishes these properties.

Proposition 12 ([2]). *Let $\mathcal{S}$ and $\mathcal{Q}$ be two VPAs over an alphabet A, with n and m states, respectively, then we can construct*

1. *a VPA $\mathcal{P}$ over A with mn states that can accept $L(\mathcal{P}) = L(\mathcal{S}) \cap L(\mathcal{Q})$. Moreover, if $\mathcal{S}$ and $\mathcal{Q}$ are deterministic, then $\mathcal{P}$ is also deterministic.*
2. *a non-blocking VPA $\mathcal{P}$ over A with at most $(n+1)(m+1)$ states and such that $L(\mathcal{P}) = L(\mathcal{S}) \cup L(\mathcal{Q})$. Moreover, if $\mathcal{S}$ and $\mathcal{Q}$ are deterministic, then $\mathcal{P}$ is also deterministic and has no ε-moves.*
3. *a non-blocking and deterministic VPA $\mathcal{P}$ over A with no ε-moves, with $n+1$ states, and such that $L(\mathcal{P}) = \overline{L(\mathcal{S})} = \Sigma^* - L(\mathcal{S})$.*

Proof. All constructions and detailed proofs can be found in [2].

2.5   Input/Output VPTSs

The VPTS formalism can be used to model systems with a potentially infinite memory and with a capacity to interact asynchronously with an external environment. In such situations, we may want to treat some action labels as symbols that the VPTS "receives" from the environment and some other action labels as symbols that the VPTS "sends back" to the environment. The next VPTS variation differentiates between input action symbols and output action symbols.

Definition 13. *An Input/Output Visibly Pushdown Transition System (IOVPTS) over an alphabet L is a tuple $\mathcal{I} = \langle S, S_{in}, L_I, L_U, \Gamma, T \rangle$, where*

– L_I *is a finite set of* input actions, *or* input labels;
– L_U *is a finite set of* output actions, *or* output labels;

– $L_I \cap L_U = \emptyset$, and $L = L_I \cup L_U$ is the set of actions or labels; and
– $\langle S, S_{in}, L, \Gamma, T \rangle$ is an underlying VPTS over L, which is associated to $\mathfrak{I}$.

We denote the class of all IOVPTSs with input alphabet L_I and output alphabet L_U by $\mathfrak{IOVP}(L_I, L_U)$. Notice that in any reference to an IOVPTS model we can substitute it by its underlying VPTS. So if $\mathfrak{S}$ is an IOVPTS with $\mathfrak{Q}$ as its underlying VPTS, then the VPA induced by $\mathfrak{S}$ is the VPA induced by $\mathfrak{Q}$, according to Definition 10. Likewise for any formal assertion involving IOVPTSs.

Next we define the semantics of an IOVPTS as the set of its observable traces, that is, observable traces of its underlying VPTS.

Definition 14. Let $\mathfrak{I} = \langle S, S_{in}, L_I, L_U, \Gamma, T \rangle$ be an IOVPTS. The semantics of $\mathfrak{I}$ is the set $otr(\mathfrak{I}) = otr(\mathfrak{S}_{\mathfrak{I}})$, where $\mathfrak{S}_{\mathfrak{I}}$ is the underlying VPTS associated to $\mathfrak{I}$.

Also, when referring an IOVPTS $\mathfrak{I}$, the notation $\xrightarrow{}_{\mathfrak{I}}$ and $\Rightarrow_{\mathfrak{I}}$ are to be understood as $\xrightarrow{}_{\mathfrak{S}}$ and $\Rightarrow_{\mathfrak{S}}$, respectively, where $\mathfrak{S}$ is the underlying VPTS associated to $\mathfrak{I}$.

Example 15. Recall Example 3. Now, Fig. 1 represents an IOVPTS that describes a machine that dispenses drinks. Again we have $L_c = \{b\}$, $L_r = \{c, t\}$ and $L_i = \emptyset$, with the initial state s_0, but here we also have $L_I = \{b\}$ and $L_U = \{c, t\}$. In this context, symbol b stands for a button where an user can press when asking for a drink, a cup of coffee or a cup of tea, represented by the labels c and t, respectively. The user can hit the b button while the machine stays at state s_0. Each time the b button is activated, the machine pushes a symbol Z on the stack, so that the stack is used to count how many times the b button was hit by the user.

At any instant, after the user has activated the b button at least once, the machine moves to state s_1 and starts dispensing either coffee or tea, indicated by the c and t labels. It decrements the stack each time a drink is dispensed, so that it will never deliver more drinks than the user asked for.

A move back to state s_0, over the internal label ς, may interrupt the delivery of drinks, so that the user can, possibly, receive less drinks than originally asked for. In this case, when the next user will operate the machine with residual number of Z symbols in the stack he could, eventually, collect more drinks than asked for. But the machine will never dispense more drinks than the total number of solicitations. An alternative could be to use one more state s_2 to interrupt the transition from s_1 to s_0 and install a self-loop at s_2 that empties the stack.

3   Visibly Pushdown Conformance Checking

In this section we define a more general conformance relation based on Visibly Pushdown Languages [1], a proper subset of the more general class of context-free languages [10], but a proper superset of the regular languages. Here we define fault models for VPTSs using this more general relation and study the notion of test suite completeness under this setting. In sequel we give a method to check conformance between an IUT and its specification, both given by VPTS models, and using the more general conformance relation over VPLs.

3.1   A General Conformance Relation for VPTS Models

The more general conformance relation is defined on subsets of words specified by a tester. Informally, consider a language D, the set of "desirable" behaviors, and a language F, the set of "forbidden" behaviors, of a system. If we have a specification VPTS S and an implementation VPTS J we want to say that J *conforms* to S according to (D, F) if no undesired behavior in F that is observable in J is specified in S, and all desired behaviors in D that are observable in J are specified in S. This leads to the following definition.

Definition 16. *Let L be an alphabet, and let $D, F \subseteq L^\star$. Let S and J be VPTSs over L. We say that J (D, F)-visibly conforms to S, written J vconf$_{D,F}$ S, if and only if*

1. $\sigma \in otr(J) \cap F$, *then* $\sigma \notin otr(S)$;
2. $\sigma \in otr(J) \cap D$, *then* $\sigma \in otr(S)$.

Notice that this notion of conformance relation is more general in the sense that it includes classical conformance relations such as **ioco** [3,14] and **ioco-like** [4,6,7] relations. Suppose an IUT, for instance, that **ioco(-like)** conforms to its specification following the classical relations. When we set the sets D and F, even if the IUT conforms to the specification according to a specific relation, we can still detect a fault behavior specified in F, or we can confirm if a desirable behavior given by D is present in the IUT.

We note an equivalent way of expressing these conditions that may also be useful. Recall that the complement of $otr(S)$ is $\overline{otr}(S) = L^\star - otr(S)$.

Proposition 17. *Let S and J be VPTSs over L and let $D, F \subseteq L^\star$. Then J vconf$_{D,F}$ S if and only if $otr(J) \cap [(D \cap \overline{otr}(S)) \cup (F \cap otr(S))] = \emptyset$.*

Proof. From Definition 16 we readily get J **vconf**$_{D,F}$ S if and only if $otr(J) \cap F \cap otr(S) = \emptyset$ and $otr(J) \cap D \cap \overline{otr}(S) = \emptyset$. And this holds if and only if

$$\emptyset = [otr(J) \cap F \cap otr(S)] \cup [otr(J) \cap D \cap \overline{otr}(S)] = otr(J) \cap [(D \cap \overline{otr}(S)) \cup (F \cap otr(S))],$$

as desired.

Example 18. *Let S be an IOVPTS specification depicted in Fig. 2a, where $L_I = \{a, b\}$, $L_U = \{x\}$, $L_c = \{a\}$, $L_r = \{b, x\}$ and $L_i = \emptyset$. Also, $S_{in} = \{s_0\}$ and $\Gamma = \{A\}$.*

Take the languages $D = \{a^n b^n x : n \geq 1\}$ and $F = \{a^n b^{n+1} : n \geq 0\}$. This says that any behavior consisting of a block of as followed by an equal length block of bs and terminating by an x, is a desirable behavior. Any block of as followed by a lengthier block of bs is undesirable. We want to check whether the implementation J conforms to the specification S with respect to the sets of behaviors described by D and F. That is, we want to check whether J vconf$_{D,F}$ S.

First, we obtain the VPA $\overline{S}$ depicted in Fig. 3a. Since S is deterministic and all its states are final according to Definition 10, we just add a new state err

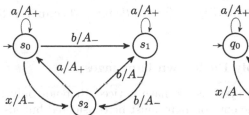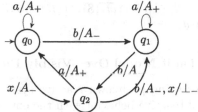

(a) An IOVPTS specification $\mathcal{S}$ with $L_I = \{a, b\}$ and $L_U = \{x\}$.

(b) An implementation IOVPTS $\mathcal{J}$ with $L_I = \{a, b\}$ and $L_U = \{x\}$.

Fig. 2. IOVPTS models $\mathcal{S}$ and $\mathcal{J}$.

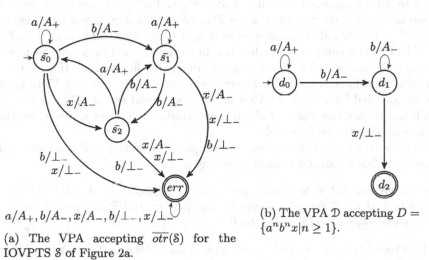

(a) The VPA accepting $\overline{otr}(\mathcal{S})$ for the IOVPTS $\mathcal{S}$ of Figure 2a.

(b) The VPA $\mathcal{D}$ accepting $D = \{a^n b^n x | n \geq 1\}$.

Fig. 3. VPA models $\overline{\mathcal{S}}$ and $\mathcal{D}$.

to $\overline{\mathcal{S}}$, and for any missing transitions in $\mathcal{S}$ we add corresponding transitions ending at err in $\overline{\mathcal{S}}$. It is not hard to see that the language accepted by $\overline{\mathcal{S}}$ is $\overline{otr}(\mathcal{S})$. Again, it is easy to see from Fig. 2a that $a^n b^{n+1} \notin otr(\mathcal{S})$, for all $n \geq 0$. So, $F \cap otr(\mathcal{S}) = \emptyset$. Also we see that the VPA $\mathcal{D}$, depicted at Fig. 3b, accepts the language D and that $D \subseteq \overline{otr}(\mathcal{S})$. Then the VPA $\mathcal{D}$ accepts the language $T = D \cap \overline{otr}(\mathcal{S}) = (D \cap \overline{otr}(\mathcal{S})) \cup (F \cap otr(\mathcal{S}))$.

Now let $\mathcal{J}$ be the implementation depicted in Fig. 2b. A simple inspection also shows that $aabbx$ is accepted by $\mathcal{J}$, and we also have $aabbx \in D$. Hence, $otr(\mathcal{J}) \cap D \cap \overline{otr}(\mathcal{S}) = otr(\mathcal{J}) \cap T \neq \emptyset$, and Proposition 17 implies that $\mathcal{J} \mathbf{vconf}_{D,F} \mathcal{S}$ does not hold.

On the other hand, if we assume an implementation $\mathcal{J}$ that is isomorphic to $\mathcal{S}$, $\mathcal{J}$ would not have the transition $q_2 \xrightarrow{x/\perp} q_1$ and then $aabbx$ would not be an observable behavior of $\mathcal{J}$. Actually, in this case, $otr(\mathcal{J}) \cap D \cap \overline{otr}(\mathcal{S}) = \emptyset$. So that *now* $otr(\mathcal{I}) \cap [(D \cap \overline{otr}(\mathcal{S})) \cup (F \cap otr(\mathcal{S}))] = \emptyset$, *and therefore* $\mathcal{I}\,\mathbf{vconf}_{D,F}\,\mathcal{S}$, *as expected.*

3.2   Fault Model Over Visibly Pushdown Languages

When testing pushdown reactive systems we have noticed that not only their natural reactive behavior with the environment must be considered but also we need to deal with a potentially infinite memory. A fault model for systems of this nature must then be able to find faults in IUTs according to their corresponding specification modeled by VPTSs, *i.e.*, the fault model must provide a fault detection in the testing process. A sequence of symbols that can detect faults in VPTS models is called a *test case*, and a set of test cases gives the notion of a *test suite*. So, a test suite T over an alphabet L is a language over L, *i.e.* $T \subseteq L^{\star}$, should be engineered to detect faulty observable behavior of any given IUT, when compared to what has been determined by a specification. In this case, T can be seen as specifying a fault model, in the sense that test cases in T represent faulty observable behaviors. In particular, if T is a VPL, then it can be specified by a VPA $\mathcal{A}$. Alternatively, we could specify T by a finite set of VPAs, so that the union of all the undesirable behaviors specified by these VPAs comprise the fault model.

Next we say that an implementation $\mathcal{I}$ passes a test suite T if no observable behavior of $\mathcal{I}$ is a harmful behavior present in T.

Definition 19. *Let T be a test suite over an alphabet L. A VPTS $\mathcal{Q}$ over L passes to T if $\sigma \notin T$ for all $\sigma \in otr(\mathcal{Q})$. Further, an IOVPTS $\mathcal{I}$ over L passes to T if its underlying VPTS passes to T.*

In a testing process we also desire test suites to be sound, *i.e.*, when $\mathcal{I}$ passes a test suite T we always have that $\mathcal{I}$-visibly conforms to $\mathcal{S}$. The opposite direction is also desirable, that is, if $\mathcal{I}$-visibly conforms to $\mathcal{S}$ then $\mathcal{I}$ passes the test suite T.

Definition 20. *Let L be an alphabet and let T be a test suite over L. Also let $\mathcal{S}$ be a specification VPTS over L, and let $D, F \subseteq L^{\star}$ be languages over L. Then*

1. *T is* sound *for $\mathcal{S}$ and (D, F) if $\mathcal{I}$ passes to T implies $\mathcal{I}\,\mathbf{vconf}_{D,F}\,\mathcal{S}$, for all VPTS $\mathcal{I}$ over L.*
2. *T is* exhaustive *for $\mathcal{S}$ and (D, F) if $\mathcal{I}\,\mathbf{vconf}_{D,F}\,\mathcal{S}$ implies that $\mathcal{I}$ passes to T, for all VPTS $\mathcal{I}$ over L.*
3. *T is* complete *for $\mathcal{S}$ and (D, F) if it is both sound and exhaustive for $\mathcal{S}$ and (D, F).*

Notice that an IUT $\mathcal{I}$ passes to a test suite T when $otr(\mathcal{I}) \cap T = \emptyset$.

Now we can show that the Proposition 17 can construct a test suite which is always complete, and also unique, for a given specification $\mathcal{S}$.

Lemma 21. *Let $\mathcal{S}$ be a specification VPTS over L, and let $D, F \subseteq L^{\star}$ be a pair of languages over L. Then, the set $[(D \cap \overline{otr}(\mathcal{S})) \cup (F \cap otr(\mathcal{S}))]$ is the only complete test suite for $\mathcal{S}$ and (D, F).*

Proof. Write $T = [(D \cap \overline{otr}(S)) \cup (F \cap otr(S))]$, and let $\mathfrak{I}$ be any implementation VPTS over L. From Definition 19, we know that $\mathfrak{I}$ passes to T if and only if $otr(\mathfrak{I}) \cap T = \emptyset$. From Proposition 17 we get that $\mathfrak{I}\,\mathbf{vconf}_{D,F}\,S$ if and only if $otr(\mathfrak{I}) \cap T = \emptyset$. Hence, $\mathfrak{I}$ passes to T if and only if $\mathfrak{I}\,\mathbf{vconf}_{D,F}\,S$. Since $\mathfrak{I}$ was arbitrary, from Definition 20 we conclude that T is a complete test suite for S and (D, F).

Now, take another test suite $Z \subseteq L^{\star}$, with $Z \neq T$. For the sake of contradiction, assume that Z is also complete for S and (D, F). Fix any implementation $\mathfrak{I}$. Since Z is complete, Definition 20 says that $\mathfrak{I}$ passes to Z if and only if $\mathfrak{I}\,\mathbf{vconf}_{D,F}\,S$. Using Proposition 17 we know that $\mathfrak{I}\,\mathbf{vconf}_{D,F}\,S$ if and only if $otr(\mathfrak{I}) \cap T = \emptyset$. Hence, $\mathfrak{I}$ passes to Z if and only if $otr(\mathfrak{I}) \cap T = \emptyset$. From Definition 19 we know that $\mathfrak{I}$ passes to Z if and only if $otr(\mathfrak{I}) \cap Z = \emptyset$. We conclude that $otr(\mathfrak{I}) \cap Z = \emptyset$ if and only if $otr(\mathfrak{I}) \cap T = \emptyset$. But $Z \neq T$ gives some $\sigma \in L^{\star}$ such that $\sigma \in T$ and $\sigma \notin Z$. The case $\sigma \notin T$ and $\sigma \in Z$ is entirely analogous. We now have $\sigma \in T \cap \overline{Z}$. If we can construct an implementation VPTS $\mathfrak{Q}$ over L with $\sigma \in otr(\mathfrak{Q})$, then we have reached a contradiction because we would have $\sigma \in otr(\mathfrak{Q}) \cap T$ and $\sigma \notin otr(\mathfrak{Q}) \cap Z$. But that is simple. Let $\sigma = x_1 x_2 \ldots x_k$, with $k \geq 0$ and $x_i \in L$ $(1 \leq i \leq k)$. Define $L_c = L_r = \emptyset$ and $L_i = L$, and let $\mathfrak{Q} = \langle Q, \{q_0\}, L, \emptyset, R \rangle$, where $Q = \{q_i \mid 0 \leq i \leq k\}$, and $R = \{(q_{i-1}, x_i, \natural, q_i) \mid 1 \leq i \leq k\}$. Clearly, $\sigma \in otr(\mathfrak{Q})$, concluding the proof.

Lemma 21 says that the test suite $T = [(D \cap \overline{otr}(S)) \cup (F \cap otr(S))]$ is complete for the specification S and the pair of languages (D, F). So, given an implementation $\mathfrak{I}$, checking if it (D, F)-visibly conforms to S is equivalent to checking if $\mathfrak{I}$ passes to T and, by Definition 19, the latter is equivalent to checking that we have $otr(\mathfrak{I}) \cap T = \emptyset$.

3.3 Visual Conformance Checking for VPTS Models

When checking conformance one important issue is the size of test suites, relatively to the size of the given specification. Let $S = \langle S, S_{in}, L, \Gamma, T \rangle$ be a VPTS. A reasonable measure of the size of S would be the number of symbols required to write down a complete syntactic description of S. Assume that S has $m = |T|$ transitions, $n = |S|$ states, $\ell = |L|$ action symbols, and $p = |\Gamma|$ stack symbols. Since any transition can be written using $\mathcal{O}(\ln(n\ell p))$ symbols, the size of S is $\mathcal{O}(m \ln(n\ell p))$. We also see that n is $\mathcal{O}(m)$ and, clearly, so are ℓ and p. Thus, the size of S is bounded by $\mathcal{O}(m \ln m)$. If we fix the stack and action alphabets, then the size of the VPTS will be bounded by $\mathcal{O}(m)$. In what follows, and with almost no prejudice, we will ignore the small logarithmic factor.[1]

Given a specification S and visibly pushdown languages, D and F, over L, Lemma 21 says that the fault model T is complete for S and (D, F), where $T = [(D \cap \overline{otr}(S)) \cup (F \cap otr(S))]$. Assume that $\mathcal{A}_D$ and $\mathcal{A}_F$ are deterministic VPAs with n_D and n_F states, respectively, such that $L(\mathcal{A}_D) = D$ and $L(\mathcal{A}_F) = F$. Also,

---

[1] It is also customary to write $\mathcal{O}(m \ln m)$ as $\widetilde{\mathcal{O}}(m)$. In the sequel, we can always replace $\mathcal{O}(\cdot)$ by $\widetilde{\mathcal{O}}(\cdot)$.

assume that S is deterministic with n_S states. Proposition 8 says that we may as well take S as a contracted and deterministic VPTS. Then Proposition 11 gives a deterministic VPA $\mathcal{A}_1$ with n_S states and such that $L(\mathcal{A}_1) = otr(S)$. Using Proposition 12(3), we can construct a deterministic VPA $\mathcal{B}_1$ with $n_S + 1$ states and such that $L(\mathcal{B}_1) = \overline{L(\mathcal{A}_1)} = \overline{otr}(S)$. Using Proposition 12(1) we can obtain a deterministic VPA $\mathcal{A}_2$ with at most $n_S n_F$ states such that $L(\mathcal{A}_2) = L(\mathcal{A}_F) \cap L(\mathcal{A}_1) = F \cap otr(S)$, and also can obtain a deterministic VPA $\mathcal{B}_2$ with $(n_S+1)n_D$ states such that $L(\mathcal{B}_2) = L(\mathcal{A}_D) \cap L(\mathcal{B}_1) = D \cap \overline{otr}(S)$. Proposition 12(2) then gives a deterministic VPA $\mathcal{J}$ with $(n_S n_F+1)(n_S n_D+n_D+1)$ states and such that $L(\mathcal{J}) = L(\mathcal{A}_2) \cup L(\mathcal{B}_2) = T$. Proposition 12(2) also says that $\mathcal{J}$ is non-blocking and has no ε-moves. Further, Lemma 21 says that $L(\mathcal{J})$ is a complete test suite for S and (D, F). Next proposition establishes the construction of a complete test suite for a given specification S relatively to a pair of visibly pushdown languages (D, F).

Proposition 22. *Let S be a deterministic IOVPTS over L with n_S states. Also let $\mathcal{A}_D$ and $\mathcal{A}_F$ be deterministic VPAs over L with n_D and n_F states, respectively, such that $L(\mathcal{A}_D) = D$ and $L(\mathcal{A}_F) = F$. Then, we can construct a deterministic, non-blocking VPA $\mathcal{J}$ with at most $(n_S n_F + 1)(n_S n_D + n_D + 1)$ states and no ε-moves, and such that $L(\mathcal{J})$ is a complete test suite for S and (D, F).*

Proof. The preceding discussion gives a deterministic and non-blocking VPA $\mathcal{J}$ with at most $n_T = (n_S n_F + 1)(n_S n_D + n_D + 1)$ states and no ε-moves, and such that $L(\mathcal{J}) = T = \left[(D \cap \overline{otr}(S)) \cup (F \cap otr(S)) \right]$.

Once we have a fault model at hand, which is complete for a given specification using visibly pushdown languages, then we can test whether IUTs conform to that specification under desirable and undesirable behaviors in a more general setting. In order to do so we will also need the notion of a *balanced run* [4]. Given a VPTS $\mathcal{V}$, and p, q two states of $\mathcal{V}$ we say that a string $\sigma \in L^\star$ induces a *balanced run* [4] from p to q in $\mathcal{V}$ if we have $(p, \bot) \xrightarrow{\sigma}_{\mathcal{V}} (q, \bot)$.

Therefore we can state the next theorem to test for visual conformance.

Theorem 23. *Let $S = \langle S_S, \{s_0\}, L_I, L_U, \Delta_S, T_S \rangle \in \mathcal{IOVP}(L_I, L_U)$ be a deterministic specification, and let $\mathcal{J} = \langle S_\mathcal{J}, I_{in}, L_I, L_U, \Delta_\mathcal{J}, T_\mathcal{J} \rangle \in \mathcal{IOVP}(L_I, L_U)$ be a deterministic IUT. Also let D, F be VPLs with their corresponding deterministic VPAs $\mathcal{A}_D$ and $\mathcal{A}_F$ such that $L(\mathcal{A}_D) = D$ and $L(\mathcal{A}_F) = F$. Then we can effectively decide whether $\mathcal{J}$ **vconf**$_{D,F}$ S holds. Further, if $\mathcal{J}$ **vconf**$_{D,F}$ S does not hold then we can find $\sigma \in L^\star$ that verify this condition (See Definition 16), i.e., $\sigma \in otr(\mathcal{J}) \cap T$ showing that $otr(\mathcal{J}) \cap T \neq \emptyset$.*

Proof. First let $L = L_I \cup L_U$. The proof of Lemma 21 shows that T is the only complete test suite for S and (D, F). From Proposition 22 we can obtain a deterministic non-blocking fault model $\mathcal{J} = \langle S_\mathcal{J}, T_{in}, L_U, L_I, \Delta_\mathcal{J}, T_\mathcal{J} \rangle$ with at most $(n_S n_F + 1)(n_S n_D + n_D + 1)$ states and no ε-moves, and such that $L(\mathcal{J})$.

Since $\mathcal{J}$ is deterministic, and using Propositions 8 and 11, we can obtain a deterministic VPA $\mathcal{A}$ with at most n_I states, and such that $otr(\mathcal{J}) = L(\mathcal{A})$. Then we can construct a deterministic VPA $\mathcal{B}$ with at most $n_I n_T$ states, and such that $L(\mathcal{B}) = L(\mathcal{A}) \cap L(\mathcal{T}) = otr(\mathcal{I}) \cap T$ since VPLs are closed under intersection [2]. From Definition 19 we know that to check whether $\mathcal{I} \textbf{vconf}_{D,F} \, \mathcal{S}$ is equivalent to checking if $L(\mathcal{B}) = \emptyset$. That is, $\mathcal{I} \textbf{vconf}_{D,F} \, \mathcal{S}$ does not hold if and only if $(b_0, \perp) \overset{\sigma}{\underset{\mathcal{B}}{\Rightarrow}} (f, \alpha \perp)$ for some $\sigma \in L^*$, where b_0 is an initial state and f is a final state of $\mathcal{B}$, i.e., $\sigma \in L(\mathcal{B})$. Then we also see that in order to check whether $\mathcal{I} \textbf{vconf}_{D,F} \, \mathcal{S}$ does not hold, it suffices to check whether a configuration $(f, \alpha \perp)$ is reachable from some initial configuration $(b_0, \perp)$ of $\mathcal{B}$.

At this point we can apply Algorithm 1 of [4], following the same steps to modify $\mathcal{B}$ in order to guarantee that the stack is empty after reaching a final state f in $\mathcal{B}$, and also that any pop move on an empty stack is eliminated from $\mathcal{B}$. Similarly, the problem is then reduced to find a balanced run σ from b_0 to f in $\mathcal{B}$ if and only if $(b_0, \perp) \overset{\sigma}{\underset{\mathcal{B}}{\Rightarrow}} (f, \perp)$. That is, we have reduced the **vconf** test to the problem of finding a string σ that induces a balanced run from b_0 to f, where b_0 is the initial state of the VPA $\mathcal{B}$ and f is a final state of it, or indicate that such a string does not exist.

Example 24. *Recall Example 18. Again, let $\mathcal{S}$ be a specification depicted in Fig. 2a, and $D = \{a^n b^n x : n \geq 1\}$ be the desirable language, where the VPA $\mathcal{D}$, depicted at Fig. 3b, accepts the language D. We also recall that the VPA $\overline{\mathcal{S}}$ depicted in Fig. 3a accepts the language $\overline{otr}(\mathcal{S})$. Since $D \subseteq \overline{otr}(\mathcal{S})$ then the VPA $\mathcal{D}$ accepts the language $D \cap \overline{otr}(\mathcal{S})$.*

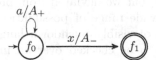

Fig. 4. The VPA $\mathcal{F}$ accepting $F = \{a^+ x\}$.

Now assume a faulty language $F \neq \emptyset$ such that $F = \{a^+ x\}$, in this case. This says that any behavior consisting of a block of as (at least one) terminating by an x, is an undesirable behavior. So the VPA $\mathcal{F}$, depicted at Fig. 4, accepts the language F and that $F \subseteq otr(\mathcal{S})$. Then the VPA $\mathcal{F}$ accepts the language $F \cap otr(\mathcal{S})$. Since the VPA $\mathcal{D}$ accepts the language $D \cap \overline{otr}(\mathcal{S})$ and the VPA $\mathcal{F}$ accepts the language $F \cap otr(\mathcal{S})$, then the language $T = (D \cap \overline{otr}(\mathcal{S})) \cup (F \cap otr(\mathcal{S})) = L(\mathcal{D}) \cup L(\mathcal{F})$.

Similarly, we want to check whether an implementation $\mathcal{I}$ conforms to the specification $\mathcal{S}$ with respect to the sets of behaviors described by D and F. That is, we want to check whether $\mathcal{I} \textbf{vconf}_{D,F} \, \mathcal{S}$.

Here also assume an implementation $\mathcal{I}$ that is isomorphic to $\mathcal{S}$. So $\mathcal{I}$ does not have the transition $q_2 \overset{x/\perp}{\rightarrow} q_1$ and then the word $aabbx$ would not be an observable behavior of $\mathcal{I}$. In this scenario, $aabbx \notin otr(\mathcal{I})$ and so $otr(\mathcal{I}) \cap [(D \cap \overline{otr}(\mathcal{S}))] = \emptyset$. The verdict means that any desirable behavior of D that is present in $\mathcal{S}$ must be a behavior of $\mathfrak{I}$. In other way around if the desirable behavior of D is not in $otr(\mathfrak{S})$ so such desirable behavior must not be in $otr(\mathfrak{I})$.

Now take the word aax. We see that aax is an observable behavior of $\mathfrak{S}$ and, clearly, it is also an observable behavior of $\mathfrak{I}$. It is easy to see that $aax \notin D$, i.e., it is not a desirable behavior. However, $aax \in F$ which means that this word represents an undesirable behavior. Hence, in this case, $otr(\mathfrak{I}) \cap [(D \cap \overline{otr}(\mathfrak{S})) \cup (F \cap otr(\mathfrak{S}))] = otr(\mathfrak{I}) \cap (D \cup F) = otr(\mathfrak{I}) \cap T \neq \emptyset$, and Proposition 17 implies that $\mathfrak{I}\,\mathbf{vconf}_{D,F}\,\mathfrak{S}$ does not hold, as expected. Noted that, in this case, the implementation does not conform to the specification, even if they are isomorphic, since an observable fault behavior is present in the specification, and consequently, in the implementation $\mathfrak{I}$.

4   Concluding Remarks

Pushdown reactive systems are more complex than traditional reactive systems because their behaviors are given by phrase structure rules in addition to their asynchronous interactions with the environment. Therefore testing activities are also more intricate when applied to systems of this nature. Several methods have been designed to treat the problem of conformance checking and test suite generation for regular reactive systems that can be specified by memoryless formal models. Few other previous approaches have addressed these same problems for pushdown reactive systems that have access to an infinite stack memory.

Here we also study the latter class of reactive systems that can make use of potentially infinite memory, but we deviated from previous works in the sense that we allow for a more wide range of possibilities to define a fault model. In this case, we make use of visibly pushdown languages to define desirable and undesirable behaviors to be checked over an implementation against its corresponding specification. That is, we treated the problem of conformance checking for asynchronous systems with a stack memory using the formalism of IOVPTS and defined a more general conformance relation for systems of this nature. So we gave a method to generate test suites that can verify whether this more general conformance relation holds between a specification and a given IUT. We have also shown that these test suites are complete, always giving a conclusive verdict, and also can be generated in polynomial time complexity.

Our approach was proved correct and reduced from the previous work [4] using an algorithm to find balanced runs to obtain verdicts of conformance. Therefore our approach exhibits an asymptotic worst case time complexity that can be bounded by $\mathcal{O}(n^3 + m^2)$, where n and m are proportional to the number of states and transitions from the product between implementations and specification models, respectively. We are currently working on an implementation of a prototype of the theoretical ideas developed in this work, and also intend to test the prototype with models that represent more practical applications.

References

1. Alur, R., Madhusudan, P.: Visibly pushdown languages. In: Proceedings of the Thirty sixth Annual ACM Symposium on Theory of Computing, STOC 2004, pp. 202–211. ACM, New York (2004). https://doi.org/10.1145/1007352.1007390
2. Bonifacio, A.L.: Conformance checking for pushdown reactive systems based on visibly pushdown languages (2023). http://arxiv.org/abs/2308.07177
3. Bonifacio, A.L., Moura, A.V.: Testing asynchronous reactive systems: beyond the ioco framework. CLEI Electron. J. **24**(10) (2021). https://doi.org/10.19153/cleiej.24.1.10
4. Bonifacio, A.L., Moura, A.V.: Conformance checking and pushdown reactive systems. CLEI Electron. J. **25**(3) (2022). https://doi.org/10.19153/cleiej.25.3.2
5. Broy, M., Jonsson, B., Katoen, J.-P., Leucker, M., Pretschner, A. (eds.): Model-Based Testing of Reactive Systems. LNCS, vol. 3472. Springer, Heidelberg (2005). https://doi.org/10.1007/b137241
6. Chédor, S., Jéron, T., Morvan, C.: Test generation from recursive tiles systems. In: Brucker, A.D., Julliand, J. (eds.) TAP 2012. LNCS, vol. 7305, pp. 99–114. Springer, Heidelberg (2012). https://doi.org/10.1007/978-3-642-30473-6_9
7. Constant, C., Jeannet, B., Jéron, T.: Automatic test generation from interprocedural specifications. In: Petrenko, A., Veanes, M., Tretmans, J., Grieskamp, W. (eds.) FATES/TestCom -2007. LNCS, vol. 4581, pp. 41–57. Springer, Heidelberg (2007). https://doi.org/10.1007/978-3-540-73066-8_4
8. Gorrieri, R.: Labeled transition systems. In: Process Algebras for Petri Nets. MTCSAES, pp. 15–34. Springer, Cham (2017). https://doi.org/10.1007/978-3-319-55559-1_2
9. Harel, D., Pnueli, A.: On the development of reactive systems. In: Apt, K.R. (ed.) Logics and Models of Concurrent Systems, vol. 13, pp. 477–498. Springer, Heidelberg (1985). https://doi.org/10.1007/978-3-642-82453-1_17
10. Hopcroft, J.E., Ullman, J.D.: Introduction to Automata Theory, Languages, and Computation. Addison Wesley, Bostpn (1979)
11. Müllerburg, M., Holenderski, L., Maffeis, O., Merceron, A., Morley, M.: Systematic testing and formal verification to validate reactive programs. Softw. Qual. J. **4**(4), 287–307 (1995). https://doi.org/10.1007/BF00402649
12. Peleska, J.: Test automation for safety-critical systems: industrial application and future developments. In: Gaudel, M.-C., Woodcock, J. (eds.) FME 1996. LNCS, vol. 1051, pp. 39–59. Springer, Heidelberg (1996). https://doi.org/10.1007/3-540-60973-3_79
13. Tretmans, G.J.: Test generation with inputs, outputs and repetitive quiescence. Technical Report TR-CTIT-96-26, Centre for Telematics and Information Technology University of Twente, Enschede (1996)
14. Tretmans, J.: Model based testing with labelled transition systems. In: Formal Methods and Testing, pp. 1–38 (2008)

Sound Test Case Generation
for Concurrent Mobile Features

Rafaela Almeida[1]($\boxtimes$) ⓘ, Sidney Nogueira[2] ⓘ, and Augusto Sampaio[1] ⓘ

[1] Centro de Informática (CIn/UFPE), Recife, PE 50740-560, Brazil
rga@cin.ufpe.br
[2] Departamento de Computação (UFRPE), Recife, PE 52171-900, Brazil

Abstract. It is well-recognised that testing concurrent systems poses challenges due to their complex interactions and behaviours, as well as the difficulty to reproduce failures. We propose a sound strategy for testing concurrent mobile applications by first extracting use cases that capture interleavings of behaviours of existing test cases for individual features. From these use cases, we generate test cases that are still sequential but exercise the execution of concurrent features. Our approach incorporates a dependency analysis to ensure a consistent execution order of test steps, avoiding incoherent sequences, like sending a message without establishing an internet connection. We introduce a conformance relation, **cspio$_q$**, based on **cspio**, but extended to consider quiescent behaviour (output absence) as in **ioco**, a widely recognised conformance relation for formal software testing. We then optimise the strategy, which involves permuting test steps without the need to generate use cases but preserving soundness. We discuss tool support and conduct an empirical evaluation to assess the effectiveness of the overall strategy in terms of test coverage and bug detection. The results indicate that our approach yields higher coverage and potential bug detection compared to the set of tests generated by Motorola engineers.

Keywords: Concurrent Features · Software Testing · CSP · Quiescence

1 Introduction

The complexity of modern software systems, especially reactive and concurrent ones like smartphones, presents challenges in testing due to their intensive and (possibly) unpredictable interactions. Moreover, manual testing is acknowledged as being time-consuming and prone to errors. Thus, automation has been increasingly adopted to balance speed and quality in software releases.

Model-Based Testing (MBT) is a software testing technique that relies on models to represent the behaviour of the system under test. These models can be used to automate the generation and execution of test cases on both sequential and concurrent systems [1]. However, relying on MBT can be a barrier because formal models are the main input for test generation. Formal notations contrast with the ones adopted by traditional software engineering approaches, such as use case models. To facilitate the adoption of MBT and make it more accessible, researchers have proposed various approaches [2–4] that use controlled natural language notations to specify input models.

In the case of concurrent systems, however, it is far from simple to capture their behaviour using natural language models, since concurrency typically involves the simultaneous interaction of multiple entities that can lead to race conditions and synchronisation issues, which is difficult to describe in natural language and processed by traditional test case generation methods.

Another challenge for testing concurrent systems is the treatment of inputs and outputs. Concurrent systems often involve multiple processes or threads that interact, culminating in more complex behaviours involving multiple sequential inputs or outputs. Regarding outputs, quiescence occurs in system states that do not generate any output response unless a new input stimulus is provided. Some inputs or states may logically result in no immediate output, which is acceptable. Conversely, lacking expected outputs in specific scenarios could indicate a potential problem.

In this paper, we propose a strategy for the automatic generation of functional test cases for concurrent features of mobile device applications. The generated test cases are sequential and exercise the GUI of concurrency applications. It is not in our scope to test classical concurrent properties like deadlock, livelock and determinism. This approach is inspired by the works in [4,5,11]. In [4], a test case generation strategy inputs use cases written in a controlled natural language, generates a (hidden) formal model in CSP [7], and then outputs test cases also in natural language. In [11] a natural language notation is proposed to express the composition of sequential and concurrent behaviour. Then, the work in [5] uses this framework but from a reverse engineering perspective: it generates a use case model from existing test cases, and then uses the approach in [4] to generate new test cases.

Here, we significantly extend both approaches to address concurrent behaviour, possibly involving quiescence and a dependent analysis mechanism that enforces a meaningful and consistent execution order of test steps; this mechanism ensures that the execution of each step is preceded by all the necessary setup for the step execution, like establishing an internet connection and opening an e-mail application before sending a message. Furthermore, we address soundness through the introduction of a new conformance relation, denoted as $\mathbf{cspio_q}$. This relation is based on $\mathbf{cspio}$ [4] (which is itself inspired by $\mathbf{ioco}$ [8]) but does not take quiescence behaviour into account, and imposes a very strong restriction that, for each input event, the system must react with a corresponding output event. Therefore, sequences of inputs or outputs are not allowed. In $\mathbf{cspio_q}$, we relax this restriction and tackle the absence of outputs (quiescence), aiming to ensure that the system can adequately handle scenarios where no further outputs or events are expected, which is common in a concurrent scenario.

Additionally, we propose an optimised test generation strategy that involves the permutation of test steps, which we denote as atoms, and simplifies the process by directly permuting the atoms, thus avoiding the need for complex reverse engineering use cases from existing test cases. We establish a link between the extended and the optimised approaches and discuss the preservation of soundness by the optimised approach. Another distinguishing feature of the strategy we propose here is its focus on automated test cases, rather than on manual test cases as considered in [4,5].

We provide tool support for most steps of the proposed approach and present the results of an empirical evaluation that analyses its effectiveness concerning code coverage and the number of uncovered bugs, compared with those resulting from the execution of test cases created by our industrial partner (Motorola Mobility) engineers, for the same features. The results reveal that the test suite produced by our approach exhibits significantly higher coverage and can potentially uncover more bugs than the suite created by Motorola engineers.

The following section provides an overview of the notation and the trace semantics of CSP, which is used for modelling use cases and for automatic test generation. Section 3 introduces our sound strategy and its optimisation, which preserves soundness. Section 4 details the preparation, operation and results of an empirical evaluation conducted in an industrial setting. Finally, Sect. 5 presents our conclusions and discusses related and future work.

2   Background

In what follows, we provide an overview of the CSP notation, its traces semantic model, and the conformance relation **cspio** that is the basis for this work.

The fundamental element of the CSP notation is a process, which represents an entity capable of exhibiting both sequential and concurrent behaviour. Processes communicate using events. The set of events that a process can communicate forms its alphabet.

The primitive CSP processes are *Stop* and *Skip*. The former represents a canonical deadlock; it does not communicate any event and does not progress. The *Skip* process represents successful termination; it communicates the special event $\checkmark$ and then behaves like *Stop*.

CSP operators are used to model both sequential and concurrent behaviour. The prefixed process $a \rightarrow P$ denotes a process that first communicates event a and then behaves as the process P. CSP allows recursive processes. For instance, the process $P1 = on \rightarrow off \rightarrow P1$ communicates the sequence of events on and off indefinitely.

In CSP, a channel represents a collection of events that share a common prefix. The notation *channel* $c : T$ is used to declare a channel c that communicates events from the set $\{c.t \mid t \in T\}$. Input communication has the form $c?t$. When synchronising with a process that communicates the event $c.v$, the effect is assigning the value v to the variable t.

Sequential composition has the form $P; Q$. It behaves like process P until it terminates successfully (behaving as *Skip*), and then the control is taken by Q. The external choice between processes P and Q is represented by $P \ \square \ Q$, which behaves as P or Q; the choice is made by the environment.

The parallel composition $P \parallel[X]\parallel Q$ specifies a concurrent behaviour of processes P and Q. The events in the set X are synchronised, meaning they must occur simultaneously on both sides of the parallel composition. All other events communicate independently. The expression $P \parallel\parallel\parallel Q$ denotes the interleave of the processes P and Q, which is a special case of parallel composition with an empty synchronisation set X. A crucial aspect of parallel composition is that it only terminates when both processes in the composition have terminated (distributed termination).

The CSP operator $\setminus$ is used for hiding process communication. In the process $P \setminus X$, P might communicate all the events in its alphabet, except the events in the set X. Finally, the process $P \triangle Q$ indicates that the process Q can interrupt the behaviour of P if an event of Q is communicated.

Traces Semantics for CSP. The simplest semantic model for CSP is its traces model. The notation αP denotes the alphabet of P: the set of events it can communicate. The traces of a process P, denoted as $T(P)$, record the sequences of observable events in which the process can engage: $T(P) \subseteq \alpha P^*$, where αP^* denotes all possible (finite) sequences formed of elements of the alphabet of P. For instance, the traces model of the process $P = x \rightarrow y \rightarrow Stop$ is the set $\{\langle\rangle, \langle x\rangle, \langle x, y\rangle\}$.

Our approach for test case generation uses the FDR tool [6] to perform traces refinement verifications that yield test scenarios. A process Q refines a process P, namely $P \sqsubseteq Q$, if the traces of Q is a subset of the traces of P. If a refinement does not hold, FDR yields a counterexample trace of Q that is not in P. For instance, the process $P1 = a \rightarrow Skip$; $accept \rightarrow Stop$ is refined, in the traces model, by the process $Stop$, namely $P1 \sqsubseteq Stop$. The traces of the former process is $\{\langle\rangle, \langle a\rangle, \langle a, accept\rangle\}$ whereas $Stop$ has a single (empty) trace represented by the set $\{\langle\rangle\}$. Consider the CSP process $Q1 = a \rightarrow Skip$. The refinement $Q1 \sqsubseteq P1$ does not hold because $\langle a, accept\rangle$ belongs to the traces of $P1$ and does not belong to the traces of $Q1$, which is the set $\{\langle\rangle, \langle a\rangle, \langle a, \checkmark\rangle\}$. Thus, $\langle a, accept\rangle$ is a counterexample for $Q1 \sqsubseteq P1$. More details about the traces (and other semantic models of CSP) can be found in [7].

Input-Output Conformance Relation. The conformance relation that is the basis for this work is named **cspio** (CSP Input-Output Conformance) [4], which is itself based on **ioco** (Input-Output Conformance Testing). Its alphabet is split into input and output events, and implementation and specification are assumed to be livelock free. As *test hypothesis* it is assumed that the implementation under test (IUT) can be formalised as a CSP process. Complementary, the IUT and the specification alphabets are also assumed to be compatible. Both the specification and the implementation are represented as *I/O processes*: triples of the form (P, A_I, A_O) where P is a CSP process, A_I the input alphabet and A_O the output alphabet.

Definition 1. *(Compatible alphabets).* Let $S = (P_S, A_{I_s}, A_{O_s})$ be the specification and $IUT = (P_{IUT}, A_{I_{IUT}}, A_{O_{IUT}})$ the implementation models. The alphabets of S and IUT are compatible iff $A_{I_s} \subseteq A_{I_{IUT}}$ and $A_{O_s} \subseteq A_{O_{IUT}}$.

Another assumption on **cspio** is that the implementation is able to accept any input from the alphabet (input-enabled) and always produce some output (output-enabled). The formalisation for these concepts can be found in [4]. Consider that the function $initials(P) = \{a \mid \langle a \rangle \in \mathcal{T}(P)\}$ yields the set of events offered by the process P. Moreover, let $out(M, s)$ be an auxiliary function that provides the set of output events of the process component of the I/O process M, P_M, after the trace s. Formally, $out(M, s) = \text{if } s \in \mathcal{T}(P_M) \text{ then } initials(P_M/s) \cap A_{O_M} \text{ else } \emptyset$. The relation **cspio** is then formalised as follows.

Definition 2. *(CSP input-output conformance).* Consider implementation model $IUT = (P_{IUT}, A_{I_{IUT}}, A_{O_{IUT}})$ and $S = (P_S, A_{I_s}, A_{O_s})$ a specification, such that $A_{I_s} \subseteq A_{I_{IUT}}$ and $A_{O_s} \subseteq A_{O_{IUT}}$ (compatible alphabets). Then

$$IUT \text{ cspio } S \equiv \forall s : \mathcal{T}(P_S) \bullet out(IUT, s) \subseteq out(S, s)$$

For an implementation model to conform with its specification, **cspio** establishes that any output event observed in an implementation model IUT is also observed in the specification S, after any trace of S. Hence, IUT **cspio** S.

3   A Sound Strategy to Generate Test Cases for Concurrent Features

Due to the possible unavailability of updated testing models to apply MBT in the industrial context of this research, in a previous work [5], we conceived a strategy to generate use cases by reverse engineering existing test cases, and then generate additional test cases from the obtained use cases. As already explained, the strategy in [5] has some limitations: (i) consistency of test step sequences was informally and manually addressed; (ii) quiescent behaviour was not considered; and (iii) generating a use case model from test cases and new test cases from the use case model, by performing refinement verifications using FDR, is complex and costly.

The test case generation approach proposed here addresses these three issues, see Fig. 1. The flow at the top part of the figure extends the approach in [5] by proposing solutions to issues (i) and (ii). The flow at the bottom part of the figure is an optimisation that additionally addresses issue (iii). The input to both strategies is a set of existing test cases for individual mobile features, and the output is a set of (automated) test cases for concurrent feature execution.

First, we detail the strategy described by the flow at the top of the figure. This requires use case models that are extracted from the input test cases using a reverse engineering process. Once the use cases are extracted, the generation of test cases for concurrent features is performed by the TaRGeT tool [3], which first converts the use cases into CSP models. These models are then used to

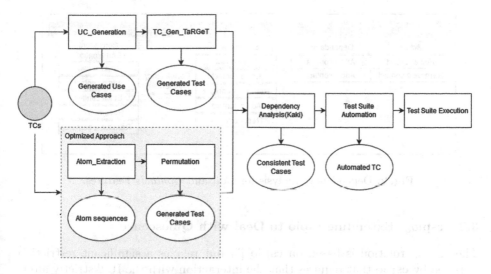

Fig. 1. Generation process with dependency analysis and optimised approach.

generate tests by running FDR refinements. The refinement verifications produce test scenarios until a stop criterion is met. Finally, the CSP events in the test scenarios are translated into natural language to create a test suite. This process is integrated with a dependency analysis tool called Kaki [12], a solution to issue (i), as detailed in Sect. 3.1. Soundness is addressed in Sect. 3.2. The optimised strategy is presented in Sect. 3.3.

3.1 Dependency Analysis Integration

For a test case given as input and, based on the information gathered in a given *Domain Model* that characterises the application domain of a mobile feature, Kaki yields a (possible reordering of the) sequence of test case steps that can be successfully executed.

We illustrate the dependence analysis using the example in Fig. 2. Consider the interaction between the features *Contacts* and *Call*. We first provide the information needed to define the *Domain Model*, along with the associations of the steps for each test case. Such associations may be expressed by dependencies (relations between actions). For instance, to execute the action *"Edit a contact"*, the contact must be added first (*"Add a contact"*). Finally, the consistency mechanism suggests a valid execution sequence, yielding a consistent test case in an optimal order. The results of applying this strategy to each test case are combined into a consistent test suite that can be automated and successfully executed.

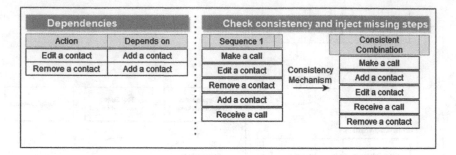

Fig. 2. Dependency Analysis for *Call* and *Contacts* Features.

3.2   cspio_q: Extending cspio to Deal with Quiescence

The **cspio_q** relation is based on **cspio** [5] but relaxes a significant restriction imposed by **cspio** that requires that the interaction with the IUT strictly alternates inputs and outputs, a property that we have previously defined as output-enabledness. This restricts the generation of tests for concurrent scenarios where the interaction of different execution flows between applications can possibly guide a test case to engage in multiple sequence of inputs without an output between them, as well as in a sequence of outputs without an input. The observation of quiescent behaviour allows this desired flexibility. In what follows, we formalise the relevant concepts to define the **cspio_q** relation.

An I/O process is input enabled when the inputs offered after each of its traces is the same as its input alphabet.

Definition 3. *(Input enabled I/O process).* Let $M = (P_M, A_I, A_O)$ be an I/O process. Then, M is input enabled *iff* $\forall t : \mathcal{T}(P_M) \bullet A_I \subseteq initials(P_M/t)$

The quiescent behaviour of a process can be inferred and annotated using the *prioritise* feature in the FDR refinement checking tool. The notation $prioritise(P, \langle X_1, ..., X_n \rangle)$ represents the process that defines priority between events. This process has a similar behaviour to P, but it prevents any event in X_i (where $i > 1$) from happening when there is a possibility of an internal event (τ), ($\checkmark$) termination, or an event in X_j (where $j < i$). We then define a process P_{qui} that captures the quiescence states of a process P as follows.

Definition 4. *(Quiescence Annotation)* Consider P is a CSP process whose output alphabet is A_O, and a special event *qui* that represents a quiescent behaviour. The process P_{qui} denotes the process P annotated with a qui-loop in the states where no event in A_O is offered. Formally,

$$P_{qui} \mathrel{\widehat{=}} prioritise(P \;|||\; RUN(qui), \langle A_O, qui \rangle)$$

where the process $RUN(s) = \square\, ev : s \bullet ev \rightarrow RUN(s)$ is a process that continuously offers the events from the set s.

The basic intuition is that quiescence happens only when there is no output event. If there is an output event, it takes priority over quiescence, and therefore quiescence is prevented from happening.

The relation **cspio$_q$** establishes a conformance notion in the context of quiescent behaviour. Consider A_I and A_O the input and output alphabets of an I/O process, and $A_{Oqui} = A_O \cup \{qui\}$ with $qui \notin (A_O \cup A_I)$.

Definition 5. *(cspio$_q$: CSP input-output conformance with quiescence)* Consider $IUT_{qui} = (P_{IUTqui}, A_{I_{IUT}}, A_{O_{IUTqui}})$ an implementation model and a specification $S_{qui} = (P_{Squi}, A_{I_S}, A_{Osqui})$, such that $A_{I_S} \subseteq A_{I_{IUT}}$ and $A_{O_S} \subseteq A_{O_{IUT}}$ (compatible alphabets). Then

$$IUT \textbf{ cspio}_q\ S \triangleq \forall s : T\ (P_{Squi}) \bullet out(IUT_{qui}, s) \subseteq out(S_{qui}, s)$$

In this relation, after every trace of the specification model, the output events observed in an implementation model (including quiescence) are a subset of the output events allowed by the specification.

Constructing Sound Test Cases. We present the steps to generate sound test cases for **cspio$_q$**. Let TC, S and IUT be I/O processes that are models for the test case, the specification and implementation, respectively. Additionally, the alphabet of the IUT is assumed to be compatible with the alphabet of the specification. A test case $TC = (P_{TC}, A_{I_{TC}}, A_{O_{TC}} \cup VER)$ generated from S to test IUT is an I/O process which inputs events from $A_{I_{TC}} \subseteq A_{O_{IUTqui}}$ and outputs events from $A_{O_{TC}} \subseteq A_{I_S} \cup VER$, with $VER = \{pass, fail, inc\}$, such that $VER \cap (A_{I_{IUT}} \cup A_{O_{IUT}}) = \emptyset$.

The parallel composition $P_{IUTqui} \|[A_{I_{IUT}} \cup A_{O_{IUTqui}}]\| P_{TC}$, say $EXEC_{qui}$, captures the execution of a test against an implementation with the observation of quiescence. Such a composition can result in the communication of a verdict event that defines the execution result: when a system behaves as expected, it behaves as $PASS = pass \rightarrow Stop$, meaning the test passes in the execution. Otherwise, if the system behaves as $FAIL = fail \rightarrow Stop$, the execution fails. Finally, if the system behaves as $INC = inc \rightarrow Stop$, the execution has an inconclusive verdict.

The refinement below verifies the presence of a verdict event $v \in VER$ in the traces of the CSP model for a test execution $EXEC_{qui}$. On the right-hand side of the refinement, input and output events are hidden from $EXEC_{qui}$, so the unique events communicated are verdicts. If the result of the refinement is successful (the refinement holds), the trace which represents the verdict (v) is present in the traces of the execution; otherwise, if the refinement does not hold, the verdict event will not be communicated and thus is not part of the traces of the test execution.

$$EXEC_{qui} \setminus (A_{I_{IUT}} \cup A_{O_{IUTqui}}) \sqsubseteq_t v \rightarrow Stop$$

A generated test is said to be sound if, and only if, whenever the test fails in its execution, it is guaranteed that the IUT does not conform to the specification. In other words, the generated tests do not reject correct implementations. Definition 6 formalises soundness according to the **cspio$_q$** theory.

Definition 6. *(Sound test case).* Let IUT be an implementation I/O process, S the specification, TC a test case I/O process and $EXEC_{qui}$ the execution of TC against IUT with the observation of quiescence. Then TC is a sound test case if the following holds.

$$\langle fail \rangle \in \mathcal{T}(EXEC_{qui} \setminus (A_{I_{IUT}} \cup A_{O_{IUT_{qui}}}) \Rightarrow \neg (IUT \text{ cspio}_q S)$$

The steps to build a process component of a test case TC (P_{TC}) in order to test the IUT are as follows. First, the output events offered by the specification after each event of the test case must be known. These outputs are recorded in an annotated trace (*atrace*) that is obtained by recording the outputs expected at the point each event of the test scenario (*ts*) is offered. The procedure for constructing an annotated trace is detailed in [4], so we omit the details. Moreover, events and outputs are associated as $\langle (ev_1, outs_1), ..., (ev_{\#ts}, outs_{\#ts}) \rangle$, with ev_i from *ts* and $outs_i$ being the outputs after the trace $\langle ev_1, ..., ev_{i-1} \rangle$. If $ev_i \in A_O$, then $outs_i = out(S, \langle ev_1, ..., ev_{i-1} \rangle) - ev_i$, else $outs_i = \emptyset$, for $1 \le i \le \#ts$ and $\langle ev_1, ..., ev_{i-1} \rangle$ is a prefix of *ts*.

Next, the function $TC\_BUILDER(atrace)$ uses the annotated trace (*atrace*) as a parameter, which recursively behaves like the process $SUBTC$ for each pair $(ev, outs)$. If the last element of a trace is reached, $TC\_BUILDER$ yields the process $PASS$. The process $SUBTC$ is responsible for creating the body of a test and initially offers the event ev to the implementation and then behaves like $Skip$ to mark the successful termination of the process.

$$TC\_BUILDER(\langle\rangle) = PASS$$
$$TC\_BUILDER(\langle (ev, outs) \rangle \frown tail) = SUBTC((ev, outs)); \; TC\_BUILDER(tail)$$

where

$$SUBTC((ev, outs)) = ev \rightarrow Skip \; \Box$$
$$(ev \in A_{O_S} \; \& \; ANY(outs, INC) \; \Box \; ANY(A_{O_{IUT_{qui}}} - outs, FAIL))$$

When ev is a test output (implementation input), it is communicated to the implementation, and the test fragment terminates successfully. Due to the input-enabled behaviour, the implementation is always ready to accept inputs. On the other hand, if ev is a test input (implementation output) and because the test cannot block implementation outputs, the process must be ready to synchronise with any output response of P_{IUT}. The test reaches an inconclusive verdict for the cases where an output event is communicated by the implementation ($P_{IUT_{qui}}$) that is not expected by the test scenario (ev) but is an output of the specification. Otherwise, the test reaches the verdict *fail* when P_{IUT} communicates an output event not in the specification or presents a quiescent behaviour.

A test cannot choose between input and output to avoid controllability conflicts [9]. The process $TC\_BUILDER$ does not allow such kind of choice; thus, it is free of controllability conflicts. A test case yielded by $TC\_BUILDER$ is sound according to Theorem 1.

Theorem 1. *(TC_BUILDER is sound). Let $S = (P_{Squi}, A_{I_S}, A_{O_{Squi}})$ be a specification, ts a test scenario from S and $IUT = (P_{IUTqui}, A_{I_{IUT}}, A_{O_{IUTqui}})$ an implementation model, such that $A_{I_S} \subseteq A_{I_{IUT}}$ and $A_{O_S} \subseteq A_{O_{IUT}}$. If atrace is an annotated trace obtained from ts, then $TC = (TC\_BUILDER(atrace), A_{I_{TC}}, A_{O_{TC}})$, with $A_{I_{TC}} = A_{O_{IUTqui}}$ and $A_{O_{TC}} = A_{I_S}$, is a sound test case.*

Proof. Consider $\langle fail \rangle \in \mathcal{T}(EXEC_{qui} \backslash (A_{I_{IUT}} \cup A_{O_{IUTqui}})$, thus, by the definition of $EXEC_{qui}$, there is a trace $t \frown \langle fail \rangle$ that belongs to the traces of $P_{IUTqui} \| A_{I_{IUT}} \cup A_{O_{IUTqui}} \| TC\_BUILDER(atrace, A_{I_{TC}}, A_{O_{TC}})$. Moreover, from the definition of the parallel composition operator and the definition of the process $TC\_BUILDER$, we have that t equals $s \frown \langle o \rangle$, such that s belongs to the traces of the processes P_{IUTqui} and to the traces of P_{Squi}. Furthermore, the output o belongs to $A_{O_{IUT_{qui}}} - outs(S_{qui}, s)$. It implies the implementation process P_{IUTqui} produces a trace $s \frown \langle o \rangle$ where s belongs to the traces of P_{Squi}, $o \in A_{O_{IUT_{qui}}}$, and $o \notin outs(S_{qui}, s)$. Consequently, o represents an output (or a quiescence) that belongs to $out(IUT_{qui}, s)$ and does not belong to $out(S_{qui}, s)$, which falsifies IUT **cspio$_q$** S.

3.3   Optimised Test Generation Strategy

As an alternative to the test generation strategy detailed in the previous sections (top level flow of Fig. 1), which involves reverse engineering existing test cases to obtain a use case model, we propose an optimised test generation strategy via permutation of atoms aiming to simplify the process by directly extracting relevant information without the need for complex reverse engineering, as depicted in the bottom level flow of Fig. 1.

As illustrated in the highlighted grey area in Fig. 1, firstly, we extract the necessary information (units) from the original test case by the syntactical identification of one (or more) actions within a step of a test case. An action, commonly expressed using a verb, denotes an act or occurrence of a fact. Some steps may contain more than one action. Thus, more than one atom may be extracted from each step. For instance, as exhibited in Fig. 3 from the test case step *Add, edit and remove a contact* one can observe the occurrence of three actions: **add**, **edit** and **remove**. Intuitively, it is possible to associate each verb with an action and, consequently, we would have three possible testable units referred to as atoms. The same applies to the *Make a call* test step, from which we can derive an atom related to the action **call**. These atoms are then systematically interleaved to produce test cases for concurrent features (**Permutation** step), which are automatically executed.

We claim that, simplifying test generation in this way preserves soundness.

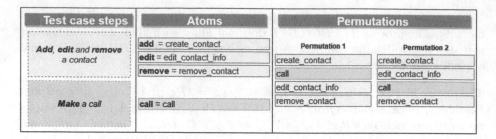

Fig. 3. Extraction and permutation of atoms.

Proposition 1

$$\forall\ TCs \bullet TC\_Gen\_TaRGeT(UC\_gen(TCs)) = Permu(Atom\_Extraction(TCs))$$

The justification is as follows. The use cases generated by `UC_generation()` captures sequences of the original test steps. These are input to the TaRGeT tool (function `TC_Gen_TaRGeT()`) that explores such sequences to generate test cases. However, each of such sequences generated by TaRGeT is a permutation of atoms extracted from these test cases in the optimised approach.

4   Evaluation

This section discusses the outcomes of a hands-on evaluation to assess the efficiency of the suggested approach compared to the conventional test case generation method used by Motorola's Mobility Test Team. We focus on two assessment criteria, namely bug detection and coverage, to substantiate our conclusions.

Concerning bug detection, we applied a Mutation technique to evaluate the effectiveness of the generated test suites by checking their ability to identify faults injected in the code (Sect. 4.1). The coverage assessment was supported by the ATP tool [14], with the goal of evaluating the extent to which an application source code has been exercised by the test suites generated by the proposed approach compared to the coverage resulting from running the original Motorola's test suites (Sect. 4.2). In the final section, we also briefly report on an evaluation of a real scenario, not involving mutation.

4.1   Number of Uncovered Bugs Using Mutation Testing

As the software attains more excellent stability, uncovering new bugs and assessing the effectiveness of the test suite in detecting potential defects becomes progressively challenging as the incidence of bugs diminishes over time. In such cases, mutation testing helps create artificial faults (mutations) in the software, allowing developers to evaluate the ability of the test suite to identify and isolate the injected faults. The motivation for using the mutation technique is primarily driven by the scarce number of known defects in Motorola's applications considering the time frame when this evaluation was conducted (end-of-cycle of the operational tests for the Android 11 [22], before its commercial release).

The steps undertaken to conduct the mutation testing evaluation encompasses five stages: (1) selection of a suitable APK and mutation operators (2) Unpacking an APK, which involves extracting its contents to analyse or modify the elements inside the package; (3) generation of mutants using a pre-selected mutation tool (MutAPK) (introduced in the sequel); (4) digitally sign the APK with a certificate using an upload key after recompiling the modified resources to ensures its integrity and authenticity and install it on a smartphone; (5) evaluate the effectiveness of the proposed approach in comparison with the original Motorola test cases in terms of bug uncovering.

To support the generation of mutants, we opted for a public academic mutation testing tool to avoid conflicts of interest with our industrial partner. After extensively analysing some alternatives, [18–21] we chose to use MutAPK [18]. MutAPK is an open-source tool for mutation testing that allows the use of Android Application Packages (APKs) as input for this purpose. The tool has a set of 38 mutation operators that emulate possible defects in Android applications.

The initial step of the evaluation is the selection of a suitable Motorola software application for the purpose of mutant injection. For this validation, we chose the *FM Radio* application, influenced by the feedback from Motorola testers who identified it as a potentially flawed application.

In this particular study `WrongStringResource` and `InvalidLabel` were chosen as the mutation operators. When the WrongStringResource operator is applied, a `<string . . . />` entry in `/strings.xml` file is deleted, and its string value is mutated. The same goes for the `InvalidLabel` operator, where the attribute `android:label` in the Android Manifest file is replaced with a random string.

Moreover, by using the APKTool [17], the *FM Radio* APK was decompiled. This task is also provided by the MutApk tool, however, due to compilation errors, we had to perform it manually. Then we used MutApk engine to generate the mutants based on the selected operators automatically.

Android requires all APKs to be digitally signed with a certificate before they are installed on a device or updated. Because of the hardware and software incompatibilities (protected build) from Motorola devices, we could not automatically assign the mutated apps using MutAPK's engine. Instead, we assigned them manually using the uber-apk-signer [15] software. We also had to apply changes to the tested device build code to delete the old version of the APK.

Finally, we tested the effectiveness of the proposed approach by selecting 3 Motorola test cases related to the *FM Radio* feature. They are designed to verify the configuration of the radio, manage the radio during phone calls, and ensure compatibility between the recording function and other audio players. Using the optimised proposed approach, concurrent tests were generated from the

permutation of the original Motorola tests following the workflow defined in
Sect. 3.3. The permutation-based tests were subjected to automation and exe-
cuted automatically using a proprietary tool developed by Motorola, namely
Force IDE.

As a result, it was possible to identify (kill) one of the mutations by running
the original Motorola test cases. The tool execution log indicated a failure message that was directly linked to the modification made to the *FM Radio Settings*
feature. On the other hand, when executing the permutations generated by the
proposed approach, it was possible to detect not only the same mutant that
Motorola had found but also a new mutation related to the *Sleep Timer* feature.
This was because the permutation suggested a path different from the one that
Motorola normally follows.

4.2   Coverage Rate

Coverage is assessed with the support of the ATP tool [14], dedicated to calcu-
lating updated components based on release notes. The tool examines the set
of test cases that had been executed and identifies the components that had
been covered. ATP makes use of the Android debugging tool known as LogCat
[16], which is a command-line utility that produces a record of system messages
directly from the device and registers occurrences of application events, such as
stack traces when the device exhibits an error and user-defined messages using
the Log class.

We considered two coverage criteria that could be derived from the execution logs. The initial criteria pertain to component coverage, which evaluates the
extent to which classes and code line parameters (specific lines of code associated
with the system's architecture components) are thoroughly covered and exam-
ined. On the other hand, the second criterion is class coverage, which assesses
the coverage of classes exclusively.

To address the aforementioned criteria, we have established a coverage metric.
This metric is evaluated considering two sets OTS_e and MTS_e, which stand
for the set of components covered by the optimised approach and the manual
execution carried out by a Motorola team, respectively. Hence, the coverage of
OTS is calculated by the formula

$$\frac{\#TTS_e}{\#(OTS_e \cup MTS_e)} \times 100.$$

The coverage of MTS is calculated in a similar way. This calculation represents
the relative coverage of a set of elements to the union of all elements observed.
Since we could not access the source code, we needed to use this coverage metric.

For the execution, we selected 15 Motorola test cases (MTS_e) and 43 tests
generated by the proposed approach (OTS_e). We explored Motorola's Modem
application, and the reverse engineering approach detailed in our previous work
[5] has been adopted.

Tables 1 and 2 display coverage data for component and class coverage. As
both tables have identical structures, we explain their structures simultaneously.

The first line of the text represents the sets of elements covered during the execution of the test suites. The second line indicates the cardinality of the sets, and the third line shows the relative coverage of the sets. The second to seventh columns provide information about the sets: the elements covered by the test suite MTS_e, the elements of the test suite OTS_e, the union of the elements of MTS_e and OTS_e, the elements in the intersection of MTS_e and OTS_e, the elements in MTS_e that are not in OTS_e, and the elements in OTS_e that are not in MTS_e.

Table 1. Component Coverage.

Comp.	MTS_e	OTS_e	$MTS_e \cup OTS_e$	$MTS_e \cap OTS_e$	$MTS_e \setminus OTS_e$	$OTS_e \setminus MTS_e$
Number	988	1436	1748	676	312	760
Coverage	56,52%	82,15%	100%	38,67%	17,84%	43,47%

Table 2. Class Coverage.

Class	MTS_e	OTS_e	$MTS_e \cup OTS_e$	$MTS_e \cap OTS_e$	$MTS_e \setminus OTS_e$	$OTS_e \setminus MTS_e$
Number	905	921	1155	671	234	250
Coverage	78,35%	79,74%	100%	58,09%	20,25%	21,64%

As evidenced by the data presented in Tables 1 and 2, it is clear that the set of elements covered by the Motorola team does not encompass all of the elements covered by the proposed approach, nor does it constitute a subset of them. The tests conducted by OTS_e and MTS_e exhibit coverage of numerous shared elements in addition to distinct elements. However, the tests generated using the proposed approach encompass more distinct elements than those designed by Motorola. This discrepancy is particularly pronounced when considering component coverage, whereas the disparity is more subtle regarding class coverage.

The use of the execution log is a valuable method for assessing improvements in coverage. However, it is important to consider the scope and intention of this method carefully. Merely measuring coverage based on the number of lines traversed provides a quantitative overview of gains but fails to capture a qualitative analysis of the observed elements.

Hence, we cannot draw definitive conclusions based on this evaluation, but we can discuss some initial observations. The tests generated by the proposed approach cover a greater number of distinct elements compared to the tests used by Motorola. A more detailed analysis of the logs is required to understand why there are areas covered by the Motorola tests that are not covered by the proposed approach. One possible explanation is that each tester follows the procedures differently, with each tester taking different paths to achieve the same goal. For example, one tester may navigate to the "Settings" menu by scrolling down the quick settings, while through the launcher in the main view.

Moreover, a significant portion of the recorded log is not directly associated with actions carried out during the test execution, but rather belongs to concurrent background activities. This can result in a considerable amount of unrelated information, leading to potential misinterpretations of the results.

One possible approach to produce a log containing most relevant information is to expose tags created by the developers during the coding of the automated scripts. Implementing this method makes it possible to filter log lines containing the inserted tag, thereby achieving a more accurate and precise coverage measurement.

4.3   Additional Evaluation Results

We expanded our evaluation by taking into account Motorola's actual development scenario and applying the optimised approach to several features (Camera, Home Screen, Themes, Contacts, Wallpaper) and uncovered additional 18 bugs, such as the contact name not displayed when changing the theme twice (enable and disable); it is not possible to confirm the wallpaper change after changing the display size; and, in multi-window, when taking a picture, the photo is inverted unexpectedly.

5   Conclusion

We have introduced an approach to generating sound test cases for concurrent features. We have also established its soundness, along with the incorporation of a dependence analysis tool to tackle any inconsistencies related to the ordering of test step execution.

To account for quiescent behaviour, we introduced a new relation called **cspio$_q$**, building upon the approach described in [4], for generating sound test cases that may involve quiescence.

Furthermore, we have optimised our test generation strategy to offer a more efficient alternative that closely aligns with the automation and execution environment of our industrial partner.

We conducted an empirical evaluation to gauge the effectiveness of the tests generated using our proposed approach. The evaluation measured bug and test coverage, comparing tests generated by Motorola with those from our approach. The analysis results revealed that the tests generated using our approach not only successfully identified the same bug that was found by the Motorola test suite but also uncovered additional previously unknown bugs. Moreover, the tests produced by the proposed approach provided broader coverage of implementation components compared to the tests created by Motorola.

The formal notion of conformance allows testers and developers to reason about the correctness of the generated test cases and the behaviours of the SUT. Existing theories in the field [4,8,10,13] rely on a well-defined mathematical relation between the system specification and the *IUT*.

The work in [13] presents a denotational semantics for CSP using suspension traces. This semantics also addresses the distinction between inputs and outputs. The authors establish healthiness conditions for the suspension-traces model and propose a characterisation of the conformance relation **ioco**. Additionally, they propose a strategy for automating the verification of conformance based on **ioco** and suspension-trace refinement. Furthermore, it opens up avenues for exploring algebraic laws and compositional reasoning techniques based on **ioco**. Although we share a common foundation related to the **ioco** conformance relation, there are distinctions in the specific semantics we adopt. While the work in [13] relies on suspension traces, our approach adopts the traces model annotated with a special event to represent quiescence. This allowed us to reuse the theory and test case generation strategy for sequential systems [4], in a conservative way.

Various methods have been employed to evaluate concurrent applications. A testing method outlined in [23] uses a CSP model to capture system behaviour and identify incorrect event sequences in multi-thread testing. The primary objective of this method is to identify specific event sequences that represent incorrect behaviour within a real-world multi-thread testing environment. While our approach focuses on testing the graphical user interface (GUI) of mobile applications, the work described in [23] is primarily applied in the domain of safety-critical systems.

The paper in [24] presents the design of a distributed test system tailored for testing distributed GUI applications. Unlike our approach, in that paper, graphical elements and test events (stimulus, response, stimulus/response, test system) need to be implemented as test scripts for execution on a test execution framework. Moreover, in contrast to the approach described in [24], ours focuses on handling concurrency by identifying actions within the textual scope of test cases that suggest concurrent behaviour and interaction between components.

Increasing the number of tests using the permutation approach leads to higher coverage. However, the exhaustive permutation generation is computationally infeasible for large test suites. To improve the scalability of the permutation, we intend to investigate alternative approaches that can produce valid permutations on demand.

Although we have addressed the evaluation of the proposed approach to a significant extent, we plan to extend this evaluation even further considering an automation context. Additionally, to assess code coverage, we will employ a code instrumentation technique. Finally, we plan to integrate our test case generation approach with test execution tools to facilitate the automatic execution of test cases.

Acknowledgements. We would like to thank the CIn-Motorola Teams for helping with the experiments. This work was partially founded by CNPq (grant 432198/2018-0). Rafaela Almeida was partially founded by Motorola Mobility Comércio de Produtos Eletrônicos Ltda and Fundação de Amparo a Ciência e Tecnologia do Estado de Pernambuco (FACEPE) (grant IBPG-0063-1.03/19).

References

1. Broy, M., Jonsson, B., Katoen, J.-P., Leucker, M., Pretschner, A. (eds.): Model-Based Testing of Reactive Systems. LNCS, vol. 3472. Springer, Heidelberg (2005). https://doi.org/10.1007/b137241
2. Carvalho, G.: NAT2TEST: Generating Test Cases from Natural Language Requirements Based on CSP. Federal University of Pernambuco, 2011 (2016)
3. Ferreira, F., Neves, L., Silva, M., Borba, P.: TaRGeT: a model based product line testing tool. In: Proceedings of CBSoft 2010 - Tools Panel (2010)
4. Nogueira, S., Sampaio, A., Mota, A.: Test generation from state based use case models. Formal Aspects Comput. **26**, 441–490 (2014)
5. Almeida, R.: Automatic Test Case Generation for Concurrent Features from Natural Language Specifications. Federal Rural University of Pernambuco (2019)
6. Gibson-Robinson, T., Armstrong, P., Boulgakov, A., Roscoe, A.W.: FDR3 17 a modern refinement checker for CSP. In: Tools and Algorithms for the Construction and Analysis of Systems, pp. 187–201 (2014)
7. Roscoe, A.: The Theory and Practice of Concurrency. Prentice Hall PTR, Upper Saddle River (1998)
8. Tretmans, J.: Testing concurrent systems: a formal approach. In: Baeten, J.C.M., Mauw, S. (eds.) CONCUR 1999. LNCS, vol. 1664, pp. 46–65. Springer, Heidelberg (1999). https://doi.org/10.1007/3-540-48320-9_6
9. Jard, C., Jéron, T.: TGV: theory, principles and algorithms: a tool for the automatic synthesis of conformance test cases for non-deterministic reactive systems. Int. J. Softw. Tools Technol. Transfer **7**, 297–315 (2005)
10. Carvalho, G., Sampaio, A., Mota, A.: A CSP timed input-output relation and a strategy for mechanised conformance verification. In: Groves, L., Sun, J. (eds.) ICFEM 2013. LNCS, vol. 8144, pp. 148–164. Springer, Heidelberg (2013). https://doi.org/10.1007/978-3-642-41202-8_11
11. Almeida, R., Nogueira, S., Sampaio, A.: Automatic test case generation for concurrent features from natural language descriptions. In: Massoni, T., Mousavi, M.R. (eds.) SBMF 2018. LNCS, vol. 11254, pp. 163–179. Springer, Cham (2018). https://doi.org/10.1007/978-3-030-03044-5_11
12. Arruda, F.: A Formal Approach to Test Automation Based on Requirements, Domain Model, and Test Cases Written in Natural Language. Federal University of Pernambuco (2022)
13. Cavalcanti, A., Hierons, R., Nogueira, S., Sampaio, A.: A suspension-trace semantics for CSP. In: 2016 10th International Symposium on Theoretical Aspects of Software Engineering (TASE), pp. 3–13 (2016)
14. Perrusi, L.: AutoTestCoverage: Uma Ferramenta para Cobertura de Testes de Integração no Contexto Android sem Uso de Codigo-Fonte, December 2018
15. Signer uber-apk-signer. https://github.com/patrickfav/uber-apk-signer
16. Www.android.com, L. LogCat—www.android.com. https://www.android.com
17. https://apktool.org/, APKTool—https://apktool.org/. https://apktool.org/
18. Escobar Velasquez, C., Osorio Riano, M., Linares Vasquez, M.: MutAPK source codeless mutant generation for Android apps. In: 2019 34th IEEE ACM International Conference on Automated Software Engineering (ASE), pp. 1090–1093 (2019)
19. Wei, Y.: MuDroid: mutation testing for Android apps. University of College London, London, UK, Technical report (2015)

20. Luna, E., El Ariss, O.: Edroid: a mutation tool for android apps. In: 2018 6th International Conference in Software Engineering Research and Innovation (CONISOFT), pp. 99–108 (2018)
21. Https://pitest.org/Pitest. https://pitest.org/
22. Android11. https://www.android.com/android 11/
23. Cao, Y., Wang, Y.: Concurrent software testing method based on CSP and PAT. In: 2018 IEEE/ACIS 17th International Conference on Computer and Information Science (ICIS), pp. 641–644 (2018)
24. Murthy, P., Ulrich, A.: Distributed GUI test automation. In: 2017 14th IEEE India Council International Conference (INDICON), pp. 1–6 (2017)

Verification and Validation

Automated Code Generation for DES Controllers Modeled as Finite State Machines

Tiago Possato[1,2], João H. Valentini[1], Luiz F. P. Southier[1],
and Marcelo Teixeira[1(✉)]

[1] Federal University of Technology Parana, UTFPR, Pato Branco, Brazil
joaovalentini@alunos.utfpr.edu.br, mtex@utfpr.edu.br
[2] Catarinense Federal Institute, IFC, Videira, Brazil
tiago.possato@ifc.edu.br

Abstract. *Finite State Machines* (FSMs) are the foundation to design *Discrete Event Systems* (DESs). A FSM that designs a DES model can be further processed using *Supervisory Control Theory* (SCT) to synthesize correct-by-construction software. When applied to industrial-scale DESs, FSMs face limitations in the design, synthesis, and implementation steps. Supremica is a straightforward tool that facilitates design and synthesis but does not reach the implementation phase. This requires additional tools to convert FSM models into code. This paper presents the tool DEScMaker, which receives as input an FSM model outputting from Supremica and converts it into implementable C code. Our approach complements Supremica with code generation and allows taking advantage of its intuitive interface, useful simulator, and safe algorithms while automating a task that, in practice, consists of complex manual programming. An example illustrates the tool and quantifies its advantages.

Keywords: Formal modeling · Model conversion · Code generation

1 Introduction

In computer systems engineering, formal methods are the foundation for the development of automatic solutions that depend, to some extent, on certain levels of quality to operate. In industrial practices, precision medicine, agriculture, cyber-physical systems, and other science domains, programming a computational solution requires a solid level of formalism to guarantee that the integration between technology, people, and the environment occurs safely, within the expected time, and with the desired synchrony [11,14,15].

This research was supported by the Brazilian National Council of Scientific and Technological Development (CNPq), under grant number 309946/2020-4, by CAPES (Coordination for the Improvement of Higher Level or Education Personnel), Brazil, financial code 001, FINEP (Funding Authority for Studies and Projects), Brazil, Araucária Foundation, Brazil, and IFC (Catarinense Federal Institute).

H. Barbosa and Y. Zohar (Eds.): SBMF 2023, LNCS 14414, pp. 113–130, 2024.
https://doi.org/10.1007/978-3-031-49342-3_7

Discrete Event Systems (DESs) [6] models have contributed fairly to the mission of making correct-by-construction solutions. A DES defines a class of systems whose behavior cannot be represented by equations, as it evolves asynchronously on time. In this case, theoretical models such as *Finite State Machines* (FSMs) appear as an option that allows identifying, representing, and processing complex properties of systems, such as concurrency, distribution, and parallelism, by using intuitive interfaces that abstract solid mathematical background [9, 36].

When a system is modeled as an FSM, the objective is to synthesize sequences of events to be allowed under control. It is assumed that events occur spontaneously in the system (also known as *plant*), and they have to be externally coordinated by a properly programmed dedicated hardware (such as *microcontroller* or *Programmable Logic Controller* (PLC)). A formal approach that automates the synthesis of controllers from FSMs is the *Supervisory Control Theory* (SCT) [29], which defines a mature mathematical method for extracting controllers from higher-level models [8].

Despite its practical relevance and formal background, the SCT is limited in converting synthesized controllers into implementable code. This depends on code generation tools for different synthesis architectures and modeling resources. There are some tools for code generation, such as DESTool [20], lib-FAUDES [20], DESLAB [7], CIF [5], Nadzoru [21], UltraDES [2]. However, they work only in combination with the specific modeling tool that implements it, which in its turn does not usually gather all the resources needed to guide the entire controller project, from conception through modeling, simulation, synthesis, model-checking, code generation, implementation, and monitoring. Furthermore, existing approaches usually focus on the implementation of PLC [4, 10, 12, 13, 16, 18, 28, 32–35], and do not include outputs for higher-level data science-oriented languages, such as Python.

A tool that gathers many functionalities for the entire development of a controller is *Supremica* [1]. This tool provides an intuitive modeling environment and a complete set of synthesis algorithms either for monolithic, modular, incremental, or variable-based synthesis. Supremica also provides a modular view of how models are related so that they can be separated accordingly. Model-checking resources and simulation functions are also available to allow empirical check of the correctness of models and constraints [8, 17, 30]. Supremica also provides some output formats, such as XML, but (at least in its free release) does not export models in implementable code, such as C, Python, or other hardware-compatible forms for PLC or microcontrollers, limiting its usefulness.

This paper introduces the DEScMaker tool [22], which is designed to generate C code from correct-by-construction controllers designed, synthesized, and checked in Supremica. From the Supremica's output controller, DEScMaker reads, interprets, and organizes this file and constructs the equivalent infrastructure in C, which can be directly transferred to compatible hardware. The three-dimensional implementation architecture of [28] is adopted for the conversion of FSM into C code, where supervisors, event handling, and physical integration are addressed in a distinct way. The code resulting from DEScMaker can be compiled and tested on a computer prior to deployment, serving as a tool for simulation, validation, and previsualization of the effect of the joint solution.

An analogous tool [23] to generate Python code, with the same functionalities as DEScMaker, is in the final stages of development and will be omitted for brevity.

The remainder of the manuscript is organized as follows. Section 2 presents the background of DESs, FSMs, SCT, and LMC. Section 3 details the proposed tool, which is illustrated in Sect. 4. Finally, Sect. 5 discusses some conclusions and perspectives on future research.

2   Foundations of Discrete Event Systems

DESs are systems that evolve according to the unexpected occurrence of discrete events at irregular, possibly unknown, intervals [6]. They oppose to system whose evolution depends continuously on time. For example, a discrete event could be pushing a button, a component arrival, a disturbance or set-point change in a control system, etc.

Designing a system as DES helps to understand it and find ways to improve it. In general, DES models are created using the notion of *strings* formed with *events* taken from an alphabet Σ. Σ^* denotes the set of all finite strings formed with events in Σ, including the *empty string* ε. Any subset $L \subseteq \Sigma^*$ is called a *language*. Two strings $s, t \in \Sigma^*$ can be concatenated as st and the *prefix-closed* $\overline{L}$ of a language L is the set of all prefixes of L, that is, $\overline{L} = \{s \in \Sigma^* \mid st \in L \text{ for some } t \in \Sigma^*\}$.

FSMs are acceptable mechanisms to represent languages. An FSM is a 5-tuple $G = (\Sigma, Q, q^\circ, Q^m, \rightarrow)$, where Σ is the set of events, Q is the set of states, $\rightarrow \subseteq Q \times \Sigma \times Q$ is the transition relation, q° is the initial state, and Q^m is the set of marked states that represent tasks completed by the DES modeled by G.

It is usual for FSMs to be exposed graphically. For two any states $q_1, q_2 \in Q$, $q_1 \xrightarrow{\sigma} q_2$ denotes a transition from the state q_1 to q_2 with the event $\sigma \in \Sigma$. The same notation can be generalized to strings $s \in \Sigma^*$, that is, $q_1 \xrightarrow{s} q_2$ means that q_2 is reached from q_1 with s, while $G \xrightarrow{s} q$ means that a string s is possible in G, from its initial state.

The language generated by G is denoted by $L(G) \subseteq \Sigma^*$ and defined as $L(G) = \{s \in \Sigma^* \mid G \xrightarrow{s} q \in Q\}$. It represents the set of all strings of events that can occur in G. Differently, $L^m(G) \subseteq L(G)$ is defined as $L^m(G) = \{s \in \Sigma^* \mid G \xrightarrow{s} q \in Q^m\}$ and denotes the language marked by G, i.e., its strings that end up in completed tasks.

As a DES is usually formed by a set $J = \{1, \cdots, m\}$ of components, it is convenient to design each of them as an FSM G_j, for $j \in J$, and combine them by *synchronous composition* (denoted $\|$). Given two FSMs, $G_1 = (\Sigma_1, Q_1, q_1^\circ, Q_1^m, \rightarrow_1)$ and $G_2 = (\Sigma_2, Q_2, q_2^\circ, Q_2^m, \rightarrow_2)$, define $G_1 \| G_2 = \langle \Sigma_1 \cup \Sigma_2, Q_1 \times Q_2, (q_1^\circ, q_2^\circ), Q_m^1 \times Q_m^2, \rightarrow \rangle$, where $\rightarrow$ is constructed as follows:

- $(q_1, q_2) \xrightarrow{\sigma} (q_1', q_2')$ if $\sigma \in \Sigma_1 \cap \Sigma_2, q_1 \xrightarrow{\sigma} q_1'$, and $q_2 \xrightarrow{\sigma} q_2'$;

- $(q_1, q_2) \xrightarrow{\sigma} (q_1', q_2)$ if $\sigma \in \Sigma_1 \setminus \Sigma_2$, and $q_1 \xrightarrow{\sigma} q_1'$;
- $(q_1, q_2) \xrightarrow{\sigma} (q_1, q_2')$ if $\sigma \in \Sigma_2 \setminus \Sigma_1$, and $q_2 \xrightarrow{\sigma} q_2'$;
- undefined, otherwise.

In words, events enabled by both G_1 and G_2 are merged, while events enabled by only one FSM and unknown by the other are interleaved in any order. All other cases are undefined, e.g., an event may be enabled by one FSM, and known but not enabled by the other case, which implies that the transition is considered undefined and disabled upon composition. A state is marked in a composition if the corresponding combination of states is also marked in the source FSMs.

2.1 DES Control

A DES often includes $n \geq 1$ components that are expected to work together. Each component can be modeled by an FSM G^i, and the so-called open-loop behavior is then given by the composition $G = G^1 \| \ldots \| G^n$, which is called the *plant*. In conjunction, the FSMs G^i are expected to interact with each other, and it is the role of a controller to define how and when they do. An approach that allows DES controllers to be automatically computed from a set of FSMs is the SCT [29], as long as control specifications are provided.

Specifications are rules that restrict actions in G, such as imposing priority on one component over another. Analogously to G, a specification Ej can also be modularly exposed so that $E = E^1 \| \ldots \| E^m$, for $m \geq 1$, is the general specification model. It can be joined to G to form the *desired behavior* under control, i.e., a sub-behavior of the open-loop denoted $K = G\|E$. Observe that, therefore, E must only restrict G without creating any new behavior.

From K, a controller can be calculated (or synthesized). This operation further considers the controllable nature of the events, which is formally expressed by partitioning the set of events of G into $\Sigma = \Sigma_c \dot\cup \Sigma_u$. Events in Σ_c can be inhibited in G, while those in Σ_u cannot be prevented directly by the controller.

Then, K is said to be controllable with respect to G if, for all $s \in \Sigma_G^*$ and all $\mu \in \Sigma_u$, whenever

$$K \xrightarrow{s} x_K \text{ and } G \xrightarrow{s} x_G \xrightarrow{\mu} x_G',$$

there exists $x_K' \in Q_K$, such that

$$K \xrightarrow{s} x_K \xrightarrow{\mu} x_K'.$$

That is, K is controllable if it allows the uncontrollable events whenever they are also allowed by the plant. When the model K is not controllable, it can be reduced iteratively to its largest controllable (supremal) submodel. This computation is called *synthesis* in SCT, and $\sup\mathcal{C}(K, G)$ is the usual notation of the result. In practice, $\sup\mathcal{C}(K, G)$ represents the most permissive behavior possible to be imposed by control on G while complying with controllability and the specification. If $\sup\mathcal{C}(K, G)$ is also nonblocking [6], it is said to be *optimal*.

Implementing the FSM that models $\sup\mathcal{C}(K, G)$ has advantages compared to empirical programming because it automates manual tasks by involving modular, usually simple, design tasks, which tends to increase development and maintenance speed, especially when the control logic changes frequently.

2.2 Modular Synthesis

For many applications, it is reasonable to design the plant model of a DES as a set of independent components to be coordinated by the controller according to multiple specifications, also constructed modularly. When these multiple plants and specifications are synchronized and the result is a single controller, the solution is said to be *monolithic*.

In monolithic synthesis, the *state-space explosion* problem may become a barrier for SCT to be adopted in the industry. Modularisation [19,27,31] is an alternative to simplify synthesis by exploiting subsets of a few components, which hopefully reduces the computational effort necessary to obtain the controller.

The tool presented in this paper supports the generation of code for both monolithic and *Local Modular Controllers* (LMC) [27]. In LMC, each specification leads to a local controller, which is calculated using only plants affected by the events of the specification.

Definition 1. Let E^i, for $i \in I = \{1, \cdots, m\}$, be specifications modeled with events in Σ_{E^i}; and G^j, for $j \in J = \{1, \cdots, n\}$, be asynchronous plants designed with events in Σ_{G^j}. For $i = 1, \cdots, m$, the local plants G_i^{loc}, associated with each specification E^i, are $G_i^{loc} = \|_{j \in J_i} G^j$, such that $J_i = \{j \in J \mid \Sigma_{G^j} \cap \Sigma_{E^i} \neq \emptyset\}$.

In words, each local plant is associated only with the plants restricted by E^i. Upon synthesis, the LMC creates a set of local controllers S_i^{loc} that are individually nonblocking. However, the conjunction of controllers can be blocking, even when individually nonblocking. In this case, the controllers are said to be conflicting. In [27] and older results, there are conditions that guarantee the non-conflict of local controllers, which we hide here for the sake of brevity. When the non-conflicting condition is achieved, the joint action of local controllers over the plant is optimal. That is, if the set $\{S_i^{loc},\ i = 1, \cdots, m\}$ is non-conflicting, then $S = \|_{i=1}^m S_i^{loc}$, for S modeling $\sup\mathcal{C}(K, G)$.

3 The DEScMaker Implementation

The DEScMaker [22] is a tool programmed in Python that receives a Supremica file as input and exports a directory with a project in C. The input file must contain at least one synthesized supervisor, which implies that it also supports modular projects of control. The directory with the generated code is organized to allow the quick implementation of the project and the easy replacement of the supervisor's files in case of any modeling change. The directory and file structure generated by DEScMaker can be found in Appendix 1.

Figure 1 provides a visual representation of the flow around code generation. DEScMaker must be called from the command line, indicating the path of the Supremica file to be processed and the name of the output file. DEScMaker then scans the file, identifies the supervisors, and builds the output project. The Supremica's file is structured in XML format, although it is saved with the extension '.wmod'. This file contains elements and attributes to represent events, plants and supervisors. Within each supervisor, there are other nested elements to represent events and transitions. After identify the supervisors, events and transitions, DEScMaker use the class Template, from Python strings, to make string substitutions in the templates and save the code. The generated project can be compiled and executed. Depending on the target platform, moving the files to a specific structure may be necessary. The user can automate this task creating a custom script.

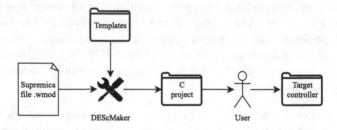

Fig. 1. Usage flow of DEScMaker, which analyses the Supremica file, fills in templates and generates a C project.

The proposed structure for code generation is based on the hierarchy presented by [28], which is adapted and shown in Fig. 2. The *automatically generated* code is separated into two main blocks, the *supervisors* and the *event handler*, which will be discussed later. In the *user defined* area, the uncontrollable events are transmitted to the event handler, and the actions associated with the events, usually controllable events, are defined.

3.1   The Supervisor Structure

Supervisors are represented through linked lists, with structures representing events, states, and transitions. These structures are linked to allow access and navigation through the automaton. A library enables operations to be performed on the supervisors, with functions to add a callback function to each event and check if an event is enabled, among other functionalities. Each event can have an associated callback function that is executed whenever the event is executed. The generated code does not perform dynamic memory allocation. Thus, it is safer to implement on microcontrollers with limited memory.

Logically, a supervisor is represented by a structure that points to an initial state, the current state, the last state, and an alphabet. The alphabet is a list

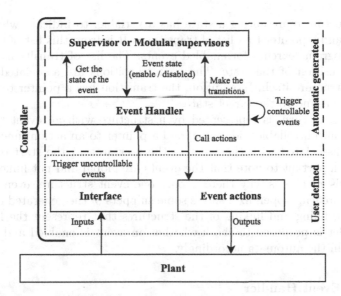

Fig. 2. Proposed structure for the operation of the generated code. At the top is the automatically generated code, highlighting the supervisors and the event handler. In the center is the user area, with functions specific to the target platform.

of all the events of the supervisor. A state has a list of transitions. A transition has the target state and an associated event. The event has a type (controllable or uncontrollable) and an associated action callback. Figure 3 illustrates these relationships.

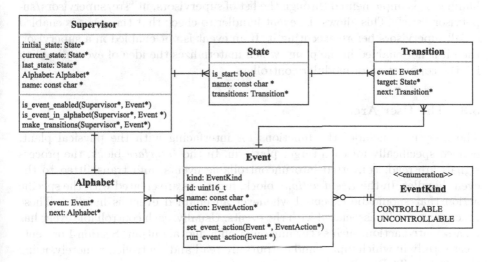

Fig. 3. Crow's foot entity relationship diagram for the structures of a supervisor.

The structure representing a state has a variable, to indicate whether it is the initial, and a pointer to a list of transitions. It is from this list of transitions that the program searches for enabled events. The list of transitions points to the first transition of the state. The next transitions are associated with the transition structure itself. In addition, the transition has a pointer to the event that triggers it and to the target state.

An event, in turn, is represented by a structure with an event type (controllable or uncontrollable), id, name, and a pointer to an action function. This function is associated with the event in the user area at the start of the program. It is important to note that the events are global and not linked directly to a supervisor. This is why there is only one event structure, even using the modular approach. Appendix 2 shows some snippets of the generated code, with the creation, filling and linking of the structures that represent the FSM. The event handler is proposed to check whether an event is enabled and make the transitions in the automata accordingly.

3.2   The Event Handler

The event handler manages the events of the controller. For the correct operation of the proposed code, every event must be submitted to the event handler through the "trigger_event" function. The event handling checks whether the event is enabled by supervisors. If enabled, it is executed. Executing an event means making the transitions in the FSM, calling the function associated with the event action, and managing the controllable events enabled in the plant. Figure 4 presents a flow chart to explain the operation of the event handler, including its interaction with plant and supervisors.

The modular control approach is incorporated into the project in the event handler. It is implemented through the list of supervisors, in "src/supervisors/supervisor_list.c". This allows the event handler to check that the event is enabled on all supervisors before executing it. If an event is not enabled in a supervisor, then it is not enabled in the plant, which materializes the idea of event disabling for the conjunction of modular controllers.

3.3   The User Area

The user area includes the functions for interfacing with the physical plant, defined specifically for each target platform. In the *Interface* block, the process signals are read, converted into uncontrollable events, and transmitted to the event handler. In the *Event actions* block, functions are created with the specific action that should be executed whenever an enabled event is handled. These functions must be associated with the events. Usually, each controllable event has an associated action, such as turning on or off a digital output. Section 4 presents a case study in which inputs and outputs are read and controlled remotely, using the Modbus TCP protocol.

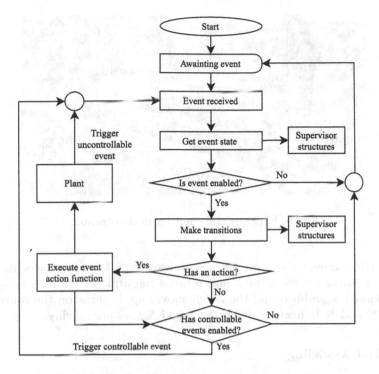

Fig. 4. Flowchart for the event handler operation.

4   Case Study

A case study was implemented to illustrate the proposed tool. The experimental plant, shown in Fig. 5, consists of conveyors, sensors, a control panel, and a Two-Axis Pick & Place arm. The arm has sensors to indicate if the axes are moving and if there is a grabbed workpiece. The Factory I/O[1] simulator was used to represent the plant and implement the controller. This tool reproduces by software the same conditions as a real plant, in terms of devices, hardware, communication channels and protocols, such as Modbus TCP used here, and many other resources. Yet, it avoids having to maintain the real infrastructure. A variety of scenarios can be constructed using the Factory I/O tool within a short period of time and at low costs, so that this becomes a viable strategy for control engineering practice and test.

The operation consists of moving the workpieces from one conveyor to another. When the start (S_3) button is pressed, the conveyor 1 (G^1) turns on. When sensor 1 (S_1) detects an item, conveyor 01 is turned off. Then the arm moves down the Z-axis (G^3). When the sensors grab (S_5) detects the item, it activates the grab (G^5), moves up the Z-axis and moves the item to the other conveyor via the X-axis (G^4). When it reaches the destination, it turns off con-

---

[1] https://factoryio.com.

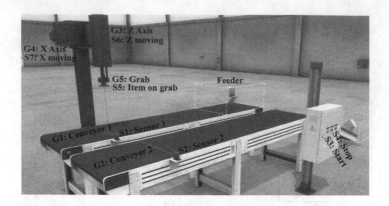

Fig. 5. Experimental plant for demonstration.

veyor 2 (G^2), moves the item down to sensor 2 (S_2), and releases it. When released, it turns on conveyor 2 and returns the arm. In parallel, as soon as the workpiece is grabbed and the Z-axis moves up, it turns on the conveyor 1. Sensors S_6 and S_7 indicate whether the Z and X axes are moving.

4.1   Plant Modeling

Figure 6 shows the automata modeling each equipment of the system presented in Fig. 5. Models G^{S_I}, for $I = 1, 2, 3, 4, 5$, represent the behavior of the respective sensor S_I. The models G^{S_J}, for $J = 6, 7$, represent the respective sensor S_J, which indicates, respectively, whether the Z and X axes are moving and paused. Finally, each G^K, for $K = 1, 2, 3, 4, 5$, models of the respective actuator or motor K. Event t_I indicates that sensor S_I has been triggered; events m_J represents that the axis is moving, while p_J indicates that the axis is paused; events s_K represent the commands that activate actuators K and events f_K represent their switching off. It has been assumed that $\Sigma_c = \{s_K, f_K\}$, while $\Sigma_u = \{t_I, m_J, p_J\}$. The composition $G = G^{S_I} \| G^{S_J} \| G^K$ is an automaton with 128 states and 1536 transitions.

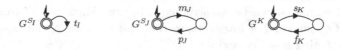

Fig. 6. Plant models.

4.2   Specification Modeling

The following specifications (see Fig. 7) are considered to coordinate the plant.

E^1: Coordinate the start of conveyor 1 according to the start button.
E^2: Turn off conveyor 1 every time an item arrives at sensor 1.
E^3: Disable the activation of the Z-axis whenever the X-axis is moving.
E^4: Coordinate the Z-axis drive to pick up and drop the workpiece on the conveyors.
E^5: Elevate the Z-axis as the grab picks up or releases a workpiece.
E^6: Move the X-axis forward as a workpiece is picked up and the Z-axis rises.
E^7: Move the X-axis back as a workpiece is released and the Z-axis rises.
E^8: Grab a workpiece whenever the grab sensor detects it.
E^9: Release a workpiece whenever sensor 2 detects it.
E^{10}: Turn on conveyor 2 whenever a workpiece is dropped on it.
E^{11}: Turn off conveyor 2 whenever the Z-axis moves down to unload a workpiece.

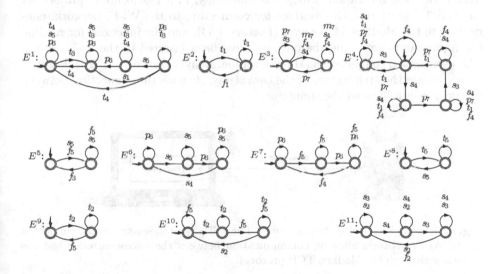

Fig. 7. Specification models.

The composition $E = \|_{i=1}^{11} E^i$ results in an automaton with 37344 states and 447784 transitions.

4.3 Synthesis

For the synthesis of the controller, the input model $K = G\|E$ resulted in 2507796 states and 22774582 transitions. This gives an idea of the computational complexity to compute the controller, as the synthesis algorithm iterates through the state space searching for controllability and non-blocking violations. Although this operation is polynomial on the state space of K, the model K itself grows exponentially with the size of the systems, which justifies LMC as a much simpler non-exponential strategy.

In this example, we first apply the monolithic synthesis over K. It turns out that, for the example, K reveals to be controllable and non-blocking, so the synthesized supervisor is the K model itself. Due to the high number of states and transitions, which would complicate the implementation, its maintainability, and make the hardware solution more expensive, LMC was adopted. This resulted in 11 local supervisors, where the worst-case modular synthesis explored 40 states, in comparison with 2507796 in the monolithic case. It turns out that the composition $\|_{i=1}^{11} S^i$ returned 2507796 states, therefore the same as in the monolithic case, which means that the LMC solution is optimal, i.e. $\|_{i=1}^{11} S^i = K$.

4.4 Conversion and Control of the Plant

After synthesizing the supervisors, the Supremica file was uploaded to DESc-Maker for code generation, which was embedded in a PlatformIO[2] project for the ESP32[3] platform. The routines for connecting to the Wi-Fi network, connecting to the Modbus TCP server (Factory I/O), and the functions for reading the inputs and controlling the outputs have been inserted in the user section. The user section completes the three-level hierarchy according to Fig. 2. Figure 8 demonstrates the architecture of the case study, showing the connection between the microcontroller and the simulator.

Fig. 8. Diagram illustrating the case study. The ESP32 and the computer are connected to the Wi-Fi network, allowing communication between the microcontroller and the simulator through the Modbus TCP protocol.

The average real time $(n = 10)$ to generate the files, measured with the Linux 'time' tool, was 373 ms. The ESP32 application's memory usage consists of: The supervisor library, which uses 214 bytes of flash, and the event handler, which occupies 176 bytes of flash and is independent of the size of the FSM. The events occupy 344 bytes of flash and 344 bytes of RAM. The supervisors, in total, consume 9964 bytes of flash and 9964 bytes of RAM. Totaling 10698 bytes of flash and 10308 bytes of RAM.[4]

---

[2] https://platformio.org.

[3] https://espressif.com/en/products/devkits.

[4] In order to measure the use of memory, the Inspect functionality of PlataformIO was used, available at: https://docs.platformio.org/en/stable/home/index.html#project-inspect.

The complete case study code can be found in [24], which also includes the Factory I/O simulation file and the file with the supervisor modeled in Supremica. In "application/src/main.cpp," it can be seen that there is no control logic, only the reading of the digital inputs, with the triggering of the respective uncontrollable events and the functions to control the outputs associated as "action function" to the controllable events. A video of the plant operation under control can be accessed at [25].

This case study illustrates how DEScMaker converts a FSM into functional code. Additional steps were required for the practical application of the generated code in the proposed scenario, such as the connection via Modbus TCP to the simulator and the Wi-Fi connection. This additional effort is necessary since the code generated is generic and only deals with supervisors and event handling. If the actuators and sensors were connected directly to the microcontroller board, other adjustments would be required for implementation.

5   Discussions and Perspectives

This paper presented DEScMaker, a tool for creating C code from controllers that have been designed, synthesized, and verified in Supremica. It is capable of generating code for monolithic and LMC controllers. To demonstrate its practicality, a case study was conducted.

Compared to [3], DEScMaker has a more straightforward structure and is more intuitive to use. It is also easier to integrate with existing projects as it does not rely on third-party libraries. The design of the project also facilitates the implementation of hybrid control by allowing the user to control the execution of the control algorithms in the user area.

The event handler is a good way to interconnect the supervisor and the physical plant. At the same time, it acts as an interface between these two layers, which allows replacement, for example, the implementation structure of the supervisors without the need for user code refactoring. In the case of a decentralized architecture, with the supervisors' state machines deployed on different hardware, the event handler is the agent that communicates with these external devices.

The tool that generates code in Python [23] has the structure of operation and use similar to DEScMaker. The same use case presented in Sect. 4 was also implemented in Python [26], and the same results were achieved. The Python implementation is easier to handle, test, and debug since the code compilation step is suppressed. Furthermore, it is data science-oriented and can straightforwardly gather cognitive skills for SCT.

Due to the execution nature of the event handler, interleaving is not yet addressed in this paper and is recommended for future work. The DEScMaker, as presented, is only designed to deal with ordinary automata. Other concepts, such as timed automata, FSM delay, or statecharts, are not yet part of the scope of this work and may be added in the future. Finally, the use of tables instead of linked lists to represent transitions will be investigated and compared.

Appendix 1   Directory Tree of Generated Code

Figure 9 shows the representation of the directory and file structure generated by DEScMaker.

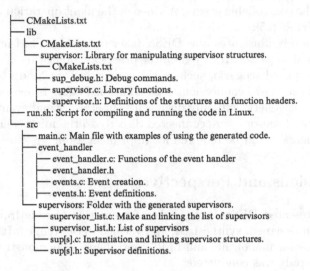

```
├── CMakeLists.txt
├── lib
│   ├── CMakeLists.txt
│   └── supervisor: Library for manipulating supervisor structures.
│       ├── CMakeLists.txt
│       ├── sup_debug.h: Debug commands.
│       ├── supervisor.c: Library functions.
│       └── supervisor.h: Definitions of the structures and function headers.
├── run.sh: Script for compiling and running the code in Linux.
└── src
    ├── main.c: Main file with examples of using the generated code.
    ├── event_handler
    │   ├── event_handler.c: Functions of the event handler
    │   ├── event_handler.h
    │   ├── events.c: Event creation.
    │   └── events.h: Event definitions.
    └── supervisors: Folder with the generated supervisors.
        ├── supervisor_list.c: Make and linking the list of supervisors
        ├── supervisor_list.h: List of supervisors
        ├── sup[s].c: Instantiation and linking supervisor structures.
        └── sup[s].h: Supervisor definitions.
```

Fig. 9. Directory tree of generated code.

In this case, the input file has only one supervisor, named "sup", which results in the files "sup.c" and "sup.h" under "src/supervisors/". If the file has two or more supervisors, as in the modular approach, all code files and headers are placed in the folder "supervisors".

Appendix 2   Code Generation Example

Consider the FSM in Fig. 10, corresponding to a supervisor with four states, seven transitions, and three different events. The Supremica file with this automaton was submitted to the DEScMaker, which created the code structure and saved it in "src/supervisors/sup.c".

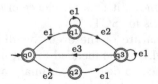

Fig. 10. Simple example of FSM for code generation.

Variables of type Alphabet are declared to create the list of events observed by the supervisor. This creates a variable with reserved memory space for an Alphabet structure, but its fields have no values assigned yet. Next, the alphabet variables are initialized and linked. This creates a list where it is possible to navigate from the first to the last event in the alphabet. In this example, the last element of the 'sup_e3_evt2' variable is NULL because there are no more elements in the list. This pattern also repeats when creating the other lists. The listing 1.1 shows the code for declaring, initializing, and linking the alphabet.

Listing 1.1. Alphabet creation and initialization.

```
#include "../event_handler/events.h"
#include "sup.h"
// Declares the Alphabet variables
const Alphabet sup_e1_evt0;
const Alphabet sup_e2_evt1;
const Alphabet sup_e3_evt2;
// Initializes and links Alphabet variables.
const Alphabet sup_e1_evt0 = {&e1, &sup_e2_evt1};
const Alphabet sup_e2_evt1 = {&e2, &sup_e3_evt2};
const Alphabet sup_e3_evt2 = {&e3, NULL};
```

Then the variables of type State, for representing the FSM states, are declared as in Listing 1.2.

Listing 1.2. States creation.

```
const State sup_q0;
const State sup_q1;
...
```

Once the alphabet and states are defined, the transition lists can be created and linked. Listing 1.3 exemplifies the transitions of the states $q0$ and $q1$.

Listing 1.3. Creating and linking transitions.

```
//Transitions for state q0
const Transition sup_q0_t0;
const Transition sup_q0_t1;
const Transition sup_q0_t0 = {&e1, &sup_q1, &sup_q0_t1};
const Transition sup_q0_t1 = {&e2, &sup_q2, NULL};
//Transitions for state q1
const Transition sup_q1_t0;
const Transition sup_q1_t1;
const Transition sup_q1_t0 = {&e1, &sup_q1, &sup_q1_t1};
const Transition sup_q1_t1 = {&e2, &sup_q3, NULL};
...
```

The states are initialized in Listing 1.4, now filled with all the necessary information, especially the pointer to the corresponding list of transitions.

Listing 1.4. Filling in the states.

```
const State sup_q0 = {true,  SUP_DEBUG_STR("q0"), &sup_q0_t0};
const State sup_q1 = {false, SUP_DEBUG_STR("q1"), &sup_q1_t0};
...
```

Finally, Listing 1.5 shows the structure of the supervisor, which will compose the list of supervisors (in the file "src/supervisors/supervisor_list.c") used by the event handler to query the event status and perform transitions. The variable of type 'Supervisor' is declared and initialized with pointers to the initial state, the current state, the last state (NULL because it has not yet been executed), the first item in the event list, and the supervisor's name.

Listing 1.5. Creating and linking the supervisor.

```
Supervisor sup = {&sup_q0, &sup_q0, NULL, &sup_e1_evt0, "sup"};
```

References

1. Akesson, K., et al.: Supremica (2019). http://www.supremica.org/
2. Alves, L.V., Martins, L.R., Pena, P.N.: UltraDES - a library for modeling, analysis and control of DES. IFAC-PapersOnLine **50**, 5831–5836 (2017). https://doi.org/10.1016/j.ifacol.2017.08.540
3. Assmann, J.V., Gotz, M., Muller, I., Rettberg, A.: Distributed embedded platform for controllers following the SCT. In: International Conference on Electrical, Communication, and Computer Engineering, pp. 1–6. IEEE (2021). https://doi.org/10.1109/ICECCE52056.2021.9514113
4. Basile, F., Chiacchio, P.: On the implementation of supervised control of discrete event systems. IEEE Trans. Control Syst. Technol. **15**, 725–739 (2007). https://doi.org/10.1109/TCST.2006.890281
5. van Beek, D.A., et al.: CIF 3: model-based engineering of supervisory controllers. In: Ábrahám, E., Havelund, K. (eds.) TACAS 2014. LNCS, vol. 8413, pp. 575–580. Springer, Heidelberg (2014). https://doi.org/10.1007/978-3-642-54862-8_48
6. Cassandras, C.G., Lafortune, S.: Introduction to Discrete Event Systems, 3rd edn. Springer, Cham (2021). https://doi.org/10.1007/978-3-030-72274-6
7. Clavijo, L.B., Basilio, J.C., Carvalho, L.K.: DESLAB: a scientific computing program for analysis and synthesis of discrete-event systems. IFAC Proc. Vol. **45**, 349–355 (2012). https://doi.org/10.3182/20121003-3-MX-4033.00056
8. Fokkink, W., Goorden, M., van de Mortel-Fronczak, J., Reijnen, F., Rooda, J.: Supervisor synthesis: bridging theory and practice. Computer **55**, 48–54 (2022). https://doi.org/10.1109/MC.2021.3134934
9. Fokkink, W., Goorden, M., van de Mortel-Fronczak, J., Reijnen, F., Rooda, J.: Supervisor synthesis: bridging theory and practice. Computer **55**(10), 48–54 (2022)
10. Gobe, F., Timmermanns, T., Ney, O., Kowalewski, S.: Synthesis tool for automation controller supervision. In: International Workshop on Discrete Event Systems, pp. 424–431. IEEE (2016). https://doi.org/10.1109/WODES.2016.7497883
11. Harrison, R., Vera, D., Ahmad, B.: Engineering methods and tools for cyber-physical automation systems. Proc. IEEE **104**(5), 973–985 (2016)
12. Hasdemir, I.T., Kurtulan, S., Goren, L.: An implementation methodology for supervisory control theory. Int. J. Adv. Manuf. Technol. **36**, 373–385 (2008). https://doi.org/10.1007/s00170-006-0843-5
13. Leal, A.B., da Cruz, D.L.L., da S. Hounsell, M.: Supervisory control implementation into programmable logic controllers. In: International Conference on Emerging Technologies and Factory Automation, pp. 1–7. IEEE (2009). https://doi.org/10.1109/ETFA.2009.5347090
14. Litchfield, S., Formby, D., Rogers, J., Meliopoulos, S., Beyah, R.: Rethinking the honeypot for cyber-physical systems. IEEE Internet Comput. **20**(5), 9–17 (2016)
15. Liu, Y., Peng, Y., Wang, B., Yao, S., Liu, Z.: Review on cyber-physical systems. IEEE/CAA J. Automatica Sinica **4**(1), 27–40 (2017)

16. Ljungkrantz, O., Akesson, K., Richardsson, J., Andersson, K.: Implementing a control system framework for automatic generation of manufacturing cell controllers. In: Proceedings 2007 IEEE International Conference on Robotics and Automation, pp. 674–679. IEEE (2007). https://doi.org/10.1109/ROBOT.2007.363064
17. Malik, R., Åkesson, K., Flordal, H., Fabian, M.: Supremica an efficient tool for large-scale discrete event systems. IFAC-PapersOnLine **50**, 5794–5799 (2017)
18. McCarthy, D., McMorrow, D., O'Dowd, N.P., McCarthy, C.T., Hinchy, E.P.: A model-based approach to automated validation and generation of plc code for manufacturing equipment in regulated environments. Appl. Sci. **12**, 7506 (2022). https://doi.org/10.3390/app12157506
19. Mohajerani, S., Malik, R., Fabian, M.: Compositional synthesis of supervisors in the form of state machines and state maps. Automatica **76**, 277–281 (2017)
20. Moor, T., Schmidt, K., Perk, S.: libFAUDES - An open source C++ library for discrete event systems. In: 2008 9th International Workshop on Discrete Event Systems, pp. 125–130. IEEE (2008). https://doi.org/10.1109/WODES.2008.4605933
21. Pinheiro, L.P., Lopes, Y.K., Leal, A.B., Junior, R.S.U.R.: Nadzoru: a software tool for supervisory control of DES. IFAC-PapersOnLine **48**, 182–187 (2015). https://doi.org/10.1016/j.ifacol.2015.06.491
22. Possato, T.: Automated code generator from Supremica to C (2023). bit.ly/3DTs-CEu
23. Possato, T.: Automated code generator from Supremica to Python (2023). bit.ly/3saIY99
24. Possato, T.: DEScMaker case study (2023). bit.ly/47w3zoA
25. Possato, T.: DEScMaker case study video (2023). bit.ly/3KFqELY
26. Possato, T.: DESPythonMaker case study (2023). bit.ly/3OD0haF
27. Queiroz, M.H.D., Cury, J.E.R.: Modular multitasking supervisory control of composite discrete-event systems. In: 16th IFAC World Congress (2005)
28. de Queiroz, M., Cury, J.: Synthesis and implementation of local modular supervisory control for a manufacturing cell. In: International Workshop on Discrete Event Systems, pp. 377–382. IFAC (2002). https://doi.org/10.1109/WODES.2002.1167714
29. Ramadge, P., Wonham, W.: The control of discrete event systems. Proc. IEEE **77**(1), 81–98 (1989). https://doi.org/10.1109/5.21072
30. Reniers, M., van de Mortel-Fronczak, J.: An engineering perspective on model-based design of supervisors. IFAC-PapersOnLine **51**, 257–264 (2018). https://doi.org/10.1016/j.ifacol.2018.06.310
31. Rosa, M., Teixeira, M., Malik, R.: Exploiting approximations in supervisory control with distinguishers. In: International Workshop on Discrete Event Systems. Sorrento, Italy (2018)
32. Silva, Y.G., de Queiroz, M.H.: Formal synthesis, simulation and automatic code generation of supervisory control for a manufacturing cell. In: Symposium Series in Mechatronics, pp. 418–426. ABCM (2010). https://www.abcm.org.br/anais/cobem/2009/pdf/COB09-1992.pdf
33. Uzam, M.: A general technique for the plc-based implementation of RW supervisors with time delay functions. Int. J. Adv. Manuf. Technol. **62**, 687–704 (2012). https://doi.org/10.1007/s00170-011-3817-1
34. Vieira, A.D., Cury, J.E.R., de Queiroz, M.H.: A model for PLC implementation of supervisory control of DES. In: International Conference on Emerging Technologies and Factory Automation, pp. 225–232 (2006). https://doi.org/10.1109/ETFA.2006.355436

35. Vieira, A.D., Santos, E.A.P., de Queiroz, M.H., Leal, A.B., de Paula Neto, A.D., Cury, J.E.R.: A method for PLC implementation of supervisory control of DES. IEEE Trans. Control Syst. Technol. **25**, 175–191 (2017). https://doi.org/10.1109/TCST.2016.2544702
36. Yang, J., Tan, K., Feng, L., El-Sherbeeny, A.M., Li, Z.: Reducing the learning time of reinforcement learning for the supervisory control of discrete event systems. IEEE Access **1**, 1–14 (2023)

AutomaTutor: An Educational Mobile App for Teaching Automata Theory

Steven Jordaan, Nils Timm$^{(\boxtimes)}$, and Linda Marshall

Department of Computer Science, University of Pretoria, Pretoria, South Africa
{sj.jordaan,nils.timm,linda.marshall}@up.ac.za

Abstract. Automata theory is one of the core theories in computer science because it allows scientists and practitioners to understand the complexity of computational problems, and thus, to develop efficient solutions to them. Several formal methods such as model checking are based on automata theory. Automata theory has traditionally been taught on a theoretical level. Students learned to define abstract machines via pen and paper without the possibility to actually run these machines. Over the years several automata simulators have been introduced and employed in teaching automata theory. These tools offer rich features for designing and manipulating automata, but do not provide pedagogical guidance to the user. In this paper we present the AutomaTutor, an educational tool on automata theory that particularly targets learners without prior knowledge of theoretical computer science. The tool is a mobile application that offers guided learning by solving interactive exercises. Exercises can be randomly generated or customised by an educator. The user-friendly touch interface allows learners to solve exercises by constructing finite automata or regular expressions that match with given languages. Learners receive immediate feedback. The application's focus on user experience and visualisation aims to make it accessible regardless of the technological background of the user. Our target is that the tool stimulates the students in their learning activities, and thus, leads to an improved understanding of automata theory and an increased interest in formal and theoretical aspects of computer science.

1 Introduction

Automata theory is the study of abstract machines and problems that can be solved by them. It is one of the core theories in computer science because it allows scientists and practitioners to understand the complexity of computational problems, and thus, to develop efficient hardware or software solutions to them. Several formal methods such as model checking are based on automata theory.

An integral part of teaching practical computer science is to make use of technology such as software development kits and tools for the visualisation of software components. Automata theory has traditionally been taught on a theoretical level. Students learned to define abstract machines via pen and paper without the possibility to actually run these machines. Over the years several

H. Barbosa and Y. Zohar (Eds.): SBMF 2023, LNCS 14414, pp. 131–140, 2024.
https://doi.org/10.1007/978-3-031-49342-3_8

automata simulators have been introduced and employed in teaching automata theory [15, 18, 19, 21]. These tools offer rich features for designing and manipulating automata, but do not provide pedagogical guidance to the user. This may overwhelm novice learners and discourage them from using the tools in their learning activities.

In this paper we present the AutomaTutor, an educational tool on automata theory that particularly targets learners without prior knowledge of theoretical computer science. The tool is a mobile application that offers guided learning by solving interactive exercises. It brings abstract automata to life and allows students to get a practical experience of theoretical computer science. The application's focus on user experience and visualisation aims to make it accessible regardless of the technological background of the user. The tool is split into two major components: the tutorial and the sandbox.

The tutorial offers interactive exercises on finite automata and regular languages on different levels of difficulty. Exercises can be randomly generated or customised by an educator. The user-friendly touch interface allows learners to solve exercises by constructing automata or regular expressions that match with given languages. Learners receive immediate feedback on each exercise. For incorrect solutions feedback is provided in the sense of counterexample strings that are incorrectly accepted or rejected. The tool generates such counterexamples automatically. The tutorial also offers hints during exercises, providing users with additional guidance without revealing the full solution.

The sandbox provides similar functionalities as existing automata editors. While being less feature-rich than existing editors, the sandbox was designed with a focus on simplicity and user-friendliness. The purpose of the sandbox is to also offer a platform for experimental learning of automata theory. Learners can create their own finite automata in an easy touch-based manner and they can simulate runs of the automata for input strings. The sandbox visualises simulation runs by highlighting the taken transitions and indicating whether the run is accepting or rejecting.

From 2024 on the AutomaTutor will be officially used in teaching the undergraduate module "Theoretical Computer Science" at the University of Pretoria. The set of tutorial exercises will be further populated and aligned with the lecture content. By using the application, students will have the opportunity to enhance their understanding of automata theory without additional guidance by an instructor. Our target is that the AutomaTutor stimulates the students in their learning activities, and thus, leads to an improved understanding of automata theory and an increased interest in formal and theoretical aspects of computer science.

2   Related Work

The development of automata simulation tools started in the early 1960s [4]. A review of tools that have been developed since then can be found in [2]. Simulators can be classified into language-, table- and canvas-based tools. Language-based tools [1, 9, 11] present automata as programs of a programming language.

In table-based tools [7,8] automata can be constructed by means of a transition table. While these two kinds of tools lack visual features, the technological advances in the 1990s allowed to introduce canvas-based simulators [5,12,14] where users can draw automata as state-transition diagrams. Today canvas-based tools are still the most popular ones with prominent examples such as JFLAP [15] and JFAST [21]. Most simulators are desktop applications where user input is performed via mouse and keyboard. In recent years, a number of mobile applications for automata simulation has been introduced. CMSimulator [3], FLApp [13] and Automata Simulator [18] are mobile applications that allow a touch-based construction and simulation of automata. Each of the above-mentioned tools comes with a particular range of supported automata types, such as finite automata, pushdown automata, Turing machines and transducers. Educators have reported on successfully using simulation tools in teaching automata theory at university level [16]. Using the tools required an instructor-guided approach where the instructor had to manually create exercises to be solved with the tool. In contrast, our AutomaTutor offers guidance by the tool itself. The exercises are already integrated into the tool. They can be automatically generated and graded, and the learner receives immediate feedback. Currently, our AutomaTutor is limited to finite automata and regular expressions, and thus, does not offer as rich features as alternative tools. During the development of the AutomaTutor particular emphasis was put on following usability guidelines [6,10] in order to make the application as user-friendly as possible, which is an aspect that is typically not addressed in related work. Our work is loosely related to game-based approaches to learn automata theory [17,20]. The approaches integrated automata aspects into classical games such as Mastermind and Tower Defence. In the proposed games the focus is more on the fun aspect than on comprehensive learning.

3   The AutomaTutor

In this section we present the AutomaTutor, a mobile application for teaching and learning automata theory. The application was designed with the purpose to provide computer science students a guided and engaging learning experience. In the design of the application particular emphasis was put on *usability* and *feedback* features. Moreover, *generation* features were integrated into the application which include the automatic generation of random exercises. After a brief tool overview we discuss the features of these types in separate subsections. The AutomaTutor can be accessed via the following link: https://sj-jordaan.github.io/masters-tool/. We recommend to use the application on a mobile phone. The source code of the AutomaTutor is available under https://github.com/SJ-Jordaan/masters-tool.

3.1   Overview

Upon first accessing the application, users are presented with a landing page (Fig. 1a) that emphasises the tool's experimental status and conveys appreciation for their engagement. They are then guided to a profile customisation interface (Fig. 1b), which hints at forthcoming personalisation enhancements. Subsequently, users are ushered into the Tutor segment, where they receive a descriptive overview of the 'Experiment' category (Fig. 1c). From here, they have the option to transition to the 'Exercises' tab (Fig. 2a) to select their desired level. Upon selecting their avatar located at the top right corner, users are directed to their profile page (Fig. 2b). From this interface, they have the option to either revert to the Tutor segment or proceed to the Sandbox environment (Fig. 2c). As users delve deeper into the application, they encounter one of its most essential features:

(a) Landing page   (b) Add profile   (c) Description

Fig. 1. Initial Application Journey.

Finite Automata Editor. The Finite Automata Editor is a pivotal feature of the mobile application, meticulously designed to provide an intuitive and efficient interface for users to interact with finite automata. The editor is implemented in two distinct contexts within the application: the exercise interface and the sandbox interface. Each interface encapsulates a range of functionalities, each contributing to the overall usability of the application.

Exercises. Exercises are a crucial component of the tool, providing users with opportunities to apply their knowledge and understanding of finite automata and

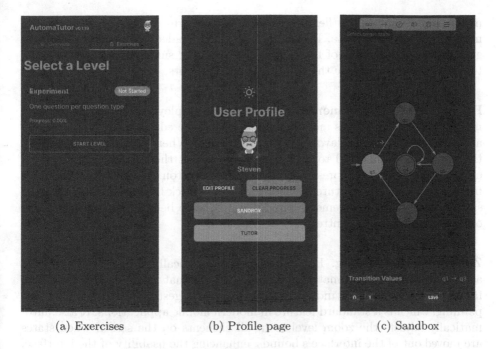

(a) Exercises	(b) Profile page	(c) Sandbox

Fig. 2. Navigating to Sandbox.

regular expressions. The exercises are designed to be diverse and challenging, offering a range of question types that cater to different learning styles and objectives. The tool supports exercises that involve providing a regular language, either textually, as a regular expression, or as an automaton, and asking the user to construct a corresponding regular expression, automaton, or perform a conversion between the two. Another variant of the exercise requires the user to provide a string that is contained within the given language. These exercises are designed to test the user's understanding of the core concepts and their ability to apply this knowledge in practical scenarios.

3.2 Usability

Prioritising user experience, the application combines intuitive design with efficiency. This section highlights features that enhance interaction with finite automata and foster a conducive learning environment.

Adding, Removing, and Modifying Components. Both the exercise and sandbox interfaces facilitate users to seamlessly add and modify transitions of an automaton. In the exercise interface, the states, including initial and accepting states, are predefined, and users can add or modify transitions between these states by labeling them with appropriate symbols. In contrast, the sandbox interface allows users to add, alter, and delete states and transitions using a context menu, providing a more flexible and advanced environment for creating and modifying finite automata. Both interfaces provide adequately sized touch targets for the components of the automaton, ensuring sufficient spacing between touch targets to minimise the risk of accidental inputs.

Re-Arranging Components. Both interfaces employ an automatic arrangement algorithm for states and transitions within the editor to create a visually appealing and organised layout for the automaton. When a state is repositioned, the transitions connected to it automatically adjust their paths to maintain a clear and uncluttered representation of the automaton. The sandbox interface further enhances this feature by allowing users to lock the layout once they are satisfied with the arrangement, providing a balance between automatic layout optimisation and user control.

Zooming and Panning. Both interfaces automatically adjust the zoom level and position of the automaton diagram to ensure that it fits nicely and is legible on the screen. The sandbox interface supports gesture-based zooming and panning, which is a standard feature in modern mobile applications. It also automatically adjusts the zoom level to fit all elements on the screen when states are moved out of the interface's bounds, enhancing the usability of the interface, especially when working with larger automata.

Progress Tracking: The tool implements a progress tracking feature which includes a timeline at the top of the exercise interface that shows users how far they have progressed and how many questions they have answered correctly. This feature allows users to gauge their progress, manage their time effectively, and stay motivated.

3.3   Feedback

Feedback in this application serves as more than just a response, it is a proactive tool that guides and informs the user's learning journey. This section details the feedback modalities, each designed to offer timely and constructive insights.

Hints. Hints, designed to scaffold problem-solving skills and alleviate user frustration, play a crucial role within the application. The application presents hints as textual prompts via a pop-up interface as seen in Figs. 3a. These hints, drawn from a manually curated pool, offer users a variety of suggestions to guide their problem-solving process.

Simulation. The Simulation (Fig. 3c) feature in the application is primarily integrated within the sandbox. This allows users to construct automata and simulate string inputs against them, fostering an active learning experience. The

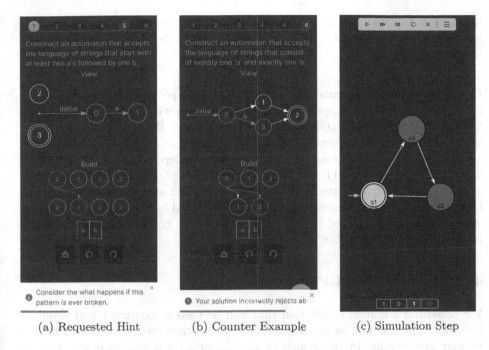

(a) Requested Hint   (b) Counter Example   (c) Simulation Step

Fig. 3. Examples of Feedback.

automata simulation in the application utilises colour highlighting to indicate the active state and transitions during the simulation. The application also incorporates an animation that signifies the reading of the next input symbol. An accepted or rejected input is highlighted in green or red, respectively, providing clear feedback to the user.

Performance Feedback: Upon completing an exercise, users are presented with a summary of their performance. This feedback includes basic metrics such as the number of submission attempts, time taken, and percentage correct (in case some questions were left incorrect or unanswered). This information helps users identify areas where they excelled and those where improvement is needed, guiding their future learning efforts.

3.4   Generation

The generation features of the application encompass the creation of exercises and the generation of counterexamples.

Random Exercise Generation. The tool employs algorithms to generate random yet solvable exercises, ensuring a diverse range of tasks and providing users with new challenges each time they engage with the exercises. Users have the option to select the difficulty scale and the number of questions, as well as the types of questions to generate, allowing for a personalised and targeted learning experience.

Counterexample Generation. The counterexample generation feature is a critical component of the application, providing users with immediate, constructive feedback upon the submission of their solutions. By comparing the user's solution to the memorandum solution, the application can generate counterexamples that highlight discrepancies in the user's understanding of the problem. This feedback is presented to the user in a clear, concise manner, accompanied by audio-visual cues to indicate an incorrect solution. The application generates two types of counterexamples: strings incorrectly accepted by the user's solution and strings incorrectly rejected by the user's solution. A generated counterexample is shown as a pop-up at the bottom of Fig. 3b.

4   Conclusion and Future Work

We presented a mobile application that can be used to construct and simulate finite automata as well as to solve interactive exercises on automata theory and regular expressions. In the design of the AutomaTutor emphasis was put on usability and feedback features. The application guides users in their learning activities without the need for additional intervention by an instructor. The question pool of the AutomaTutor is currently small but the implemented generation features allow to automatically generate random questions of several types. In preliminary user experiments we asked computer science students at the University of Pretoria to solve automata theory exercises via pen and paper, via the classical simulators as well as by using the AutomaTutor and to report on their experiences and preferences. The majority of students favoured the guided learning approach offered by the AutomaTutor. A more extensive experimental evaluation of the tool is in progress. From 2024 on the AutomaTutor will be officially used in teaching the undergraduate module "Theoretical Computer Science". Our conjecture is that the use of the tool will allow students gain a better understanding of the abstract topics of theoretical computer science. Although automata theory is not a formal method on its own, it it one of the core theories that is employed in several formal methods. Thus, with introducing our app we also intend to motivate and prepare students to study formal methods at postgraduate level.

In its current version the AutomaTutor only includes exercises on finite automata and regular expressions. As future work we are planning to extend the application such that further types of automata such as pushdown automata and Turing machines are supported. It is also planned to include Kripke structures and Büchi automata such that model checking subjects can be taught via the tool. Moreover, based on student feedback the usability, feedback and generation features of the AutomaTutor will be further improved.

References

1. Chakraborty, P.: A language for easy and efficient modeling of Turing machines. Prog. Nat. Sci. **17**(7), 867–871 (2007)
2. Chakraborty, P., Saxena, P.C., Katti, C.P.: Fifty years of automata simulation: a review. ACM Inroads **2**(4), 59–70 (2011)
3. Chuda, D., Trizna, J., Kratky, P.: Android automata simulator. In: Proceedings of the International Conference on e-Learning, pp. 80–4 (2015)
4. Coffin, R.W., Goheen, H.E., Stahl, W.R.: Simulation of a Turing machine on a digital computer. In: Proceedings of the November 12–14, 1963, Fall Joint Computer Conference, pp. 35–43 (1963)
5. Cogliati, J.J., Goosey, F.W., Grinder, M.T., Pascoe, B.A., Ross, R.J., Williams, C.J.: Realizing the promise of visualization in the theory of computing. J. Educ. Resour. Comput. (JERIC) **5**(2), 5–es (2005)
6. Google LLC.: Material design guidelines (2023). https://m3.material.io/
7. Hamada, M.: Supporting materials for active e-learning in computational models. In: Bubak, M., van Albada, G.D., Dongarra, J., Sloot, P.M.A. (eds.) ICCS 2008. LNCS, vol. 5102, pp. 678–686. Springer, Heidelberg (2008). https://doi.org/10.1007/978-3-540-69387-1_79
8. Hannay, D.G.: Interactive tools for computation theory. ACM SIGCSE Bull. **34**(4), 68–70 (2002)
9. Harris, J.: Programming non-deterministically using automata simulators. J. Comput. Sci. Coll. **18**(2), 237–245 (2002)
10. Inc., A.: Human interface guidelines (2023). https://developer.apple.com/design/human-interface-guidelines/
11. Knuth, D.E., Bigelow, R.H.: Programming language for automata. J. ACM (JACM) **14**(4), 615–635 (1967)
12. LoSacco, M., Rodger, S.: FLAP: a tool for drawing and simulating automata. Media **93**, 310–317 (1993)
13. Pereira, C.H., Terra, R.: A mobile app for teaching formal languages and automata. Comput. Appl. Eng. Educ. **26**(5), 1742–1752 (2018)
14. Robinson, M.B., Hamshar, J.A., Novillo, J.E., Duchowski, A.T.: A java-based tool for reasoning about models of computation through simulating finite automata and turing machines. In: The Proceedings of the Thirtieth SIGCSE Technical Symposium on Computer Science Education, pp. 105–109 (1999)
15. Rodger, S.H., Finley, T.W.: JFLAP: An Interactive Formal Languages and Automata Package. Jones & Bartlett Learning, Burlington (2006)
16. Rodger, S.H., Wiebe, E., Lee, K.M., Morgan, C., Omar, K., Su, J.: Increasing engagement in automata theory with JFLAP. In: Proceedings of the 40th ACM Technical Symposium on Computer Science Education, pp. 403–407 (2009)
17. Silva, R.C., Binsfeld, R.L., Carelli, I.M., Watanabe, R.: Automata defense 2.0: reediçao de um jogo educacional para apoio em linguagens formais e autômatos. In: Brazilian Symposium on Computers in Education (Simpósio Brasileiro de Informática na Educaçao-SBIE), vol. 1 (2010)
18. Singh, T., Afreen, S., Chakraborty, P., Raj, R., Yadav, S., Jain, D.: Automata simulator: a mobile app to teach theory of computation. Comput. Appl. Eng. Educ. **27**(5), 1064–1072 (2019)
19. Traoré, M.K.: SimStudio: a next generation modeling and simulation framework. In: 1st International ICST Conference on Simulation Tools and Techniques for Communications, Networks and Systems (2010)

20. Vieira, M., Sarinho, V.: Automatamind: a serious game proposal for the automata theory learning. In: van der Spek, E., Göbel, S., Do, E.Y.-L., Clua, E., Baalsrud Hauge, J. (eds.) ICEC-JCSG 2019. LNCS, vol. 11863, pp. 452–455. Springer, Cham (2019). https://doi.org/10.1007/978-3-030-34644-7_45
21. White, T.M., Way, T.P.: JFAST: a java finite automata simulator. In: Proceedings of the 37th SIGCSE Technical Symposium on Computer Science Education, pp. 384–388 (2006)

ESBMC v7.3: Model Checking C++ Programs Using Clang AST

Kunjian Song[1]($\boxtimes$), Mikhail R. Gadelha[2]($\boxtimes$), Franz Brauße[1]($\boxtimes$),
Rafael S. Menezes[1]($\boxtimes$), and Lucas C. Cordeiro[1]($\boxtimes$)

[1] The University of Manchester, Manchester, UK
{kunjian.song,rafael.menezes}@postgrad.manchester.ac.uk,
{franz.brausse,lucas.cordeiro}@manchester.ac.uk
[2] Igalia, A Coruña, Spain
mikhail@igalia.com

Abstract. This paper introduces ESBMC v7.3, the latest Efficient SMT-Based Context-Bounded Model Checker version, which now incorporates a new Clang-based C++ front-end. While the previous CPROVER-based front-end served well for handling C++03 programs, it encountered challenges keeping up with the evolving C++ language. As new language and library features were added in each C++ version, the limitations of the old front-end became apparent, leading to difficult-to-maintain code. Consequently, modern C++ programs were challenging to verify. To overcome this obstacle, we redeveloped the front-end, opting for a more robust approach using Clang. The new front-end efficiently traverses the Abstract Syntax Tree (AST) in-memory using Clang APIs and transforms each AST node into ESBMC's Intermediate Representation. Through extensive experimentation, our results demonstrate that ESBMC v7.3 with the new front-end significantly reduces parse and conversion errors, enabling successful verification of a wide range of C++ programs, thereby outperforming previous ESBMC versions.

Keywords: Formal Methods · Model Checking · Software Verification

1 Introduction

C++ is one of the most popular programming languages used to build high-performance and real-time systems, such as operating systems, banking systems, communication systems, and embedded systems [1,2]. However, memory safety issues remain a major source of security vulnerabilities in C++ programs [3]. Fan et al. [4] created a dataset of C/C++ vulnerabilities by mining the Common Vulnerabilities and Exposures (CVE) database [5] and the associated open-source projects on GitHub, then curated the issues based on Common Weakness Enumeration (CWE) [6]. According to their findings, two out of the top three vulnerabilities are caused by memory safety issues: Improper Restriction of Operations within the Bounds of a Memory Buffer (CWE-119) and Out-of-bounds Read (CWE-125) [4].

© The Author(s), under exclusive license to Springer Nature Switzerland AG 2024
H. Barbosa and Y. Zohar (Eds.): SBMF 2023, LNCS 14414, pp. 141–152, 2024.
https://doi.org/10.1007/978-3-031-49342-3_9

The limitation of software testing resides in the user inputs [7]. Only a limited number of execution paths may be tested since test cases involve human inputs in the form of concrete values [8]. Unlike testing, formal verification techniques can be used more systematically to reason about a program, although they suffer from the state-space explosion problem [9]. There is an increasing adoption of formal verification techniques for C programs in the industry, e.g., Amazon has been using model-checking techniques to prove the correctness of their C-based systems in Amazon Web Services (AWS); this has positively impacted their code quality, as evidenced by the increased rate of bugs found and fixed [10].

Formal verification of C++ programs is more challenging than C programs due to the sophisticated features, such as the STL (Standard Template Libraries) containers, templates, exception handling, and object-oriented programming (OOP) paradigm [1]. The existing state-of-the-art verification tools for C++ programs only have limited feature support [11]. For ESBMC, Ramalho et al. [12] and Monteiro et al. [11] initiated the support for C++ program verification. Since then, ESBMC has undergone heavy development.

This research presents a significant improvement to ESBMC's C++ verification capabilities by introducing a new Clang-based front-end. Particularly, the original contributions of this work are as follows:

- **Complete Redesign**: ESBMC's C++ front-end has undergone a complete overhaul and now relies on Clang [13]. By leveraging Clang's parsing and semantic analysis capabilities [14,15], we check the input program's Abstract Syntax Tree (AST) using a production-quality compiler. This eliminates the need for static analysis logic and ensures enhanced accuracy and efficiency.
- **Object Models Details**: We provide comprehensive insights into the object models used to achieve seamless conversion of C++ polymorphism code to ESBMC's Intermediate Representation (IR). This improvement allows ESBMC to handle C++ growth and its variants like CUDA [16].
- **Simplified Type Checking for Templates**: The new Clang-based front-end greatly simplifies type checking for templates, streamlining ESBMC's ability to adapt to C++ advancements. Furthermore, this enhancement facilitates the incorporation of C++ variants like CUDA.

By introducing these advancements, our work significantly enhances ESBMC's C++ verification capabilities, paving the way for more robust and efficient verification of C++ programs and their variants.

2   Background

ESBMC's verification for C++03 programs reaches its maturity in version v2.1, presented by Monteiro et al. [11]. ESBMC v2.1 provides a first-order logic-based framework that formalizes a wide range of C++ core languages, verifying the input C++ programs by encoding them into SMT formulas. Since C++ Standard Template Libraries (STL) contain optimized assembly code not verifiable using ESBMC, ESBMC v2.1 tackled this problem using a collection of C++

operational models (OM) to replace the STL included in the input program. The OMs are abstract representations mimicking the structure of the STL, adding pre- and post-conditions to all STL APIs [17]. Combining these approaches, ESBMC v2.1 outperformed other state-of-the-art tools evaluated over a large set of benchmarks, comprising 1513 test cases [11]. Nonetheless, ESBMC v2.1 employs a Flex and Bison-based front-end from CBMC [18], which leads to hard-to-maintain code and can hardly evolve to support modern C++11 features.

Limitations of the Old C++ Front-End. The version of ESBMC in Monteiro et al. [11] uses an outdated CPROVER-based front-end [18] with the following limitations.

1. For the type-checking phase, ESBMC could not provide meaningful warnings or error messages.
2. It is inefficient at generating a body for default implicit non-trivial methods in a class, such as C++ copy constructors or copy assignment operators.
3. The parser of the old front-end needs to be manually updated to cover the essential C++ semantic rules [19], which leads to hard-to-maintain code to keep up with the C++ evolution.
4. The old front-end contains excessive data structures and procedures auxiliary to scope resolution and function type checking.
5. The type checker [19] of the old front-end only works with a CPROVER-based parse tree and supports up to C++03 standard [20]. We find adapting it to the new C++ language and library features difficult.
6. The old front-end uses a speculative approach to guess the arguments for a template specialization and a map to associate the template parameters to their instantiated values, which leads to hard-to-maintain and hard-to-debug code in the case of recursive templates. Additionally, owing to its limited static analysis, the old front-end could not provide any early warning when there is a circular dependency on the templates.

These limitations combine to a point where the old front-end is too laborious to maintain and extend for formal verification of modern C++ programs. We propose the Clang-based approach to convert an input C++ program to ESBMC's IR to overcome these limitations.

3   Model Checking C++ Programs Using Clang AST

Figure 1 illustrates ESBMC's verification pipeline for C++ programs. The new Clang-cpp front-end typechecks and converts the input C++ program (along with the corresponding OMs) into the GOTO program representation [21, 22]. Then the GOTO program will be symbolically executed to generate the SSA form of the program, thus generating a set of logical formulas consisting of the constraints and properties. An SMT solver is used to check the satisfiability of the formulas, giving a verdict *VERIFICATION SUCCESSFUL* if no property violation is found up the bound k or a counterexample in case of property violation.

3.1   Polymorphism

The traditional approach for achieving polymorphism makes use of virtual function tables (also known as *vtables*) and virtual pointers (known as *vptrs*). While
the Clang AST, to the best of our knowledge, does not include information about
virtual tables or virtual pointers of a class, it nonetheless provides users with
enough information to enable them to create their *vtables* and *vptrs*. In the new
Clang-based C++ front-end, we reimplemented the *vtable* and *vptr* construction
mechanism following a similar approach from ESBMC v2.1, but with significant
simplifications based on the information provided in the Clang AST. Figure 2
illustrates an example of C++ polymorphism.

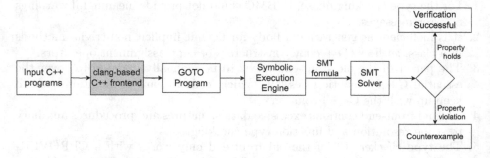

Fig. 1. ESBMC architecture for C++ verification. The grey block represents the new
Clang-based C++ front-end integrated into ESBMC v7.3.

```
1   class Bird {
2     public:
3       virtual int doit(void) { return 21; }
4   };
5
6   class Penguin: public Bird {
7     public:
8       int doit(void) override { return 42; }
9   };
10  int main(){
11    Bird *p = new Penguin();
12    assert(p->doit() == 42);
13    delete p;
14    return 0;
15  }
```

Fig. 2. Example of C++ classes with virtual functions.

Figure 3 illustrates the object models for the Bird and Penguin classes. The
new front-end adds one or more *vptrs* to each class. The *vptrs* will be initialized

in the class constructors, which set each *vptr* pointing to the desired *vtable*. The child class contains an additional pointer pointing to a *vtable* with a thunk to the overriding function. The thunk redirects the call to the corresponding overriding function. In the case of multiple inheritances, the child class would have multiple *vtprs* "inherited" from multiple base classes. The new front-end can also manage a virtual inheritance, such as the diamond problem, which avoids duplicating *vptrs*, referring to the same virtual table in an inheritance hierarchy. Line 2–4 in Fig. 4a illustrates the dynamic dispatch is achieved using the *vptr* calling the thunk, which in turn calls the desired overriding function in Fig. 4b Line 9–11. Note that the *override* specifier is a C++11 extension that the old front-end could not support.

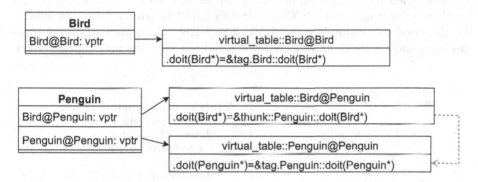

Fig. 3. Object models for Bird and Penguin classes.

```
1  int return_value;
2  return_value =
3  *p->Bird@Penguin
4      ->doit(p)
5  assert(return_value == 42)
```

(a) GOTO program of the dynamic dispatch in Line 12 of Figure 2.

```
1   thunk::Penguin::doit(Bird*):
2       int return_value;
3       return_value =
4       Penguin::doit(
5          (Penguin*)this)
6    RETURN: return_value
7    END_FUNCTION
8
9    Penguin::doit(Penguin*):
10      RETURN: 42
11   END_FUNCTION
```

(b) thunk redirecting the call to the overriding function.

Fig. 4. GOTO conversions of the overriding methods and dynamic dispatch.

3.2 Template

Template is a key feature in C++, allowing type to be passed as a parameter. The template allows STL containers and generic algorithms to work with different C++ data types [23, 24]. The old front-end in ESBMC v2.1 implements the template specialization based on Siek et al. [11, 25]. However, it produces a "CONVERSION ERROR" for the test case illustrated in Fig. 5a. This benchmark is based on the *Friend18* example from the GCC test suite [26], which was added for Bug 10158 on GCC Bugzilla [27]. ESBMC v7.3 successfully verified this benchmark and found the assertion's property violation in Fig. 5a. The verification result is illustrated in Fig. 5b. The example in Fig. 5a contains a C++20 extension. The *foo* function is defined in *struct X*, but gets called using an unqualified name with explicit template arguments in *main*. ESBMC v2.1 failed to verify it due to the "CONVERSION ERROR symbol "'foo' not found". We also tried this example with CBMC 5.88.1 [28], which aborted during type-checking, and cppcheck v2.11.1 [29], which did not give any verification verdict.

```
1   #include <cassert>
2   template <int N> struct X
3   {
4     template <int M>
5     friend int foo(X const &)
6     {
7       return N * 10000 + M;
8     }
9   };
10  X<1234> bring;
11
12  int main() {
13    assert(
14      foo<5678> (bring)
15        !=12345678);
16  }
```

(a) Example of C++ class template

```
1   Violated property:
2     file tmp2.cpp
3     line 13 column 3
4     function main
5     assertion
6       foo <5678>(bring)!=12345678
7     return_value!=12345678
8
9   VERIFICATION FAILED
```

(b) Verdict for the template example

Fig. 5. ESBMC verified the *Friend18* example from the GCC test suite [26].

4 Experimental Evaluation

We used some benchmarks from Monteiro et al. [11] to evaluate ESBMC v7.3. These benchmarks were used to assess ESBMC v2.1 in Monteiro et al. [11].

We did not evaluate the test cases (TCs) that depend on the operational models (OMs) in each benchmark. We only ran the TCs for core C++ language features because the OMs for the new Clang-based C++ front-end are still under development, e.g., exception handling support. Otherwise, running test cases for sure to fail would be pointless due to a feature still being developed. Hence each benchmark is a subset of the original benchmark, which only comprises TCs for verifying core C++ language features. There are 352 benchmarks in total over 6 sub-benchmarks. The *cpp-sub* contains example programs from the book *C++ How to Program* [30]. The inheritance and polymorphism sub-benchmarks are extracted from [11]. There are three sub-benchmarks for template specialization - *cbmc-sub* comes from the CBMC regressions [31]; *gcc-template-tests-sub* were extracted from the GCC template test suite [26]; *template-sub* is also from benchmarks used in [11]. *cpp-sub* contains programs with mixed use of various C++ language features combined with inheritance, polymorphism, and templates.

4.1 Objectives and Setup

Our evaluation framework is based on Python's *unittest* [32]. For each TC in the test suite, we check whether the verification verdict reported by each tool matches the expected outcome. TC passes when the tool reports a verdict of "VERIFICATION SUCCESSFUL" on a program without any violation of properties or reports "VERIFICATION FAILED" on an unsafe program that violates a property. Such properties include arithmetic overflows, array out-of-bounds, memory issues, or assertion failures. Our evaluation aims to answer the following experimental questions:

EQ1 (soundness): Can ESBMC give more correct verification results and a higher pass rate than its previous versions?

EQ2 (performance): How long does ESBMC v7.3 take to verify C++ programs?

EQ3 (completeness): Does the tool complete the future work specified by Monteiro et al. [11]?

The experiment was set up in Ubuntu 20.04 with 32GB RAM on an 8-core Intel CPU. The dataset, scripts, and logs are publicly available in Zenodo [33]. The accumulative verification time represents the CPU time elapsed for each tool finishing all sub-benchmarks.

4.2 Results

Table 1 shows our experimental results. With a higher pass rate than ESBMC v2.1 over 5 out of 6 sub-benchmarks, ESBMC v7.3 successfully verified all benchmarks and passed all test cases, confirming **EQ1**. As for ESBMC v2.1, the failed TCs in *cpp-sub* are due to parsing or conversion errors, meaning the previous tool version is unable to properly typecheck the input programs, probably due to the weak parser, as described in Sect. 2. The failed TCs in *inheritance and polymorphism-sub* contain a common feature of dynamically casting a pointer of a child class with a base class containing virtual methods. ESBMC v2.1 could not handle this type of casting, giving conversion errors.

ESBMC v2.1 has limited support for C++ templates, matching our expectations as reported by Monteiro et al. [11]. The failed test cases in *cbmc-template-sub* are the results of ESBMC v2.1 not able to handle the default template type parameter or explicit template specialization combined with C++ *typedef* specifier. The low pass rate of ESBMC v2.1 on *gcc-template-tests-sub* indicates that the old version cannot verify test cases used by an industrial compiler. **EQ3** is affirmed through the experiment, as none of these problems persist in ESBMC v7.3. Since one of the test cases in *cpp-sub* timed out against ESBMC v2.1 after 900 seconds, the actual verification time has been rectified to 149s; otherwise, the cumulative verification time would be 1049s. As for the performance **EQ2**, ESBMC v7.3 could verify all sub-benchmarks in 128s, faster than its previous version, which affirms **EQ2**.

Overall, we have enhanced the template support in ESBMC v7.3, which completed the future work by Monteiro et al. [11]. In comparison to its previous version, ESBMC v7.3 can provide more accurate results faster.

In addition to the pass rate and verification time in Table 1, we also assessed each tool's memory usage. Table 2 shows the cumulative maximum RSS (Resident Set Size) for each benchmark using each tool under evaluation. Our metrics collection approach is based on Python's *resource* module, *subprocess* module and *unit test framework* [32]. Compared to ESBMC v2.1, ESBMC v7.3 can verify more test cases and uses less memory. The lower memory usage of v2.1 than v7.3 is due to lower pass rates for the TCs using templates, mainly because of v2.1's inadequacy to handle C++ templates. Many TCs failed due to CONVERSION ERROR in ESBMC v2.1's front-end and never even reached the solver in the back-end. As a result, no verification effort was made for those TCs and hence less memory was used.

Table 1. Experimental results showing the pass rate for each sub-benchmark and accumulative verification time. This experiment uses ESBMC with Boolector SMT solver.

Sub-Benchmarks	ESBMC-v2.1 pass rate	ESBMC-v7.3 pass rate
cpp-sub	91%	100%
inheritance-sub	79%	100%
polymorphism-sub	87%	100%
cbmc-template-sub	92%	100%
gcc-template-tests-sub	39%	100%
template-sub	100%	100%
Total verification Time	149.94 s	128.796 s

Table 2. Experimental results showing the cumulative maximum RSS (Resident Set Size) for each sub-benchmarks. This experiment uses ESBMC with Boolector SMT solver.

Sub-Benchmarks	ESBMC-v2.1	ESBMC-v7.3
cpp-sub	31477 MB	19385 MB
inheritance-sub	231 MB	845 MB
polymorphism-sub	722 MB	2373 MB
cbmc-template-sub	650 MB	2295 MB
gcc-template-tests-sub	395 MB	1387 MB
template-sub	207 MB	727 MB
Total memory	33682 MB	27012 MB

4.3 Performance Using Different SMT Solvers

ESBMC supports multiple SMT solvers in the back-end, such as Z3 [34], Bitwuzla [35], Boolector [36], MathSAT [37], CVC4 [38], and Yices [39]. We also evaluated ESBMC v7.3 with various solvers over the same set of benchmarks. Table 3 shows the total verification time and memory consumption for ESBMC v7.3 using different solvers.

Table 3. Experimental results showing the total verification time and memory consumption for ESBMC using different solvers.

Sub Benchmarks	Boolector	CVC4	MathSAT	Yices	Z3	Bitwuzla
Time	128.796 s	637.988 s	131.934 s	182.327 s	162.848 s	152.442
Memory	27012 MB	72281 MB	161608 MB	35589 MB	44028 MB	27124 MB

Overall, ESBMC v7.3 with Boolector is the fastest configuration that also consumes the minimum amount of memory to verify all benchmarks. Among the other solvers, the memory consumption of ESBMC v7.3 with Bitwuzla comes near the Boolector configuration.

4.4 Threats to Validity

While developing the new C++ front-end, we found that the Clang AST does not fully describe the correct order of constructors or destructors to be called in the most derived class in a complex hierarchical inheritance graph, e.g., crossed diamond hierarchy. We documented it under an umbrella issue, which is currently in our backlog [40] on ESBMC GitHub repository [41]. ESBMC v2.1 mimics the semantics of the APIs of C++ STL libraries using a set of operational models (OMs). The C++ front-end of ESBMC has been completely rewritten, and the back-end has also undergone significant development and evolution since v2.1 was published in [11], therefore it is questionable whether those OMs still work. Our technical report [42] provides a summary of the pass rates.

5   Conclusion and Future Work

We present a new Clang-based front-end that converts in-memory Clang AST to ESBMC's IR. In our evaluation of ESBMC v7.3, we compared it to ESBMC v2.1, specifically focusing on a subset of benchmarks to cover core C++ language features. The results demonstrate significant progress with ESBMC v7.3, as it successfully parses real-world C++ programs, including those from the GCC test suite. Notably, it significantly reduces the number of conversion and parse errors compared to the previous version, showcasing improved performance over the sub-benchmarks for core language features.

While ESBMC effectively mimics the semantics of APIs of the STL libraries using the OMs from ESBMC v2.1, we recognize the need for continuous improvement. As we endeavor to verify modern C++ programs, these OMs require regular review and updates to align with the C++ standard used in the input program. Accurate OMs are essential, as any approximation may lead to incorrect encoding and invalidate the verification results. To further enhance our front-end coverage and reduce the number of OMs we maintain, our future work will focus on handling more C++ libraries.

Additionally, we aim to integrate various checkers, such as cppcheck [29], into our testing framework to facilitate future evaluations. Our previous success verifying a commercial C++ telecommunication application using ESBMC v2.1 has inspired further goals [11,43]. With ESBMC v7.3 and beyond, we plan to verify the C++ interpreter in OpenJDK as part of the Soteria project [44] and contribute to benchmarks for the International Competition on Software Verification (SV-COMP) [45].

Acknowledgements. The ESBMC development is currently funded by ARM, Intel, EPSRC grants EP/T026995/1, EP/V000497/1, EU H2020 ELEGANT 957286, and Soteria project awarded by the UK Research and Innovation for the Digital Security by Design (DSbD) Programme.

References

1. Deitel, P.J., Deitel, H.M.: C++ How to Program: Introducing the New C++14 Standard. Prentice Hall (2016)
2. Cordeiro, L.C., de Lima Filho, E.B., de Bessa, I.V.: Survey on automated symbolic verification and its application for synthesising cyber-physical systems. IET Cyper-Phys. Syst. Theory Appl. **5**(1), 1–24 (2020). https://doi.org/10.1049/iet-cps.2018.5006
3. Miller, M.: Trends and challenges in the vulnerability mitigation landscape. USENIX Association (2019)

4. Fan, J., Li, Y., Wang, S., Nguyen, T.N.: A C/C++ code vulnerability dataset with code changes and CVE summaries. In: Proceedings of the 17th International Conference on Mining Software Repositories, pp. 508–512 (2020)
5. Common Vulnerabilities and Exposures database. https://cve.mitre.org/
6. Common Weakness Enumeration. https://cwe.mitre.org/about/index.html
7. Quadri, S., Farooq, S.U.: Software testing-goals, principles and limitations. Int. J. Comput. Appl. **6**(9), 1 (2010)
8. Ammann, P., Offutt, J.: Introduction to Software Testing. Cambridge University Press, Cambridge (2016)
9. Monteiro, F.R., Garcia, M., Cordeiro, L.C., de Lima Filho, E.B.: Bounded model checking of C++ programs based on the Qt cross-platform framework. Softw. Test. Verification Reliab. **27**(3), e1632 (2017). https://doi.org/10.1002/stvr.1632
10. Chong, N., et al.: Code-level model checking in the software development workflow. In: 2020 IEEE/ACM 42nd International Conference on Software Engineering: Software Engineering in Practice (ICSE-SEIP), pp. 11–20. IEEE (2020)
11. Monteiro, F.R., Gadelha, M.R., Cordeiro, L.C.: Model checking C++ programs. Softw. Test. Verification Reliab. **32**(1), e1793 (2022)
12. Ramalho, M., Freitas, M., Sousa, F., Marques, H., Cordeiro, L., Fischer, B.: SMT-based bounded model checking of C++ programs. In: 2013 20th IEEE International Conference and Workshops on Engineering of Computer Based Systems (ECBS), pp. 147–156. IEEE (2013)
13. LLVM clang. https://clang.llvm.org/
14. Lopes, B.C., Auler, R.: Getting Started with LLVM Core Libraries. Packt Publishing Ltd. (2014)
15. Pandey, M., Sarda, S.: LLVM Cookbook. Packt Publishing Ltd. (2015)
16. Pereira, P.A., et al.: SMT-based context-bounded model checking for CUDA programs. Concurr. Comput. Pract. Exp. **29**(22), e3934 (2017). https://doi.org/10.1002/cpe.3934
17. Dos Reis, G., García, J.D., Logozzo, F., Fähndrich, M., Lahiri, S.: Simple contracts for C++(R1) (2015)
18. Clarke, E., Kroening, D., Lerda, F.: A tool for checking ANSI-C programs. In: Jensen, K., Podelski, A. (eds.) TACAS 2004. LNCS, vol. 2988, pp. 168–176. Springer, Heidelberg (2004). https://doi.org/10.1007/978-3-540-24730-2_15
19. ESBMC L312–L359. https://github.com/esbmc/esbmc/blob/master/src/cpp/cpp_typecheck_compound_type.cpp
20. C++03 standard. https://www.iso.org/standard/38110.html
21. Cordeiro, L., Fischer, B., Marques-Silva, J.: SMT-based bounded model checking for embedded ANSI-C software. IEEE Trans. Softw. Eng. **38**(4), 957–974 (2011)
22. Cordeiro, L.C., Fischer, B.: Verifying multi-threaded software using SMT-based context-bounded model checking. In: Taylor, R.N., Gall, H.C., Medvidovic, N. (eds.) Proceedings of the 33rd International Conference on Software Engineering, ICSE 2011, Waikiki, Honolulu, HI, USA, 21–28 May 2011, pp. 331–340. ACM (2011). https://doi.org/10.1145/1985793.1985839
23. Prata, S.: C++ Primer Plus. Pearson Education India (2012)
24. Stroustrup, B.: The C++ Programming Language, 4th edn (2013)
25. Siek, J., Taha, W.: A semantic analysis of C++ templates. In: Thomas, D. (ed.) ECOOP 2006. LNCS, vol. 4067, pp. 304–327. Springer, Heidelberg (2006). https://doi.org/10.1007/11785477_19
26. GCC test suite. https://gcc.gnu.org/git/?p=gcc.git;a=blob_plain;f=gcc/testsuite/g%2B%2B.dg/template/friend18.C;hb=649fc72d2

27. GCC bugzilla bug 10158. https://gcc.gnu.org/bugzilla/show_bug.cgi?id=10158
28. CBMC 5.88.1. https://github.com/diffblue/cbmc/releases/tag/cbmc-5.88.1
29. cppcheck. https://cppcheck.sourceforge.io/
30. Deitel, P.: C++ How To Program, 6th edn. Prentice Hall Press (2007)
31. CBMC regression test suite. https://github.com/diffblue/cbmc/tree/develop/regression/cbmc-cpp
32. Python unittest. https://docs.python.org/3/library/unittest.html
33. ESBMC v7.3 evaluation archive on Zenodo. https://zenodo.org/record/8233714
34. de Moura, L., Bjørner, N.: Z3: an efficient SMT solver. In: Ramakrishnan, C.R., Rehof, J. (eds.) TACAS 2008. LNCS, vol. 4963, pp. 337–340. Springer, Heidelberg (2008). https://doi.org/10.1007/978-3-540-78800-3_24
35. Niemetz, A., Preiner, M.: Bitwuzla. In: Enea, C., Lal, A. (eds.) CAV 2023, Part II. LNCS, vol. 13965, pp. 3–17. Springer, Cham (2023). https://doi.org/10.1007/978-3-031-37703-7_1
36. Brummayer, R., Biere, A.: Boolector: an efficient SMT solver for bit-vectors and arrays. In: Kowalewski, S., Philippou, A. (eds.) TACAS 2009. LNCS, vol. 5505, pp. 174–177. Springer, Heidelberg (2009). https://doi.org/10.1007/978-3-642-00768-2_16
37. Bruttomesso, R., Cimatti, A., Franzén, A., Griggio, A., Sebastiani, R.: The MATH-SAT 4 SMT solver. In: Gupta, A., Malik, S. (eds.) CAV 2008. LNCS, vol. 5123, pp. 299–303. Springer, Heidelberg (2008). https://doi.org/10.1007/978-3-540-70545-1_28
38. Barrett, C., et al.: CVC4. In: Gopalakrishnan, G., Qadeer, S. (eds.) CAV 2011. LNCS, vol. 6806, pp. 171–177. Springer, Heidelberg (2011). https://doi.org/10.1007/978-3-642-22110-1_14
39. Dutertre, B.: Yices 2.2. In: Biere, A., Bloem, R. (eds.) CAV 2014. LNCS, vol. 8559, pp. 737–744. Springer, Cham (2014). https://doi.org/10.1007/978-3-319-08867-9_49
40. ESBMC CPP support feature coverage and backlog. https://github.com/esbmc/esbmc/wiki/ESBMC-Cpp-Support
41. Github: ESBMC issue 940: Umbrella issue for the order of ctors/dtors. https://github.com/esbmc/esbmc/issues/940
42. Song, K., Gadelha, M.R., Brauße, F., Menezes, R.S., Cordeiro, L.C.: ESBMC v7.3: model checking C++ programs using clang AST. arXiv preprint arXiv:2308.05649 (2023)
43. Sousa, F.R.M., Cordeiro, L.C., de Lima Filho, E.B.: Bounded model checking of C++ programs based on the Qt framework. In: IEEE 4th Global Conference on Consumer Electronics, GCCE 2015, Osaka, Japan, 27–30 October 2015, pp. 179–180. IEEE (2015). https://doi.org/10.1109/GCCE.2015.7398699
44. UKRI: Sotereia project. https://soteriaresearch.org/
45. Beyer, D.: Competition on software verification and witness validation: SV-COMP 2023. In: Sankaranarayanan, S., Sharygina, N. (eds.) TACAS 2023. LNCS, vol. 13994, pp. 495–522. Springer, Cham (2023). https://doi.org/10.1007/978-3-031-30820-8_29

Author Index

Printed in the United States
by Baker & Taylor Publisher Services